*f*P

THE POWER OF
PRODUCT PLATFORMS

Building Value and Cost Leadership

MARC H. MEYER
ALVIN P. LEHNERD

THE FREE PRESS

THE FREE PRESS
A Division of Simon & Schuster Inc.
1230 Avenue of the Americas
New York, NY 10020

Manufactured in the United States of America

10   9   8   7   6

Library of Congress Cataloging-in-Publication Data

Meyer, Marc H.
    The power of product platforms: building value and cost leadership /
Marc H. Meyer, Alvin P. Lehnerd.
        p.   cm.
    Includes bibliographical references and index.
    ISBN 0-684-82580-5
    1. New products—Management.   2. Product management.
I. Lehnerd, Alvin P.   II. Title.
HF5415.153.M49   1997
658.5'75—DC20   96-33508
                                                            CIP

"If wishes were horses, beggars would ride." But of course wishes are not realities. Simply wishing for an escape from chaos and crisis to a more harmonious future will never get you there.

We dedicate this book to our mentors and colleagues from whom we have so richly learned, and to our readers who we hope will use the lessons conveyed herein to transform their own wishes into a more productive, prosperous future for themselves and their corporations.

Contents

Preface

When a company's products are robust—highly functional, elegant in their design, fairly priced, and a pleasure to use—the corporation itself will be equally robust. It will grow in the good times, weather the bad times, and make the difficult transition from one generation of technology to the next.

This book is about creating and managing extraordinary products. While many companies have great difficulty mastering this activity, we have been fortunate to work with firms in a range of industries that have successfully developed new products and integrated manufacturing processes with new product designs. Those experiences, which have complemented our academic research, have been the source of our insights. As authors, we wish to share this information with all those responsible for the vitality of the enterprise: the chief executive, his or her management team, and the Board. We believe this book will be highly useful for both large corporations and those of smaller size, including entrepreneurs, all of whom depend on the excellence of their new products for growth.

For many companies, the road to growth, admiration, and customer loyalty has been built on excellence in new product development. Only a handful, however, have been able to sustain that excellence through eras of changing technology and leadership. Motorola, which began as a maker of car radios in the 1930s, switched to making walkie-talkies during World War II and then redefined itself again, this time in the field of consumer electronics. As that field matured, Motorola's leadership successfully guided the company into exciting new markets for semiconductors, pagers, and cellular communications. Each transition enriched existing competencies with new technologies and business skills. Hewlett Packard, too, started during the 1930s, as a maker of electronic testing devices. Over the years it successfully changed direction as new markets and new technologies appeared, branching into high-end calculators, plotters and printers, medical equipment, workstations, PCs, and systems integration services. Similarly, Intel charges forward year after year with new and better microprocessors that make its existing designs obsolete. Microsoft must also be listed among this elite group of companies; it continues to enhance its technology for the desktop, the corporate network, and, most recently, the Internet. Each of these companies has recognized and responded to new market opportunities by leveraging core skills and technologies in the form of new products.

The industrial roadway is also littered with the wreckage of companies that have left their products unattended. Those companies lost their technological edge, industry leadership, and customers. The list of the fallen extends far back in industrial history. In the nineteenth century, for example, Boston was known for its preeminence in harvesting ice from local ponds and shipping it at great profit to the far corners of the world.[1] When mechanical ice manufacturing was invented by an Englishman during the time of the American Civil War, the great Boston ice companies collectively said, "That is not the ice business" and continued to invest heavily in traditional ice harvesting and distribution technologies. Within just a few decades, their customers had abandoned them for manufactured ice, which could be produced more reliably and at lower cost. A century later, the same tragedy replayed itself with many of the Boston area minicomputer manufacturers, who believed their own proprietary operating systems could withstand the onslaught of "open systems."

What makes companies like Motorola, Hewlett Packard, Intel,

and Microsoft different from those that fail to advance their products? Why is it that they continue to offer exciting new products while others do not? It cannot be for lack of desire. What manager would not want to hold the keys to the future, the technologies that render existing ways of doing things obsolete? Nor can it be for a lack of new management ideas. Consider QFD (quality functional deployment), stage-gate control systems, reengineering, ISO 9000, core competencies, and mass customization. Such innovations are often tried one year and abandoned the next. While each may have value, taken together they consume an enormous amount of the organization's energy. Too often their net effect is organizational upheaval, a plague of meetings, countless reports, exorbitant consulting bills, and unmanageable complexity in downstream activities such as manufacturing and support. Perhaps most damaging is that the implementation of these management fads can divert attention from the renewal of products and services. Management's eye gets taken off the ball, away from its customers and products. Tocqueville noted in the nineteenth century that Americans had a tendency to become "slaves to slogans." If he were observing the corporate scene today, he might well come to the same conclusion.

Fads and slogans notwithstanding, what differentiates innovative companies from others is the constancy of their devotion to strong products. Their managers need no lectures about the need to constantly improve products over time and to find new markets for their core technologies. Further, they understand that long-term success *does not hinge on any single product.* They know they must generate a *continuous stream* of value-rich products that target growth markets. Such products form the product family, individual products that share common technology and address related market applications. It is those families of products that account for the long-term success of corporations.

Product families do not have to emerge one product at a time. In fact, they are planned so that a number of derivative products can be efficiently created from the foundation of common core technology. We call this foundation of core technology the "product platform," which is *a set of subsystems and interfaces that form a common structure from which a stream of derivative products can be efficiently developed and produced.* A platform approach to product development dramatically reduces manufacturing costs and provides significant economies in the procurement of components and materials, because so many of these are shared among individual products. Perhaps as important, the building blocks of product platforms can be integrated with *new* components to address new market opportunities rapidly.

Product platforms must be managed. If a platform is not rejuvenated, its derivative products will become dated and will fail customers in terms of function and value. If a company's platforms are renewed periodically, however, redesigned to incorporate new functions, components, and materials, the product family will remain robust through successive generations.

Robust product platforms do not happen by accident. They are the result of a unique methodology and of strategies for designing, developing, and revitalizing them over time. These are described in the following chapters and are highlighted through case examples that include traditional consumer products, industrial equipment, and computers, as well as "nonphysical" products, such as software and information products distributed through the Internet. As different as physical and nonphysical products may appear, they in fact share a number of conceptual elements when viewed through the lens of platform thinking.

In a nutshell, this book is about how to create powerful, elegant solutions that set the standard for product excellence. It is guided by a simple metaphor: an arch spanning the chasm of uncertainty that every company faces (Figure P–1). Like other arches, this one is constructed from fitted building blocks. What holds the blocks in place and gives the arch its strength, of course, is the keystone. As applied to corporate renewal, the building blocks are the concepts and methods for developing product platforms and families. The keystone, the most critical block, is the dedication and enthusiasm of senior management for the principles that create and renew those families.

FIGURE P-1
Bridging the Chasm

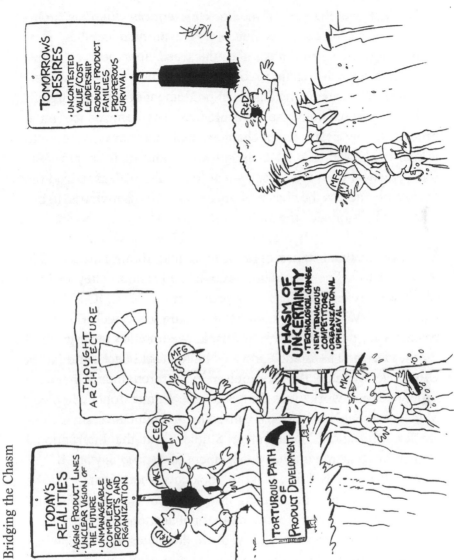

The first two chapters of the book present our "thought architecture," a set of concepts that embrace product families, platforms, derivative products, and the need for their collective renewal. Successive chapters offer specific rules and tools: platform-market strategy, the design of product platforms, the organization of teams, and the measurement of performance on a product family basis. Later chapters apply platform concepts to nonphysical products, such as software. The final chapter sets forth practical ways for management to use these ideas to lead the corporation across the chasm of uncertainty; in other words, to become the keystone for the arch.

We wish to thank those organizations that allowed us to study them and to refine our ideas through application. They include Black & Decker, Boeing, Compaq, CorpTech, EMC, Hewlett Packard, IBM, Lincoln National Reinsurance, Steelcase, Sunbeam, Visio, and Ziff Davis/Softbank. We are also most grateful for the ideas and assistance provided by Richard Luecke and James Utterback. We thank the three university research centers that have supported our work over the years: the Center for Technology Management at Northeastern University, Lehigh University's Center for Innovation Management Studies, and the International Center for Research on the Management of Technology at MIT.

We believe you will find that this book covers ideas relative to the management of product-making firms in a way that is useful, distinctive, and not readily found in other publications. In sharing our concepts and experiences with you, we hope you will enriched by them. We hope you will then be able to approach your own work with renewed vigor and a keener vision of how you can create a better future for yourself, your company, and your customers.

—Marc Meyer and Al Lehnerd
Boston, Massachusetts

1

The Power of Product Platforms

Product-making enterprises—the ones that survive, that is—are evolutionary entities. Their product portfolios change through periodic enhancements to basic product and manufacturing technologies. Some of the changes are true breakthroughs, while others are merely incremental. The appropriate changes lead to market success; those that are not appropriate lead to failure.

The long-term success of an enterprise depends on a stream of new products—some replacing older ones, others pioneering new markets. As the world economy becomes more integrated, many new products have to be global products, satisfying worldwide customer needs and regulatory requirements. The stream of new global products, exploiting advances in both product technologies and technologies used to manufacture, distribute, and provide support, is what provides the fuel for corporate growth and renewal.

FOCUSING ON SINGLE PRODUCTS

Regardless of the importance creating streams of new products, traditional methods for managing this vital business function usually fail to deliver in the long run. That is because companies typically design new products *one product at a time*. The single product must compete for resources against other projects in the corporation's portfolio. Every product team must justify its own existence repeatedly throughout the process of development and commercialization. Approval gates swing open and shut as single development projects move forward. Budget, break-even, and cycle-time measures are all typically calculated on the basis of single products.

The end result of this single-product focus is a failure to embrace commonality, compatibility, standardization, or modularization among different products and product lines. For a given company, the evidence for lack of commonality is found in the products themselves and their component parts. One will observe that the products use different materials for the same purposes; different switches when one kind of switch would do; a technology developed in-house at great expense to serve a single product; components with the same technical specifications but different sizes (so they cannot be interchanged); and on and on. That is where a product portfolio can easily end up when it is developed and managed one product at a time.

Now ask yourself: Would it not be better to build an entire family of products that leverage a common market understanding, common product technologies, and a common set of highly automated production processes? Rather than have separate development teams each working on single products, wouldn't it be better to have them join forces in building a common *platform* or a design from which a host of *derivative products* could be effectively and efficiently created? In short, might not the entire product portfolio of a business segment be tackled *en masse?*

To see that this alternative to a single-product mentality is not so far-fetched, but rather highly feasible and operationally viable, let us reach back to the experience of Black & Decker. Most readers probably own a Black & Decker power tool. There is a very good reason for this. Black & Decker drove most of its competitors out of the consumer segments of the power tools business by developing effective product platforms for its major product families.

RENEWING THE PRODUCT PORTFOLIO
AT BLACK & DECKER

In the early 1970s Black & Decker's consumer power tool product portfolio was broad and deep, consisting of eighteen power tool groups. Eight groups contributed 73 percent of sales and 91 percent of units sold: drills, jigsaws, shrub and hedge trimmers, power hammers, circular saws, grinders and polishers, finishing sanders, and edgers—122 different models in all.

As with most established companies, Black & Decker's product portfolio had evolved over many years; by 1970 it was a collection of uncoordinated designs, materials, and technologies. Its power tools relied on thirty different motors, each manufactured by a different set of tooling. Sixty different motor housings were needed to accommodate variations in power and application (e.g. a drill versus a saw or sander). Besides, the company relied on 104 different armatures, the part that connects the motor to the "business end" of the tool (e.g., to the drill bit or the saw blade). Each of those armatures, in turn, required its own tooling. Dozens of different switches and buttons populated the company's parts bins and bills-of-materials.

The vast majority of Black & Decker's products had crept into the power tool portfolio one at a time, with little thought given to how economies might be achieved through shared components and manufacturing processes. The thousands of parts needed for the products required thousands of square feet of stockroom space and hundreds of people to order, shelve, and inventory them. Each unique product design required either a dedicated production line or frequent and time-consuming line changeovers. Inelegant designs translated into high labor inputs.

Despite those impediments, Black & Decker had grown into a major player in consumer power tools, perhaps because its competitors also followed the same one-at-a-time approach to product development. Its products worked as well as those of rivals and were priced competitive with those of other domestic manu-facturers. Circa 1970, Black & Decker controlled about 20 per-cent of market share worth about $200 million annually in revenue. Despite its comfortable situation, management saw three dark clouds on the horizon:

- Offshore manufacturers were making inroads into the North American market and attacking emerging markets overseas.
- Inflation and the rising cost of labor, materials, services, and capital goods were devouring Black & Decker's margins. To maintain constant labor-cost content in its products, manage-ment calculated that about one-third of the labor cost would have to be removed from products over the next three to four years. While that would be difficult for any single product, it would be impossible for the company's entire power tool line without making use of design standardization, automation, better use of materials and floor space, and intelligent capital planning.
- Consumers and regulators would be requiring higher standards of safety—specifically, adding a backup barrier of insulation around the power tool motors to protect the users from electri-cal shock if the existing insulation system failed. Regulatory mandates for double insulation had already taken hold in Europe and were expected to surface in the American market. This would create havoc for Black & Decker's production process. Its management estimated that redesigning all its power tools for double insulation one product at a time would take nearly a decade.

Black & Decker's Board and its management team understood that those threats could not be met with small measures. They also un-derstood that their competitors faced the same problems. "If we can respond more rapidly and effectively," they reasoned, "the threats we face as an enterprise might be turned into opportunities to dominate our industry."

The Double Insulation Program

The need to adopt double insulation turned out to be the catalyst for renewal of the entire Black & Decker power tool portfolio.[1] Management started the Double Insulation Program with a clear mission: (1) redesign all consumer power tools at *the same time;* (2) redesign manufacturing simultaneously so that all the new products could be manufactured at substantial cost advantage; and (3) offer double insulated products at no increase in price to the consumer. The implication of this mission was that current consumer power tool lines would have to be abandoned!

Management established five powerful objectives for its power tool renewal:

- Develop a clear, distinctive "family" look across all products so that the customer could pick up any given product and, without reading the label, know that it was a "Black & Decker."
- Simplify product offerings, replacing customized gadgetry with standardized parts, interfaces, couplings, and connections.
- Dramatically reduce per unit manufacturing costs through automation and the use of new materials. While a number of other power tool companies had already introduced double insulated products, they had done so at a 20 percent premium in material and labor costs. Black & Decker would aim to introduce double insulation at less than the single insulation costs of its current product line..
- Use design to improve power tool performance and make it possible to add new features (such as more power or variable speeds) with minimal costs.
- Make global products—i.e., products that would meet worldwide customer needs and regulatory requirements.

Getting Started

The most important decision made by the company's senior managers was made at the beginning of the effort: The resources of the company would be concentrated on the Double Insulation Program until the transition was complete. Only a token force would be left to carry out development efforts on existing power tool designs. That was clearly a high-risk, "bet-the-company" decision. The best talent and the weight of capital investment would be shifted to the new program. One retired Black & Decker executive remarked, "We bet the company, but if we hadn't, there wouldn't have been a company by the end of the decade."

Development of new products was placed temporarily on hold while a focused "hit team" sought to create a new common product platform for all the company's major power tool groups. They began to search the industrial world for the best product components and new advances in both materials and manufacturing processes.

Since manufacturing was to be the key enabler of a radical new product platform design, the traditional company barrier between engineering and manufacturing would have to be bridged. Black & Decker established that link by placing advanced manufacturing engineers in residence at headquarters where they would work elbow to elbow with the product design group. The manufacturing engineers were directly involved from the start in tooling machine development, process development, value and cost product design engineering, purchasing decisions, and packaging. A "war room" was created where people from many functions could meet to hammer out new product designs over the three-year duration of the project.

The basic structure of the company was also changed to prevent higher level organizational politics from interfering with the renewal effort. Instead of having one general manager of the consumer power tools business with two vice presidents for engineering and manufacturing respectively, a new "vice president of operations" position was created to combine product development, manufacturing engineering, and manufacturing operations under one vice president.

Perhaps as important as anything, management and Board members committed themselves to a long-term planning horizon. They allocated $17.1 million (in 1971 dollars)—a substantial investment for the company at that time—and break-even was not anticipated until nearly seven years after the program's launch. Capital expenditures, largely for new plant and equipment, were $6 million. Tooling, i.e., setting up the production facilities, was another $6.5 million. Manufacturing technology engineering and development engineering were each to receive $1.7 million. Inventory and other miscellaneous expenditures were budgeted at $1.2 million.

Building a Common Product Platform

Black & Decker had the good fortune to possess an unbridled fascination with the details of creating better product function and price for the consumer power tools user. The Double Insulation initiative supported that fascination with resources and direction. Its goal was to create a *product platform* to support a new generation of power tools. A product platform is a set of common components, modules, or parts from which a stream of derivative products can be efficiently created and launched. The most common part across all power tools is the motor. Key product parts, such as the motor in a power tool, represent a major *subsystem* of the product platform. Figure 1–1 illustrates the before and after design of the universal motor field assembly, one of the key subsystems of Black & Decker's universal motor.

To appreciate just how inelegant product designs were in Black & Decker's power tools prior to the Double Insulation Program, note the various wires. These wires were the connections between the motor field and the power supply. We refer to connections such as these as the *interfaces between subsystems* in a product platform. Across its major product groups, the company manufactured thirty different motors. They were not simply variations of a single design, but specific architectures developed for different power requirements within and across the power tool groups. Each motor had a unique manufacturing process, and those processes were only semiautomated. For example, technicians manually attached the wires between the motor fields and the power supply.

FIGURE 1–1

Black & Decker's Universal Motor Field Assembly Before and After Design

To solve that problem, a team went to work designing a universal motor, one that could serve a broad range of products: drills, sanders, saws, grinders, and so forth. The team was guided by the principles of standardization and modularization. The principle of scalability was also important. Their goal was to create a single basic motor design that could be adapted to produce a broad range of power to serve infrequent household users, frequent household users, and even professional tradesmen.

The result of their work is shown in the "after" part of Figure 1–1. Note the simpler interface architecture of the redesigned motor—"plug-in" connections that could be inserted automatically into the power tool housing. Manual wiring of the motor to the power supply was eliminated. The motor design was fixed in its axial diameter, allowing variation only in length. Such standardization offered several important advantages. First, designers could create a common housing for the motor. The fixed diameter of the entire motor assembly also allowed engineers to create a standardized housing diameter for all power tools in the product family. The housing of the power tool would be the same for a drill, a sander, a jigsaw, or a grinder.

Another advantage of the new motor design was that power could be increased by simply adding length. By increasing the length of the motor from .8" to 1.75", as shown in Figure 1–2, stacking and wrapping more copper and steel around the laminations, a range of 60 watts to 650 watts could be achieved.

The standardization and modularization achieved in redesign of the basic motor platform made it possible for Black & Decker engineers to make important breakthroughs in manufacturing automation. The team designed a single process wherein variations (in length) of the basic motor could be produced untouched by

FIGURE 1–2

Stack Length and Power Range of the Universal Motor Field

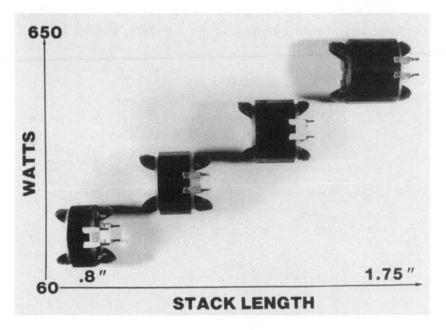

human hands. The laminations (the backbone of the motor) could be placed at the head of a mechanized line and then stacked, welded, insulated, wound, varnished, terminated, and tested automatically.

Figure 1–3 shows that at the 1974 volumes of 2,400 motors per hour, the new double-insulated motor system required sixteen operators, whereas the previous motor design required 108 operators—an 85 percent reduction in labor costs! Material, labor, and overhead costs were 31 cents per unit in the new design, as against 51 cents in the old design, a 39 percent reduction. The labor content itself was only 2 cents per unit in the new, down from 14 cents per unit in the old! Further, all motors could be produced on the same line because of the fixed axial dimension. Labor cost was therefore the same for a 650 watt motor as it was for a 60 watt motor. The only costs that varied were lamination steel and copper wire. The company realized savings of $1.28 million annually (in 1974 dollars) in making its power tool motors. That more than covered the capital investment of $1.22 million to purchase and integrate new equipment.

While the new motor design was under way, several members of the team turned their attention to the armature, another key sub-

FIGURE 1–3

Motor Field Cost Comparison (at 2,400 units per hour)

	Old Design and Manufacturing Process	New Design and Manufacturing Process	Improvement
Operators to produce	108	16	85%
Cost to insulate (materials, labor, overhead)	$0.51	$0.31	39%
Labor cost/unit	$0.14	$0.02	85%
Capital to produce	$400,000	$1,222,000	
Annual savings (labor and material)		$1,280,000	

system in the structure of the product platform for power tools. The armature connects to a set of gears, which in turn drive the "business end" of the power tool, be it a drill bit, saw blade, or sanding surface. The armature rotates between 20,000 and 30,000 revolutions a minute in a typical power tool. Thus, anything connected to it has to be attached very securely. The armature consists of iron, laminations to the iron, more copper wrapping, a commutator, a shaft leading to the gears that drive the drill bit, sander, or blade, and insulating end caps. The armatures must also be balanced, like a car wheel.

Another layer of insulation had to be added around the armature shaft to meet the double insulation requirement. In the old armature design, the laminations had to be fitted precisely onto the shaft. The shaft and the laminations would be assembled with special fixtures. The layer of insulation would also have to be measured and then pressed onto the shaft. Defects in the insulation were experienced when the armature had to be balanced and tested.

The manufacturing engineers wanted to simplify this process to enable increased volumes. They searched the world across a wide range of industries, looking for a process that would make it possible to avoid mechanically fastening the laminations to the shaft. Fortunately, one engineer identified a new adhesive called Loctite, made by a small firm in Connecticut. Loctite had the unique feature of curing in the absence of air and in the presence of metal. That was precisely what the team needed to automate armature production fully. All subassemblies could be attached to the shaft with Loctite and, as the Loctite was curing, could be aligned properly.

Machines were developed to automate the entire process, including the fine art of balancing the entire subassembly—a first in the power tools business. The team also developed a unique double insulating material, a special type of paper tube that was formed into a sleeve placed around the armature with Loctite adhesive. The new automated process of armature production made it possible to produce the same number of armatures with one-fourth as many operators. Costs were reduced to one-fifth of their former levels. Key aspects of the new armature design were patented by Black & Decker.

Motors and the armatures were just the start. Standardization, modularization, and automation became the pervasive thought architecture guiding the team. Each major subsystem of the power tools product platform was attacked by the Black & Decker team. Gears were standardized. The decision was made to switch from beveled gears to spur gears made from powdered metal. That eliminated the need for gear cutting, heat treating, and gauging, all of which added labor cost and material cost, as well as high levels of materials waste in the old process. Subsequent volumes soon allowed the company to vertically integrate, bringing the fabrication of powdered-metal gears in-house at a lower cost.

Even the lowly drill "chuck" became an object of the design team's scrutiny. The chuck is the little gear-faced device used to tighten drill bits. Despite their size and simplicity, chucks were expensive relative to the drill itself: 29 percent of the total cost of the drill. Black & Decker had sourced chucks from outside vendors. This cost alone made the chuck an important subsystem in the overall design. The team redesigned the chuck for cost-effective manufacturing, cutting its cost almost in half.

Purchasing was approached in a similar manner. For each purchased part, such as power cords, the team standardized selections to a narrow few and then searched the world for the best suppliers. The increased volume achieved through standardization allowed Black & Decker to secure good pricing from vendors immediately.

Quality improvements also benefited the company, its dealers, and its customers. Failure rates for all small appliances in the hands of consumers during this period had been in the range of 6–10 percent. Black & Decker's experience with field failures had fallen within that range as well; its scrap rate inside the factory took an equal toll. Thanks to the new product platform and manufacturing process design, those losses plummeted: Field failures dropped to near 1 percent, and internal scrappage fell below 5 percent!

THE BUSINESS IMPACT OF THE DOUBLE
INSULATION PROGRAM

Seventeen million dollars and three years after starting the program, Black & Decker had completed the common platform for its power tools. It proved to be a robust platform from which the company introduced a multitude of derivative products with power ranges from 60 to 750 watts. As new concepts for power tools emerged, much of the work in design and tooling was eliminated because so much of any given products had been standardized in the new platform: motors, bearings, switches, gears, cord sets, and fasteners. Designers had to concern themselves only with the "business end" of a new product, i.e., a new type of drilling, sanding, or cutting attachment, and to perfect its intended function. In other words, their job was one of understanding customer needs, integrating modular subsystems, and perfecting the incremental attachments.

Cycle times for new derivative products were greatly accelerated. For a number of years, the rate of new product introductions averaged *one per week!* Further, as those products reached maturity and had to be dropped, massive writeoffs and scrapping of special tools and equipment was avoided simply because there were minimal special tools or equipment for any single product. Such flexibility allowed marketers and managers to pivot quickly and avoid being tied to dying products.

The financial payoff from the program was substantial. In a retrospective review done in 1976, management estimated that the 1976 requirements for motor manufacturing would have been nearly six hundred people, whereas the new production system required only 171 people. The labor cost difference in motor manufacturing alone was $4.6 million (in 1976 dollars).

Black & Decker took its cost advantage directly to the marketplace in the form of aggressive pricing. A customer could go to his local store and buy a great drill for less than $10.[2] The company

FIGURE 1–4

Price Comparison of Black & Decker's Power Tools, 1958 Versus 1973

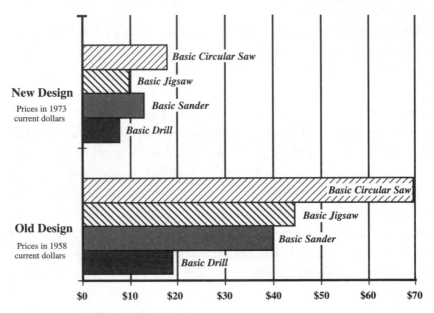

Source: 1974 Black & Decker Annual Report.

played its price advantage to the hilt, and between 1971 and the early 1980s its market share soared. Figure 1–4 shows the end-user prices of Black & Decker's newly designed power tools compared to prices for the older designs in constant 1973 dollars. The price reductions were over 50 percent in some instances. Demand soared, fueled by a strong advertising campaign. Even at those low price points, however, Black & Decker consistently maintained a gross margin of 50 percent over its cost of goods sold.

Competitors in consumer tools were blind-sided by Black & Decker's innovations. Competitors' product designs and manufacturing processes were costly. Attempts to match Black & Decker's prices diluted their profitability and undercut their ability to fund fundamental product redesign of their own. Furthermore, Black & Decker had patented many of its product and process innovations, making reverse engineering difficult if not impossible. Competitors would have to figure out their own proprietary solutions and the vast majority had neither the time nor the resources to do so. One competitor charged Black & Decker with unfair pricing practices, claiming that its tools were being dumped onto the market below the cost of production to gain market share. A plant tour of Black & Decker's motor and armature production line quickly laid that charge to rest. That competitor soon exited the consumer segment of the business.

Over the next five years a great shakeout occurred. Stanley, Skil, Pet, McGraw Edison, Sunbeam, General Electric, Wen, Thor, Porter Cable, and Rockwell all left the consumer power tool business. Only Sears Roebuck was able to stay in the domestic consumer market with Black & Decker. Foreign competitors such as Bosche and Makita were buoyed by their brand names in their own domestic markets, but even there Black & Decker competed aggressively with them. Black & Decker's breakeven period for the product line renewal, initially expected to be seven years, turned out to be about half that time.

A THOUGHT ARCHITECTURE FOR EFFECTIVE PRODUCT LINE RENEWAL

Black & Decker's approach to revitalizing its consumer power tools brought it tremendous success in the marketplace. In effect, Black & Decker did three things right:

- It avoided a piecemeal, single-product focus. Instead, management dealt with the power tool product line as a whole.
- It bridged the traditional divide between engineering and manufacturing with the result that both products and the processes for creating them were simultaneously redesigned.
- Senior management adopted a long-term horizon and made the initiative a top priority.

We believe that these approaches represent a "thought architecture" for management that is powerful and generalizable for any product-making company. That thought architecture has five basic principles.

Principle 1. Product Family Planning and Platforms

Companies should plan and manage on the basis of the *product family,* which we defined in the Preface as a set of products that share common technology and address a related set of market applications.

The Black & Decker case illustrates the concept of product families very well. We can see the same product family principle at work in some of today's leading companies. Intel's dominant share of the microprocessor market has grown through successive generations of chip designs, each more powerful than the last. Each basic design, be it the 8086 developed and marketed almost twenty years ago or the Pentium or its successors that come to our attention today, has then been tailored to provide different speeds at different price points. The automobile industry is also noteworthy for its product family successes. Honda's Accord and Civic lines have kept their edge through a combination of new "platform" designs from which three or four derivatives of increasing power and luxury are always made available. Microsoft excels on the desktop not only because of its operating systems but because of its continuously growing family of software applications for word processing, spreadsheets, database, presentations, home entertainment, software development, and Internet usage.

One can also find a product family approach in successful companies before Black & Decker's time. The venerable DC-3, for example, was first developed during the 1930s to carry passengers for the fledging commercial airlines. It was then modified to serve as a troop carrier in the South Pacific. The DC-3 was also modified to serve as a cargo plane—three different derivative planes based on the same product platform. The remarkable part of the DC-3 story is that the lead engineers completed the basic design of the plane over the course of several weeks: two engines versus the three of earlier planes, an aluminum skin as opposed to fabric wrapped around wood structures, new navigational systems, robust landing gear, and seating capacity large enough to make commercial traffic profitable for the first time. Today, more than fifty years later, thousands of DC-3's are still in use, proving it to be an efficient and durable plane for short haul cargo traffic.[3] It is a story, we are told, that inspired the lead designers of the new Boeing 777 to "clean sheet" their own aircraft designs, embracing both commonality in components and systems, and planning in advance a multiple element product family.

Thus, developing robust product families has been and continues to be one of the cornerstones of sustained corporate success. Find a successful product-making company today, and it is hard not to find the presence of a diverse, feature-rich product family.

Product family planning means looking forward not only to the market applications for derivative products, but also planning the successive generations of the product platforms beneath those derivative products. Black & Decker embraced product family planning when it decided to redesign its entire product portfolio in a single stroke.

Principle 2: Simultaneous Design for Production

The design of new products is often constrained by existing capabilities in plant and production equipment. In high-volume manufacturing situations one frequently finds very complex, intricate machines that lack the flexibility to accommodate variations to existing product designs. It is a classic case of the tail wagging the dog: Manufacturing engineers guide product design decisions to match the capabilities of their existing factories and subcontractors. Manufacturing managers participating in reviews of new product developments heed the inner voice: "We already have millions of dollars tied up in this equipment, so design something that's like our existing products." This can be one of the greatest barriers to product innovation and helps explain the incrementalism found in many industries.

Simultaneous design for production is the early and continuous integration of product design with manufacturing design. It means getting manufacturing personnel to work elbow to elbow with product designers, engineers, and marketers, from the beginning and for the duration of the development program. Collocation is essential.

The power of simultaneous design is clear from the Black & Decker story, where such major subsystems as motors, armatures, and gears were designed in conjunction with such process innovations as Loctite, automated armature balancing, and powdered-metal fabrication.

Principle 3: Global Product Design and Market Development

Development teams must assume a global perspective for sourcing technology for new products. Teams should be intimately familiar with market research on customer needs and preferences, distribution channels, support requirements, and technical and product safety requirements beyond domestic borders. Failure to meet those requirements through design locks products out of important markets.

Standardization of subsystems is clearly a key part of the global solution. When Black & Decker redesigned its power tool line, it adopted the metric standard for all of its subsystems. That facilitated global sourcing of components and helped ensure that the common product platform could accommodate local needs for manufacturing, the addition of various accessories, and packaging.

Principle 4: Discover Latent, Unperceived Customer Needs

New product development must be the able to intuit, test, and ultimately discover latent, unperceived customer needs. Good market research can identify the perceived needs and preferences of customers. Most companies readily understand how to do this type of research. Far more difficult, but more powerful as a source of competitive advantage, is the ability to identify needs that customers have not yet learned to articulate. Finding latent needs is as much art as science in the context of product development. Management should cherish individuals who do it well. New product platforms designed to address those latent needs can generate renewed excitement and sales, even in dormant, unexciting industries. Safety concerns were a latent need in the Black & Decker power tool case. So was a $10 power drill. Discovering and acting upon latent needs will undoubtedly drive the success of companies that offer Internet applications in the years ahead.

Principle 5: Elegance in Design

The norm in industry is to add functionality to existing designs. If a product is selling, you can bet that a "new and improved" version will appear with various bells and whistles. For example, a popular software package might contain tens of thousands of lines of programming code. Each new version adds features, more code, and more complexity. In scanning the voluminous documentation required to understand all the features of the product, the user justifiably wonders, "Who is making this product, and for whom?"

Customers' resistance to complexity is observable even as companies raise the level of complexity in their products. Japanese producers of personal "organizers" and VCRs have run up against customer complaints that the products have too many features and that the effort to master them is not worth the trouble. High levels of product variety constitute another form of complexity against which consumers have rebelled in recent years. Automobile companies that ask the buyer to choose among a dozen different steering wheels, two dozen styles of wheel covers, more than a hundred carpet types, and so forth, have discovered that complexity can be a sales killer.

Simplicity, on the other hand, is a virtue. And simplicity in product design can often be attained through modular construction.

Top-flight software developers, for example, generally avoid monolithic programs in favor of functionally focused modules that are coupled through standardized interfaces. Or, the Dustbuster™, another successful consumer product, is at its essence marvelously simple yet useful.

Herb Simon, the 1978 Nobel Prize winner in economics, tells the story of two Swiss watchmakers, Bios and Mekhos, both of whom made fine, expensive watches. While their watches were in equal demand, Bios prospered while Mekhos struggled. The watches consisted of about one thousand parts each. Mekhos assembled his watches bit by bit—rather like making a mosaic floor out of small colored stones. Thus, each time he was disturbed in his work and had to put down the partly assembled watch, it fell to pieces and he had to start again from scratch. Bios, on the other hand, made watches by constructing subassemblies of about ten components, each of which held together as an independent unit. Ten of the subassemblies could then be fitted together in a subsystem of a higher order, and ten of those constituted the whole watch. If an interruption caused Bios to put down or even drop the watch he was working on, it did not decompose into its elementary bits. Instead of starting all over again, he had merely to reassemble that particular subassembly. Bios's watches were also incomparably more resistant to damage and much easier to repair.[4]

Simplicity, when combined with a richness of features, represents elegance in product design. The renewal of the Black & Decker power tool motor demonstrates this principle and indicates how elegance in product design translates into market power.

TOWARD CONTINUOUS RENEWAL

The five principles just cited represent a thought architecture to guide managers in creating powerful and profitable products and services. The chapters that follow expand on these principles and provide tools for applying them.

Victory in the contest for market leadership can be attained through these principles, but long-term success and survival require continuing innovation and renewal. While our story of Black & Decker assures us that entire families can be revitalized in a bold stroke and that financial success indeed follows, one victory is not the end of history. Renewal must become a habit of mind and action. The Double Insulation Program revitalized Black & Decker's consumer power tool business and brought the company years of prosperity. For a number of years the thought architecture was adhered to and reapplied to new situations. For example, the company identified a new opportunity in the automotive aftermarket. Using the lessons of the Double Insulation initiative, the company developed a new product family for that market that used many of the product technologies and manufacturing processes of its consumer power tools.

Unfortunately, our story does not have an entirely happy ending. The thought architecture behind Black & Decker's success did not "stick" as a way of thinking and managing. In pursuit of ever lower costs, the company sought a way to reduce the physical size of its electric motors further. That was accomplished through the development of new manufacturing equipment. But in its rush to bring out a new line of products featuring this reduction, it abandoned many of the lessons learned earlier. The shared architecture of the motor housings, handle, and gearbox interfaces was lost; every product using the new motor was required to have a unique housing and peripherals. Over time, the development of new products reverted to the old piecemeal practices. Although some of the Double Insulation Program designs can still be found in the company's products today, the preponderance of its offerings no longer share significant componentry. Even the number of fasteners in its power tools has proliferated.

Institutionalizing the rules, tools, and disciplines of shared architecture is especially difficult as organizations change and new managers come into power. If Black & Decker momentarily lost its edge, it was not the first industry leader to do so. The failure to sustain success is a story that repeats itself in every industry and with every generation. The conclusion of this story, however, is not preordained. Managers who understand the need for longer-term evolution of the product family can create a much different ending—which is what we consider in the next chapter.

2

Managing Product Platforms

The Black & Decker case in the previous chapter demonstrates the cost efficiencies, technological leverage, and market power that can be achieved when companies redirect their thinking and resources from single products to *families* of products built upon robust product platforms. Many companies have accomplished this at one time or another, but few have revitalized those families over time. More often than not, they have used their successful families as cash cows, to be milked for as long as possible. Companies have difficulty institutionalizing the thinking and action that contributed to their initial success.

In this chapter, we explore how product innovation can be maintained across multiple generations of a product family. Doing a "Black & Decker" once is not sufficient for the long term; new platform development must be pursued on a continuing basis, embracing technological changes as they occur and making each new generation of a product line more exciting and value-rich than its predecessors. To demonstrate this, we will use a contemporary case of a dynamic and successful product family, Hewlett Packard's ink jet printers.

THE HEWLETT PACKARD INK JET PRINTER FAMILY

The market for home and office computer peripherals—laser printers, ink jet printers, scanners, and various storage devices—has paralleled the burgeoning sales of personal computers. In the early 1980s the low-end printer market was dominated by products made by several Asian companies. Over the course of that decade, however, Hewlett Packard developed an ink jet product design, associated component technologies, and manufacturing processes to establish an expanding beachhead in that market.[1] HP has constantly improved the cost, quality, and speed of its ink jet printers so that they now dominate the low-end market. Its product family renewal has been systematic and vigorous.

According to Dave Packard, HP's interest in ink jet printing technology began with a chance discovery in its Palo Alto laboratory where researchers noted how jets of fluid could, in the presence of electrical simulation, be used for marking purposes. They reasoned that if those jets could be controlled, they might provide an alternative to the noisy, serial dot matrix printers so popular in the PC printing market. Compared to dot matrix printers, ink jet technology held out the possibility of a much quieter, higher-quality, and more cost effective method of printing.

Between 1980 and 1984 HP developed the core of ink jet printing technology—the disposable ink jet head—and introduced its first commercial product, the ThinkJet Printer. The machine was compact, quiet, and relatively inexpensive; it printed with reasonable quality on special thermal paper. However, the ThinkJet failed to sell in large numbers. Customer research indicated that customers wanted higher-quality printing on plain paper and a choice of different fonts.

Back in the lab, the "Maverick" project team met each of those customer objectives. Unfortunately, the new prototype would have been priced at about $1,500, much too high to break into the dot matrix market, where printers were being sold in the $350 range. Customers made it clear that the price would have to be *below*

$1,000. HP attacked the problem again, setting itself against a time line of twenty-two months to bring a new product to market that would crack the barriers of cost and quality. The fruits of their labors was an underlying platform architecture that would serve as the foundation for a stream of derivative products, providing an unparalleled level of function and price.

Figure 2–1 is a high-level block diagram of that platform architecture. You can see that the subsystems fall within three general groups: mechanical elements (such as the drive chain), electronics (the computer chip and memory, for example), and software embedded into chips (the "firmware" that controls printing and communications with the PC). Each of these subsystems has clear interfaces, be they physical, electronic, or software-based, to other subsystems. The design also has interfaces to the external environment such as communications protocols to computers or paper feeds accommodating ordinary paper, envelopes, transparencies, labels, and even holiday greeting cards. Even though the new architecture was developed rapidly, it is clear that the team made outstanding design decisions. The basic architecture remained in force for over a decade, albeit refreshed with new component technologies once every two or three years.

The "product family map" for HP's ink jet printers is shown in Figure 2–2 (pp. 28–29). The map has a format that we often use to portray the evolution and renewal of product families in many industries. A unique platform architecture is defined as the combination of subsystems and interfaces between subsystems that constitute a common product structure or *platform* for a series of derivative products. The three thickest lines on the map represent the three distinct platform architectures of the ink jet printer product family: the "500" platform, the "600," and the "800," respectively. Those lines begin at the start of R&D for a particular product platform and continue to the end of commercial sales of products based on that platform. Note that "600" platform and the "800" platform were developed *in parallel* with refinements to

FIGURE 2–1

Original Product Platform Architecture for the Deskjet Printers

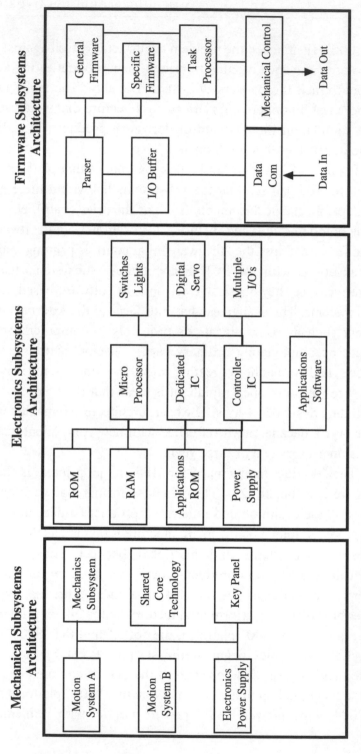

Mechanical Subsystems Architecture

Electronics Subsystems Architecture

Firmware Subsystems Architecture

Source: Hewlett Packard Corporation, 1996.

original "500" platform and that the R&D for the "800" was started before that for the "600." One finds similar parallel platform developments in Intel's microprocessor family (i.e., the Pentium, P6, and P7 projects) and in Compaq's computers (i.e., the Deskpro, Presario, and Proliant product lines.) Concurrent platform development is the essence of a company's obsoleting its own products with better ones.

The lines of medium thickness in Figure 2–2 represent major enhancements to an existing platform architecture. These occur when a company replaces one or more existing subsystems in a platform with better technology, all the while maintaining the overall structure or design of the platform. HP, for example, has made four major platform enhancements to its original Deskjet platform design: (1) a single-pen, single-cartridge color-capable design; (2) a double-pen, dual-cartridge design; (3) a portable printer design; and (4) a major cost reduction design of all the earlier models. It has also made one major platform enhancement to the more recently introduced "600" platform.

Lastly, the thinnest of the lines in Figure 2–2 represents specific derivative products based on a product platform. Product family maps quickly reveal the degree to which a firm has both created derivative products from an underlying platform and renewed the platform itself with better designs and component technologies.

The product family of the ink jet printers gives us an inside look at how HP managed a highly successful product family. The original Deskjet was strictly a black-and-white printer. Over the course of about five years, four derivatives were created from the underlying Deskjet platform: the Deskjet Plus (a combination of cost reductions and quality improvements), the first Deskwriter (for the Apple Macintosh), the Deskwriter Appletalk (using a new Macintosh communications interface), and the Deskjet 500. The combination of platform improvements and manufacturing efficiencies made it possible to drop the price of the base-level Deskjet 500 to below $400. This breakthrough sealed the fate of dot matrix printing and gave HP the opportunity to ride the wave of PC sales.

FIGURE 2–2

The Product Family Map for HP's Ink Jet Printers

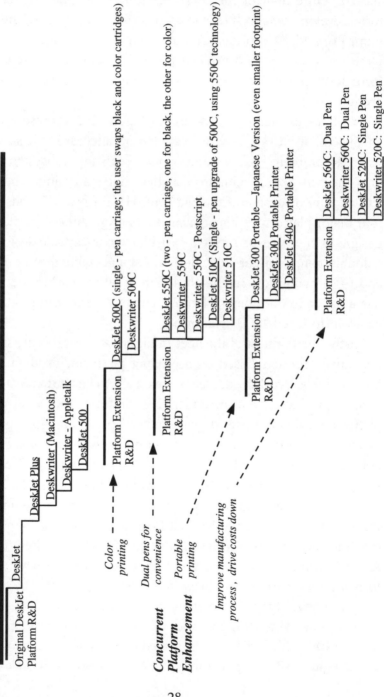

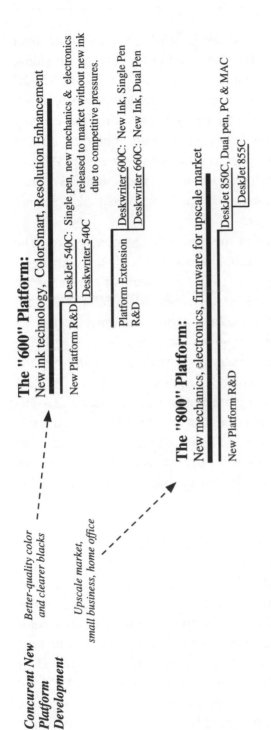

Concurrent New
Platform
Development

*Better-quality color
and clearer blacks*

*Upscale market,
small business, home office*

The "600" Platform:
New ink technology, ColorSmart, Resolution Enhancement

New Platform R&D

DeskJet 540C: Single pen, new mechanics & electronics
released to market without new ink
due to competitive pressures.

Deskwriter 540C

Platform Extension
R&D

Deskwriter 600C: New Ink, Single Pen
Deskwriter 660C: New Ink, Dual Pen

The "800" Platform:
New mechanics, electronics, firmware for upscale market

New Platform R&D

DeskJet 850C, Dual pen, PC & MAC

DeskJet 855C

Source: Hewlett Packard Corporation, 1996.

29

The First Platform Extension: Color Printing. Even as the Deskjet 500 was being developed, HP was looking forward to providing color inkjet capability—an unmet market need. The Deskjet 500C was a classic extension of an existing product platform. A *platform extension* occurs when particular subsystems within the existing platform design are substantially changed and enhanced. In this case, key subsystems in the electronics and firmware subsystems were reengineered with color capabilities. Production cost, print quality, and speed were also improved. Yet the basic platform architecture remained constant.

There was true elegance in the new color printer design: The same carriage accommodated both black and color ink cartridges. It is a "single-pen" system. When the user wants to print just in black, he or she inserts a black ink cartridge. When color is desired, the user just as easily inserts a color cartridge. Internal electronics and software automatically recognize the type of cartridge being used and communicate necessary information to and from the user's word processor, spreadsheet, or graphics program. While it took much discussion and engineering work to achieve this "universal interface," the convenience provided to users proved compelling. Add a low price of about $350, and it is no surprise that sales of the color ink jets soared. Further, as millions of printers worked their way into the hands of users, sales of highly profitable ink cartridges grew exponentially.

The Second Platform Extension: A Dual Pen System. Having achieved a high level of market success, many companies would have rested on their laurels. However, HP continued to advance the product line. Market research indicated that many color printer users would prefer not swapping in and out the black and color cartridges. Further, if a user wished to print a chart that contained both color graphics and pure black text, the "black" produced by the existing single-pen color cartridge was a composite black that to the eye was really a dark gray. Accordingly, HP began working on a double cartridge system, having both a pure black and a color cartridge together, side-by-side. This resulted in the two-pen 550 series, another platform extension that nonetheless preserved the original platform architecture. Three derivative products were introduced from this platform extension: the Deskjet 550C, the Deskwriter 550C (Macintosh version), and the Deskwriter 550C equipped with Postscript formatting language capability. HP used also the cost reductions and print quality improvements of the 550 series to reintroduce lower-cost versions of its 500 series single-pen printers (the Deskwriter and Deskjet 510).

The Third Platform Extension: Portable Printers. HP continued to make systematic platform improvements. A team inside the ink jet printer engineering group focused on making a smaller "portable" printer based on the earlier single-pen 500C design. The result of this third platform extension was the Deskjet Portable 300 and a localized version for the Japanese market. Once again, the original Deskjet platform architecture remained intact while key subsystems were substantially changed and repackaged to achieve the smaller "footprint." It would have been tempting for engineers to design a smaller print cartridge for the new portable printers. But they resisted. The beauty of the portable's design was that it employed the ubiquitous HP print cartridge, which itself had become HP's version of the Black & Decker universal motor. The cartridge's fixed geometries and electronic interfaces, which while perhaps suboptimized in the context of any given printer model, provided an *optimization of the overall system.* For example, the user could take the cartridge out of the 500C and use it on the road in the 300.

The Fourth Platform Extension: Cost Reductions. HP's success had attracted the attention of other manufacturers, particularly those using primarily cheap foreign labor. Management directed teams of product engineers and manufacturing engineers to drive cost down further in the "500" platform. Most of the effort and project cost went to improve processes for production and procurement. From this, HP introduced new versions of both its single-pen and double-pen printers (the Deskjet 520C, Deskjet 560C, Deskwriter 520C, and Deskwriter 560C). The combination of improved print quality at even lower costs made derivative products winners in the market place.

Two New Product Platforms, the "600" and "800" Series. The next progression in HP's product family came with the introduction of products based on two entirely new platforms, shown in the bottom of Figure 2–2 as the "600" and "800" platforms, respectively. Both of these new platforms were "clean sheeted." Development teams started fresh and let user needs drive their new designs. It turned out that many of the subsystems from the original "500" platform were carried forward into the "600" and "800." However, both teams introduced new subsystems, interfaces, and component technologies, as well as new packaging, to create distinct platform architectures.

The "600" platform was designed to replace HP's existing low-end ink jet products. Propelling the effort was a key innovation in the most basic of core technologies: the ink itself. A new, highly proprietary ink technology, one that produced deeper blacks and more vivid colors, was created and patented. The new ink had tremendous ripple effects through the entire platform architecture. This is shown in Figure 2–3, the hierarchy of subsystems within an ink jet printer. The new ink affected the mechanical subsystems, which in turn affected the industrial design of the printers, and then a reworking of the electronics. Any major changes to electronics then required new firmware, which itself required new applications software (the printer "drivers" that communicate with the user's own software).

The new "600" platform entailed a tremendous engineering effort. In fact, there was so much work to do, the team was forced by competitive pressures to scale back its original product plans and start by introducing a single-pen system, the 540C. This product used most of the new platform's subsystems, with the exception of the novel ink and the cartridge needed for it. However, within a

FIGURE 2–3

Hierarchy of Subsystems in the Ink Jet Printer System

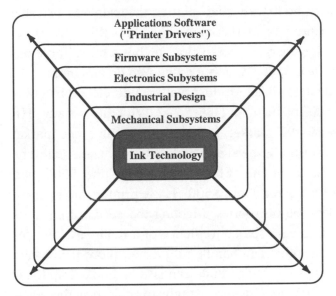

Source: Hewlett Packard Corporation.

year HP introduced derivative products that did use the new ink and cartridges (the single-cartridge 600C and the dual-cartridge 660C, with PC and Macintosh versions of each).

With the "600" platform, for the first time in a decade HP took the step of introducing a new design for its print cartridges. The existing cartridges could not satisfy pressing user needs. Users wanted their ink jet printers to print with a near comparable quality to laser printers. The new cartridges allowed the 600 series to print in black at a resolution of 600 dots per inch, and 600 * 300 dots per inch in color. HP also introduced its Resolution Enhancement technology, which manipulates the size of dots to yield smoother curves. Another pressing problem for users was that often the colors printed on paper did not exactly match those seen on the terminal display. HP incorporated into the "600" platform its new ColorSmart technology, which finely balances and tunes color mixing on the printer to match screen colors. All these innovations demonstrate a persistency by management, engineers, and marketers to maintain HP's edge in the technology. Exploiting HP's formidable manufacturing capabilities, the team was also able to bring these printers to market at highly competitive prices yet still maintain healthy margins. Today one can buy a 600C for about $250 and a dual-pen 660C for about a hundred dollars more.

The third and latest ink jet product platform developed by HP is labeled as the "800" platform in Figure 2–2. With this initiative HP targeted the upscale PC market, including the small office market where both faster printing speed and high quality are essential. The new products based on the "800" platform are the 850C and 855C, which sell today for about $500. These printers have almost twice the speed of the 600 series. Meeting the needs of business users, the 800s also have the convenience of a dual-cartridge design and paper trays that can handle 50 percent more paper than HP's other ink jet printers. The 800s can also be hooked up to either a PC or a Macintosh. Not surprisingly, to achieve all these features, the "800" team had to design new mechanics, electronics, and firmware as part of the platform development effort.

Lessons. There are compelling management lessons from HP's ink jet story. First, it is a classic case of managing product development from a product family perspective. The company's strategy has been distinctively *trimodal,* developing derivatives from existing product platforms, enhancing those platforms to address new markets niches or reduce costs, and creating wholly new platforms—*all at the same time.* Management knew that its competitors (such as Epson) would not acquiesce in its efforts to own the market. Therefore, new generations of ink jet printers would always be required at what is now a breathtaking pace. To bring these innovations to market in a timely manner meant that development work had to be started early. This approach to managing platforms has kept HP's ink jet family fresh and competitive, which customers see as a continuous stream of new and increasingly value-rich products.

The second lesson is that HP has embraced state of the art manufacturing for its new platform developments. This has made it possible for the company to operate profitably even in a market where complex machinery had to be sold for under $500, and today, well below that price.

Third, in riding the rapidly growing PC market, HP certainly chose a wonderful market for the application of its technology. One can also argue, however, that HP's ink jet printers created a new wave of demand for desktop printing, bringing excitement to what had been a rather mundane dot matrix business. As we have seen across industry, great products *can often bring new customers into a market.*

GENERALIZING A FRAMEWORK FOR MANAGING THE EVOLUTION OF A PRODUCT FAMILY

Both the HP and the Black & Decker cases suggest a conceptual framework for achieving continued vitality in product families. But first, what do we mean by a "product family"? As stated in the Preface: *A product family is a set of individual products that share common technology and address a related set of market applications.*

From the customer's vantage point, a coherent and well-planned product family is apparent from the physical appearance of the individual member products. Each has a "look" that says, for example, "This machine is a member of Hewlett Parkard's family of ink jet printers." Each has features and user interfaces that make it familiar to users of other product within the family. For example, if you have used the Deskjet 500C, the chances are that you will be able to set up the new Deskjet 600C, install an ink cartridge, and begin printing with barely a glance at the owner's manual.

The earmarks of product families are even more apparent and utilitarian from the producer's vantage point. When products are being developed in coherent families, the company stockroom has far fewer different parts and components. Line changeovers are fewer and faster, because most or all products in a family can be built on the same production line. This, in turn, results in shorter production runs and smaller finished goods inventories. Development costs of derivative products are low, making it economically feasible to produce products for small niche markets.

A general framework for considering the evolution of a product family is shown in Figure 2–4. This pattern of evolution illustrates

FIGURE 2–4

Product Family Evolution, Platform Renewal, and New Product Creation

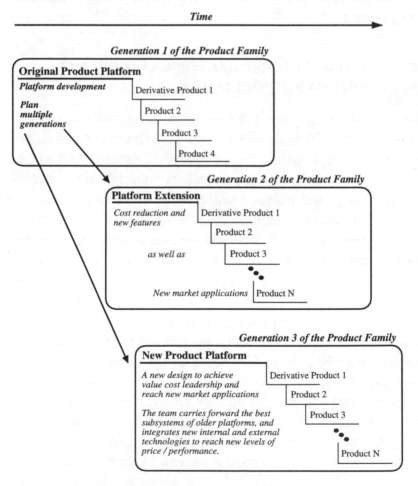

how development work that focuses resources on product platforms can carry a company into the future and across transitions in technology and market needs. The figure represents a single product family starting with the initial development of a product platform, followed by successive major enhancements to the core product and process technology of that platform, with derivative product developments within each generation.

To achieve sustained success in new product development, a firm must continuously renew its platform architectures and their manufacturing processes by integrating advances in core product and process technologies. The advances may be created internally or externally. Renewal is balanced between core product and process technology development, the integration of these technologies into successive generations of product platforms, and the creation of specific derivative products for both existing and emerging market niches. By consistently obsoleting its own products with better ones, the company keeps the heat on its competitors and ensures the perpetuity of the enterprise.

THE POWER TOWER: AN INTEGRATIVE MODEL
FOR MANAGING INNOVATION

Effectively managing the evolution of a product family requires that management consider in collective fashion three essential elements of the enterprise: (1) the market applications of technology, i.e., derivative products made for various customer groups; (2) the company's product platforms; and (3) the common technical and organizational building blocks that are the basis of product platforms.

Figure 2–5 shows how these three components fit together in a second conceptual framework, which we call the "power tower": The common building blocks are the power behind product platforms, and the platforms themselves are the power behind specific products brought to market. Let us consider each component of the framework.

FIGURE 2–5

The Power Tower: An Integrative Model of Product and Process
Innovation

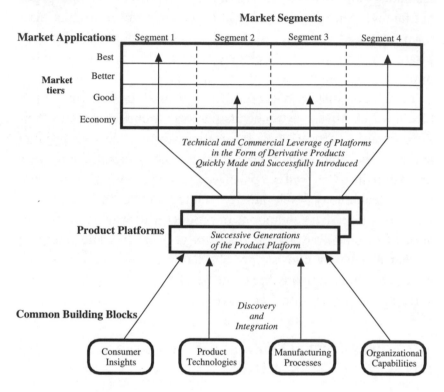

Market Applications

The market for the product family is defined in a traditional way,
i.e., through a matrix of market segments that identify particular
user groups and product price and/or performance characteristics.
The market applications of a product family take the form of derivative products based on product platforms. In the Black & Decker
case, those derivative products were the various power tools that
resulted from the Double Insulation Program. Using a common set
of motors, housings, switches, and so forth, the company was able
to spin out different power tools to address the particular needs of
different market segments: for example, a variable speed drill ver-

sus a variable speed drill with a reverse feature. HP has done the same in its ink jet printers with versions for both low-end and up-scale market segments.

Product Platforms

The term "product platform" has already entered the lexicon of most R&D and product developers, as well as many business executives. Still, we find considerable disagreement within the same company by different individuals on the meaning of platforms. To be clear, we shall repeat our definition from the Preface: *A product platform is a set of subsystems and interfaces that form a common structure from which a stream of derivative products can be efficiently developed and produced.*

For example, the subsystems and interfaces of the universal motor, the armature, and motor the housing constituted the product platform for Black & Decker's line of power tools. Our Figure 2–1 shows the subsystems and interfaces of HP's original ink jet printer platform. Every company must determine precisely the structure of the product platforms suitable for its business. For automobiles, the product platform is generally defined by a combination of chassis, engine, drive train, transmission, and other major subsystems upon which a variety of different models can be based. Honda, for example, has developed its popular Civic, DX, and LX passenger cars from a common platform. In later chapters we shall explore the meaning of platforms for nonphysical products such as software and information products.

The combination of subsystems and interfaces defines the *architecture* of any single product. Every product has an architecture; the goal is to make that architecture common across many products. Any single product's architecture therefore has the potential to become a product platform architecture if it is designed and then used as the basis for creating several more derivative products.

Each subsystem of a product platform has a specific function; when combined, they create a higher form of function for the overall product platform architecture. As we saw in the ink jet printer case, not all subsystems and interfaces are equal in their importance to the evolution of a product line. Some subsystems, if changed, will require changes in many other subsystems; others will have little ripple effect.

Subsystem Interfaces Can Be Strategic. Experience suggests the critical importance of specifying clear interfaces in new product design, standardized to the point where the interfaces may be assigned "part numbers" similar to components. The importance of interfaces is often overlooked, even though they can be the lever for long-term success. Clearly defined interfaces between subsystems of products, and between products and users, provide product designers with the degrees of freedom needed for the rapid and cost-efficient creation of derivative products. This can also translate into clear benefits for users. As we described earlier, part of the genius of HP's ink jet platform design was that it provided a single, common mechanical interface for inserting both the black and the color cartridges.

Industry standard interfaces adds clarity and flexibility. For example, personal computer manufacturers now incorporate a standard interface called PCMCIA[2] for attaching and communicating with peripherals. PCMCIA allows the same computer peripheral to be used, without change, for Intel-based and Macintosh machines.

Industry standard interfaces can be even more powerful when a company has had an active hand in creating them; with a more intimate understanding of the interfaces, its engineers can create products and systems that fully exploit the interface. Sun Microsystems is one of the best examples. Interoperability of its computers over networks has always been a strong selling point for Sun workstations. The company defined and offered a specification for networked file systems in the Unix operating system (called NFS, or networked file system). Its own workstations excelled in a technology that many other manufacturers came to offer in their own products. This story has been replayed now that Sun has developed and licensed to other vendors a software programming language that enables computers to download and execute software over the Internet on demand. This new standard—called JAVA—is sweeping across industry. The Sun story is an inspiring example of enlightened management. The company's leaders recognized the potential discontinuity of the Internet, embraced it, and invented a powerful new technology to exploit it.

Platforms Should Provide Leverage. Product platforms capable of accommodating new component technologies and variations make it possible for firms to create derivative products at incremental cost relative to initial investments in the platform itself. That is possible because the fundamental subsystems and interfaces of the platform are carried forward across derivative products. Since the costs associated with the elements carried forward are essentially sunk costs, only the incremental costs of creating variations to them accrue to the derivatives. Typically, these incremental costs are a small fraction of the cost of developing the original product platform, providing what we call "platform leverage." Product platforms can also improve development cycle times of derivative products by facilitating a more streamlined development process and more frequent model changes.[3]

Platforms Must Be Managed as Evolving Entities. While product platforms form the solid foundation from which many derivative products are developed, they should not be viewed as frozen. Successfully managed product platforms evolve as engineers integrate new market knowledge and technologies into products and manufacturing processes.

Figure 2–6 illustrates changes to product platforms in a general sense. Such changes lead to the successive generations in an evolving product family. In the top part of the figure, the initial version of the product platform comprises the key subsystems (S1, S2, S3) and the interfaces that unite them (the connecting lines). The uni-

FIGURE 2–6

Defining Changes to Product Platforms

Initial Product Platform:
Subsystems and interfaces serving as a common architecture for multiple products

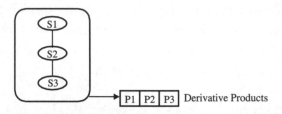

Platform Extensions:
The number and types of subsystems and interfaces remain constant,
but one or more are substantially improved with new technology.

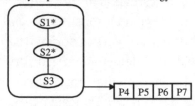

New Product Platforms:
A new architecture, i.e., a new combination of subsystems and interfaces.
Some subsystems and interfaces from prior generations may be carried forward and
combined with new subsystems and interfaces in the new composite platform design.

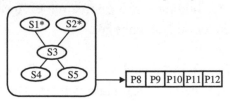

fied product structure, or platform architecture, serves as the foundation for the first generation of derivative products (P1, P2, P3).[4]

A new generation in a product family appears when the platform itself undergoes substantial enhancement (the middle region of Figure 2–6). Here, the *number and types* of subsystems and interfaces remain constant, but one or more undergo major revision (as indicated by the asterisks in Figure 2–6).. In computers, manufacturers have created ongoing generations of their basic PC families by incorporating successively more powerful microprocessors and upgrading their operating systems with new versions of Microsoft Windows.

An entirely new platform emerges only when its basic architecture—its subsystems and interfaces—changes. That is shown in the bottom region of Figure 2–6. In such "platform renewals," subsystems and interfaces from prior generations may be carried forward into the new design but are joined by entirely new subsystems and interfaces.

The Sony Walkman provides a powerful example of the generational changes that can occur within a single product platform. More than 160 variations of the Walkman were introduced from 1980 to 1990.[5] Beneath the surface of these was a robust product platform. Over time, Sony refreshed the platform with technical innovations, each addressing a major subsystem of the product: a miniature stereo headphone; a super-flat motor; an improved tape drive; and, lastly, rechargeable nickel-cadmium batteries. Each of the subsystem enhancements defined a new generation of the Walkman family. Sony engineers exploited this evolving product platform, creating a Walkman derivative on the average of one every month for a period of eleven years.

Manufacturing and Platform Design. A product platform also incorporates the manufacturing or production aspects of a product family. This includes the technologies, facilities, and processes used to produce a firm's products. For an assembled product, the process elements of a product platform include the stages of producing or sourcing of components (with intermediate testing processes), assembly of the components into the product, and final product testing. Nonassembled products such as materials and petrochemicals, in particular, require the creation and renewal of process platforms for sustained success. Consider Gillette's sensor razor cartridge, where a key challenge was to develop highly automated, fault-free manufacturing.

The Common Building Blocks: The Fuel for Product Platforms

A product platform may appear to be the bedrock of a family of products, but dig deeper and you will find that robust product platforms are themselves based on a number of building blocks. We categorize these building blocks into four general areas:

1. insights into the minds and needs of customers and the processes of customer and competitive research that uncover and validate those insights
2. product technologies in components, materials, subsystem interfaces, and development tools
3. manufacturing processes and technologies that make it possible for the product to meet competitive requirements for cost, volume, and quality
4. organizational capabilities, which include infrastructures for distribution and customer support, as well as information systems for control and market feedback

Greater power in product development can be achieved if these building blocks are leveraged across the product platforms of different product lines. For example, Intel's advances in microprocessors are leveraged into new versions of its servers and super computers. HP has created an integrated fax-printer-scanner-copier machine that utilizes technologies from across the corporation. Likewise, L. L. Bean applies its formidable organizational capabilities in the areas of consumer analysis, market segmentation, mail order merchandising, and information systems to deliver a wide variety of outdoor goods and clothing in a series of printed catalogs and an on-line catalog.

Many firms fail to leverage their capabilities across product lines. If one considers the diversified businesses of most large organizations, one finds that core technologies are typically not shared. In the customers' eyes, the products are neither related nor compatible.

Customer Insights. As a foundation of product platforms, intimate knowledge of customer needs is every bit as important as breakthrough technology. Fortunately, marketers have many techniques for determining customer needs, perceptions, and preferences.[6] Conjoint analysis, for example, asks representative customers to make tradeoffs between features and price points for different product models. However, this knowledge cannot be the exclusive property of marketers but is needed organizationwide. No one function within the enterprise can be allowed to "own the customer."

Customer needs fall into one of two categories: perceived, and unperceived or *latent*. The first represents those needs that users themselves are capable of articulating. The discovery of latent needs often takes place outside the realm of traditional marketing research. Frequently engineers are themselves the innovative *lead-users*.

A very simple but powerful process for uncovering latent needs—one that the reader may use on a product line in his or her own company—is as follows: *Imagine that you are the product; then think about how you, as the product, frustrate your users.* This simple exercise can produce powerful insights into how a more satisfying and pleasurable experience can be provided to the user. Those insights can then be validated with the techniques of market research.

The discovery of latent needs in existing or emerging markets should be a goal for R&D as well as marketing. Absent this objective, companies spend the majority of resources on "me too" products or incremental improvements to existing ones. Further, we find that too often the junior marketing staff is assigned to product development teams, be they single-product efforts or more ambitious platform initiatives. The "big guns" of marketing are off doing strategic planning, visiting customers, or closing distribution deals—standing aloof from the critical details of new product design. Their insights and experiences are sorely missed.

Product Technologies. The term "technology" has different meanings for different people. We think of technology as the implementation of knowledge with the potential to be incorporated into a product or service. Product technology takes many forms: chemistries, programming languages and algorithms, hardware or logic design, and so forth. One level up from those basic technologies are actual implementations of proprietary knowledge and skills in the form, for example, of chemicals, materials, software modules, or chips. Such implementations should be considered as essential components within the subsystems of product platforms. Product technologies also include subsystem interfaces, be they proprietary connections or those based on *de facto* or regulatory imposed standards.

Rapid platform development and renewal are facilitated by ongoing research that advances the state of basic technologies. Those advances can then be integrated into new platform designs. "Integration" is the operative word. Just as derivative products should be rapidly developed through incremental improvements to existing product platforms, new platforms should themselves be created by integrating complete component technologies, either from the firm itself or from external suppliers. To make platform renewal work, senior management must invest in the basic research and development of technology building blocks, as well as specific product development.

Consider 3M's Post It. The long-term research was on the backside adhesive; the "platform" development was on the manufacturing processes for coating paper with that adhesive; and incremental refinements have come in the different sizes and colors of Post Its. All three categories of technical work were required for success.

Essential product technologies may come from sources external to the firm. Thomas Allen, a professor at the Massachusetts Institute of Technology, has studied the communications patterns of R&D lab workers and has found that the most successful R&D groups include individuals who spend as much time communicating outside as inside the company. Such individuals search for new technologies, participate in the definition of industry standards, and bring to the lab a wealth of competitive information.[7] Management should therefore encourage engineers to search the world aggressively for breakthroughs in core technologies that may prove useful for their own product designs and manufacturing processes. "Getting to work" should also mean "getting out there" to find new approaches and breakthrough technologies that can help improve the company's products and services.

The Black & Decker case exemplifies the role of external discovery. Loctite was the adhesive that made it possible to automate armature manufacturing. Loctite's salespersons did not come knocking on Black & Decker's door; instead, the development team discovered Loctite's existence and tested its utility for their particular application.

Manufacturing Technologies. Manufacturing technologies can be as critical to the creation of powerful product platforms as the component technologies around which they are designed. In many industries—glass, refining, and so forth—the firms with the best manufacturing technologies are the clear winners. For those industries, *the process is the platform.* For a host of other industries, manufacturing is on a par with product technology in terms of creating successful product platforms.

For both assembled and nonassembled products, the tendency is to consider evolution of the process elements of a product platform as increasing volume or capacity. However, the evolution of manufacturing processes also represents an opportunity for innovation. A lack of innovation or flexibility built into the production process constrains the variety of product versions that can be derived from the basic process.[8] Flexible manufacturing has enormous implications for the design of plant and equipment, patterns of resource allocation, and the range of product variety that a company can bring to the market.

Organizational Capabilities. Organizational capabilities are the last of our common building blocks. In the context of new products and services, those capabilities include distribution, customer support, and information systems. Firms must have strong channels through which to distribute their products or services—either as a proprietary capability or through channel partners. Lacking well-developed channels between the company and customers, even the best products will sit on the shelf. For many firms, particularly those in consumer markets, *packaging* is a distinct focus of achieving competitive advantage and lies at the intersection between product design and distribution. Likewise, customer support must be available both to help customers get the full value of the firm's products and as a listening post for gathering customer insights. Remote diagnostics built into industrial and medical equipment are but one example of how product design can be used to facilitate and improve customer support. Finally, information systems are needed to capture and share the right information with the people who need it. In many industries, such as financial services, publishing, and merchandising, information is among the most valuable assets of an enterprise.

Companies might wish to consider their managements and planning processes as an essential organizational capability, too. For example, to company insiders "HP" stands for "Heavy Planning," as witnessed by five-year product family planning that is annually redone and reviewed by senior management. Lacking such planning, we doubt that the company would have robust product platforms or commercially successful derivative products.

These various organizational capabilities each have the potential to make a substantive contribution to the success of new generations of an evolving product family. They are clearly part of the mix.

THE BLACK & DECKER POWER TOWER

Having described the market applications, platforms, and common building blocks that make up the "power tower," we can see its practical application through the Black & Decker case described in Chapter 1. As shown in Figure 2–7, the company's product platforms for drills, saws, sanders, and so forth comprised common subsystems and specific design rules for making them. From the

FIGURE 2–7

Black & Decker's Power Tower

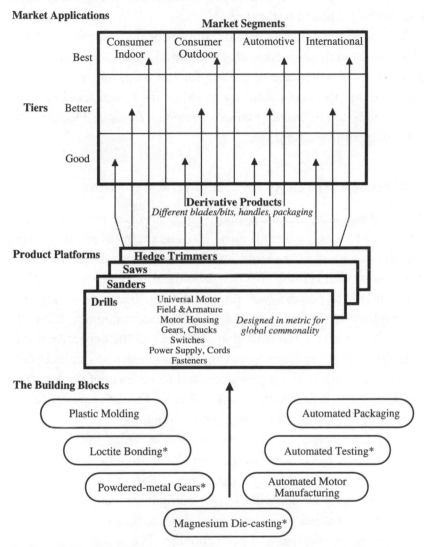

Market Applications

Market Segments

| | Consumer Indoor | Consumer Outdoor | Automotive | International |

Tiers Best / Better / Good

Derivative Products
Different blades/bits, handles, packaging

Product Platforms

Hedge Trimmers

Saws

Sanders

Drills

Universal Motor
Field & Armature
Motor Housing
Gears, Chucks
Switches
Power Supply, Cords
Fasteners

Designed in metric for global commonality

The Building Blocks

Plastic Molding

Loctite Bonding*

Powdered-metal Gears*

Automated Packaging

Automated Testing*

Automated Motor Manufacturing

Magnesium Die-casting*

*Indicates new to the industry.

platforms, derivative products were efficiently developed to serve the consumer division's principal market segments: indoor, outdoor, automotive, and international. "Good," "better," and "best" versions of many derivatives were introduced. The result was a high level of product variety targeting the needs of many market niches. Beneath the surface of this variety, however, was a small number of parts and packaging.

The common building blocks supporting the double-insulated platform were product technologies, materials, and manufacturing processes. All were state of the art for the time, and several were new to either the manufacturing world or the power tool industry. Collectively, these building blocks provided Black & Decker with clear competitive advantages.

THE POWER TOWER AS A SYSTEM FOR MANAGING

The power tower does more than simply describe the structure of evolving product families. It also serves as the intellectual foundation for a system of research and product development management—one that is more effective than the traditional tools used by executives. The power tower elevates executive attention from single products to the broader dynamics of product families. It directs energy and focus to the market applications of the derivative products the executives hope to create, to planning the product platforms that support those products, and to renewal of the building blocks on which future platforms will rest. Thus, the power tower is an integrative tool for thinking and managing.

We are now ready to move on to specific "rules and tools" that will transform the power tower framework into a process for reinvigorating your company's product lines. Chapter 3 addresses platform strategy—in particular how companies can use product platforms to extend their reach into new market segments and at different levels of price and performance. The ability to do so, of course, requires that the platforms be elegant in their design, capable of providing the functionality that users need, and sufficiently robust to accommodate variations for different customer groups. We address these issues in Chapter 4 through the methods of "composite design." Chapter 5 then explains how companies can organize those efforts for the best results.

Over the years companies have developed metrics for product development performance. Unfortunately, these are more suited for single-product, technology, or project assessment than for common platforms and their families of derivative products. Chapter 6 provides a novel set of metrics that give executives a practical handle on performance from a product family perspective.

Product development literature is heavily oriented toward assembled, physical products such as computers and automobiles. This, unfortunately, ignores the large and growing sector of the economy that produces nonphysical goods and services. Chapters 7 and 8 extend our platform and product family principles to two nontraditional areas: software and on-line information products. Chapter 9 will then summarize all of these chapters within the context of a process that corporations can use to plan and manage their new product development more effectively.

3

Platform Strategy

B uilding robust product platforms can be a market domination
strategy and can provide access to new markets. Formulating
this type of strategy is our focus in this chapter.

New product strategy is as much a mindset as a process, a fact
often lost as small companies grow larger over time. New companies are generally started when a small groups of founders discover
the "Aha!" of a new product or service. The founders of fledgling
companies maintain a hand in all important activities: new product
design, manufacturing, distribution, and customer service. Initially
those functions remain focused on products and customers, creating the company's first product family. As growth continues, however, product portfolios expand and may diversify into new
technologies and markets. A functional division of labor may also
take form, where R&D, manufacturing, sales, service, and other
functions find themselves in separate departments, in separate
buildings, and often in different cities.

Diversification is often unplanned; products and product lines
are added one product at a time and without the benefit of overar-
ching strategic principles. Typically, the additional products create
greater complexity in manufacturing, procurement, and distribution, and the attention of senior managers is consumed in manag-

ing that complexity. Once senior managers lose touch with the development of new products, new product strategy is guided by the initiatives of middle managers. The notion of a centrally rationalized product strategy guided by the top executives gets lost in the bureaucracy.

Senior managers sense their feel for the business slipping away and respond with various processes to maintain the semblance of order and control: approval committees, stage-gates, and procedural rules of various types. Unfortunately, many such measures merely reinforce the bureaucracy and make the important business of product development slower and more difficult. In such an environment it is very difficult for executives, entrepreneurial middle managers, or innovative employees to marshal the energy and resources needed to introduce common subsystems and manufacturing processes across the corporation.

To be fast-moving, to achieve competitive excellence in technology, and to leverage common assets between individual products, corporations need to recapture the entrepreneurial vigor of their early years. Platform strategy is a tool that can help them do so, serving as *a top-down planning approach to maximize market leverage from common technology.*

IDENTIFYING EXISTING PLATFORM STRATEGIES

Figure 3–1 recaps the market segmentation level of the conceptual framework developed in the previous chapter. We use a "platform-market grid" to consider a number of generic platform strategies. You may find it useful to think conceptually about your own product platforms in terms of a similar grid. Here, major market segments are arrayed horizontally, each representing the principal customer groups served by your products. In the Black & Decker power tools case, the two major market segments were consumer and professional users, with subgroups within them. HP's ink jet printers' market segments include the desktop PC user, the portable computer user, and the upscale home office or small busi-

FIGURE 3–1

Market Segmentation Grid

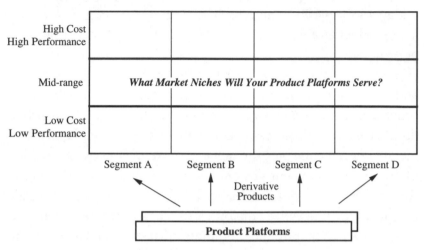

ness user. A company that makes air conditioners may have segments that include residential indoor systems, residential outdoor systems, and commercial systems.

The vertical axis of the market segmentation grid reflects different tiers of price and performance. In the figure, we use the terms "low cost, mid-range, and high cost"; many companies prefer the words "good, better, and best." Either way, stepup functions in product lines ordinarily command higher prices over base level models.

Car manufacturers typically use engine horsepower, seat materials, and other amenities to distinguish performance and pricing tiers in their product lines. For Black & Decker, a $50 drill offers variable speeds, antikickback, reverse drilling, and higher wattage, whereas a $20 drill has a single speed and lower power. Personal computers provide stepup functionality through faster microprocessors, greater memory, and larger or faster disk drives. It is rare to find a mature business without stepup functions in its product lines; the trick is to rationalize them into a consistent gradation of price-performance, as these are required to clearly plan how and where platforms will be scaled and leveraged into different regions of your market. The cells formed by the intersection of the horizontal and vertical axes are market niches.

The next step is to identify where the product family's main product platforms compete on this grid and how they might be improved to serve a variety of market niches. First, let us consider platform strategies in the context of the market segmentation grid, and the business implications of these strategies.

Strategy 1: Niche-specific Platforms with Little Sharing of Subsystems and Manufacturing Processes

Dearborn, Michigan, March 1996. Two years into a major reorganization, Ford Motor Company announced plans to radically alter its product development activities. The centerpiece of its plan was to reduce the number of vehicle platforms from twenty-four to sixteen. Many observers noted that Ford's product development activities were terribly complex and that the reduction would save the company enormous sums of money and make its dealings with suppliers less difficult, even as it would provide the means to design and manufacture a multitude of vehicle types and models for the company's global markets. "What we are striving for," one person familiar with auto maker's plans said, "is under-the-skin commonality, and more vehicle products."[1]

Platform strategy can be used to simplify portfolios. Like Ford, many companies suffer from having too many platforms, sharing too little technology. Each market niche is served by a different platform architecture. The result is a myriad of product families, with few shared subsystems or manufacturing technologies, higher costs, and lower margins. That strategy typically creates products that look and feel very different to the customer.

Figure 3–2 shows a fragmented platform strategy for a manufacturer focused on high-end and mid-range market niches. Here, low-end niches are left uncovered, creating tempting targets for offshore manufacturers. For this company, each product develop-

FIGURE 3–2

Niche-specific Platforms with Little Sharing of Subsystems and Manufacturing Processes

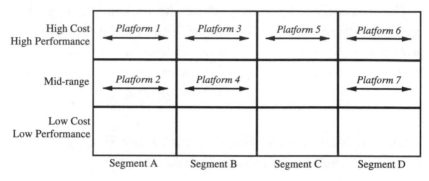

ment group and manufacturing plant is totally focused and dedicated to serving the needs of a very specific niche. While such a strategy may have its benefits, it can be a very expensive way to do business. R&D can easily be duplicated, and discoveries made by one team may remain unknown to other groups. Capital investments in manufacturing would be expected to be far higher than if production capacity were shared between product lines. Fundamental improvements to manufacturing introduced by one group may not be adopted by others. Lastly, the potential for synergy in market development between product lines, i.e., a common brand supported by shared advertising and promotional campaigns, is largely forgone.

Unfortunately, this fragmented platform approach is common in industry. Seeking to build the perfect product for each new customer group, engineers lead the corporation away from commonality. Each time a new customer request is formalized, new parts are added to achieve the optimum solution without consideration of the downstream costs of the decision. The engineer, or the engineering manager, rarely gets wind of those costs. As the components of the firm's products proliferate—be they motors, fasteners, or whatever—opportunities to achieve economies in procurement diminish.

Component variety also makes manufacturing unnecessarily complex. Each plant, focused on making particular product lines, becomes enamored with its own processes, machines, and materials, and enjoys the liberty to pursue its own initiatives. Substantial changes to processes or materials fly in the face of existing plant and equipment and the need to amortize the investment in them.

Strategy 2: Horizontal Leverage of Key Platform Subsystems and Manufacturing Processes

An alternative strategy is one in which a product platform, or one of its key elements, is leveraged from one market niche to the next within a given tier of price-performance. A representation of this horizontal leverage platform strategy is shown in Figure 3–3. The figure also shows the two basic variations of the strategy, based on the tier of price-performance that is the company's primary focus. Many companies have successfully leveraged product platforms from one premium market segment to the next. For example, the A. T. Cross Company leverages common components and manufacturing processes across its high-end pen product lines.[2] In contrast to these high-end players, other companies have successfully leveraged their platforms across a related set of low-end market seg-

FIGURE 3–3

Horizontal Platform Leverage

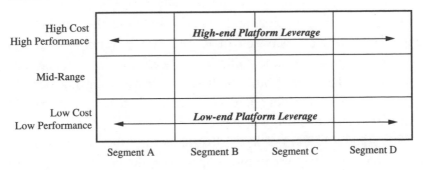

ments. Pentel is the counterexample to Cross, branching across different segments in the low-end of the writing instrument market with common product platforms and manufacturing processes.

Either way, the benefit of the horizontal leverage strategy is that a company introduces streams of new products across a series of related customer groups without having to reinvent the wheel for each group. The primary benefit for R&D is that new products can be developed more rapidly. Further, if particular subsystems can be designed to provide a distinctive functional advantage over competitors, the entire product family will benefit. Manufacturing, procurement, and retooling costs can be minimized when new products are introduced into the line.

Leverage can be achieved even if the platform *as a whole* is not used in adjacent segments. Key subsystems of the platform not only will suffice, but are the most common form of horizontal leverage of common technology. We saw this, for example, in the universal motor used across Black & Decker's power tool groups, and in the ink cartridge used in HP's ink jet printers.

Leverage occurs to the degree that the major subsystems of a product platform are adapted for use within different market segments. Figure 3–4 presents this concept. Within a given tier of price-performance, a number of major subsystems are adapted for use in a second market segment. This is a classic extension of a particular product platform into a new market segment where one subsystem, noted as S5 in the figure, is replaced with S6 to meet customer requirements. All other subsystems are adapted to the new market application. Consider the Gillette Sensor-Excel razor systems. The shape, color, and general design of the handles are completely different between male and female versions, but the razor cartridge is the same. Gillette has been able to use those cartridges as a key lever point, both for improving shaving performance and for achieving low costs through a common, highly automated manufacturing process.

The standardization of key subsystems (and their components) across a product family can thus improve product performance and

FIGURE 3-4

Reusing Subsystems Across Market Segments

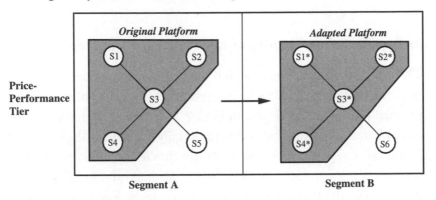

*Subsystem adapted, enhanced to serve new market application.

reduce costs. The horizontal leverage concept applies as well to nonmanufacturers. For example, in software companies, crucial modules containing decision-making algorithms or user interfaces are often leveraged across a range of customer groups. Financial services organizations likewise have successfully applied common approaches to risk management for different types of risks encountered in various financial product categories, including loans, insurance, and financial instruments.

Horizontal leverage is not risk-free. If the platform or any of its key subsystems are flawed, then a broader array of products will feel the pain. Also, responsibility for platform renewal can become problematical if each market segment is "owned" by a different business unit—a common circumstance in many corporations. We observe, for example, that separate business control of different international markets is the norm for global enterprises. That tends to produce a diversity of platforms, subsystems, and manufacturing processes in different regions—even within single product categories. Who would force one business unit owner to accept, and thus depend on, platform technology coming from another business unit? However, if analysis finds the opportunities offered by sharing platforms between groups to be compelling, executives are obliged to revisit the organization and integrate different business units.

Strategy 3: Vertical Scaling of Key Platform Subsystems

This third strategy is one in which the firm seeks to address a range of price-performance tiers within a market segment with common product platforms. As shown in Figure 3–5, one basic variation occurs when a company that has traditionally excelled in the high end of a market segment scales its platform down into lower price-performance tiers. In its simplest form, certain functionality is removed from the high-end product set to achieve lower price points for customers, or else major subsystems from the high-end platform are used in a distinct low-end platform design.

A second basic variation of vertical scaling is when low-end product platforms are scaled upward into higher price-performance tiers through the addition of more powerful component technologies or new modules to meet the demands of functionality and performance for higher level market tiers.

FIGURE 3–5

Vertical Platform Scaling: Two Variations

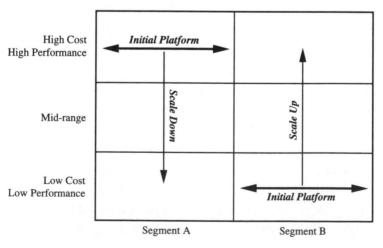

The benefit of this approach to vertical platform scaling is that the firm is able to leverage its knowledge of any particular market segment, and to do so through product development that will be less costly than if an entirely new platform had to be developed for each tier of price-performance. Once again, the risk is that a weak common platform or weak common subsystems will undermine the competitiveness of the entire product line.

A number of companies pursue both types of vertical platform scaling described above. Is one preferable to the other in terms of product development effectiveness and cost? Many American companies with strong engineering cultures have a tradition of building high-powered solutions. Meeting the needs of high-end segments is perceived as the greatest challenge for engineers. However, growth in markets invariably shifts downward over time into mid-range and lower price-performance tiers. Engineers go to work to serve those growth areas. What they typically find, however, is that it is not so easy to turn a Lexus into a Civic. The expensive componentry or materials of the high-end platform condemn the new lower-priced products to low levels of profitability.

Manufacturers supplying medical equipment to the domestic health care industry provide an excellent contemporary example. Many such suppliers have historically developed high-end platforms and have scaled them down to mid-range or lower tier niches. Fee-for-service remuneration for health care once provided hospitals and physicians with the luxury to buy premium products. In the age of cost containment, however, budgets for new equipment purchases are severely constrained. Hospitals and physicians still need value-rich products, but at substantially lower prices. As a result, the highest growth areas for many manufacturers making medical equipment has shifted from high-end niches to the mid-range tiers of their respective market segments, challenging their traditional competencies and product offerings.

In response to that market discontinuity, several leading medical equipment suppliers have redesigned their platforms to address the lower price-performance tiers first. Armed with modular platform designs, those firms have added stepup functions to their entry-level products to create higher cost "flagship" products for those hospitals and physicians that can still afford the price. They have replaced special purpose componentry with general purpose components and have reworked their manufacturing processes to achieve cost efficiencies. We like to think of this approach to platform renewal as following the "sweet spot" of the market, characterized in Figure 3–6, where technical competencies are leveraged into new platforms for niches experiencing the highest rates of growth.

The goal of this strategy is to achieve healthy margins in all members of the product family, even those in low price-performance niches. That may best be achieved by first building platforms that can profitably serve low-end requirements. Then, with modular and flexible platform designs in hand, the company can scale upward into the higher market tiers, adding more powerful subsystems, better materials, and so forth. Making money in the lower price-performance tiers of the platform-market grid requires that engineers embrace this goal as a starting point in their platform designs.

FIGURE 3–6

Following the Sweet Spot of the Market

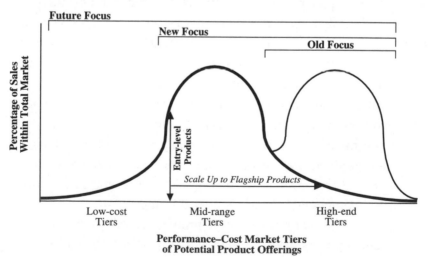

THE BEACHHEAD STRATEGY:
HORIZONTAL LEVERAGE AND VERTICAL SCALING

The power of platforms becomes all the more significant when horizontal leverage is combined with upward vertical scaling. One might call this the "beachhead strategy" (see Figure 3–7). Here, the company develops a low-cost but effective platform, and the processes for making it efficiently, for one particular segment of low-end users. From that initial market foothold, engineers then scale up the performance characteristics of the platform and add other features designed to appeal to the needs of other segments. Extensions are made to the initial platform to make it ideal for different segments; extensions are also made to provide the stepup functions required by customers in higher price-performance tiers within market segments. Leverage in creating the derivative products, and the low-cost manufacturing process developed to compete in the initial market, make it possible for the company to enter the new market niches from a superior cost position.

FIGURE 3–7

The Beachhead Strategy: Horizontal Leverage and
Vertical Scaling

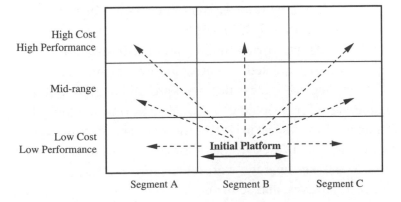

Compaq Computers

Compaq Computer Corporation provides a noteworthy example of the beachhead strategy. Compaq entered the personal computer business in 1982 with a line of portable computers and quickly established a strong foothold in that niche, surpassing $300 million in annual sales within two short years. From that base, the company introduced a stream of new products for other market segments and at many levels of price and performance, beginning with a line of desktop PCs, the Compaq Deskpro series. Sales grew apace. By 1988 annual revenues had reached $2 billion, and by year-end 1995 Compaq could boast sales nearing $15 billion, with earnings of almost $800 million.[3] Yet, despite its sales growth and abundance of product variety, Compaq's 1995 R&D spending was about 2 percent of sales.

A key source of Compaq's success was its ability to leverage platforms and key subsystems across different market niches. The initial desktop PC product platform was developed for the Deskpro line in the early 1980s and was targeted at the corporate microcomputer market, especially for networked PC environments. Figure 3–8 shows that the market focus of this platform was in the low-end tier of the corporate and small business market. Numerous derivative products were created from the Deskpro platform, including a server called the Compaq Systempro. (Servers are used as the hubs for sharing printers, storing data and programs in local area networks.) The Deskpro platform itself was upgraded throughout the 1980s with faster microprocessors, new memory components, and improved electronics.

The early 1990s was a rich time of product innovation within Compaq. Engineers created a new platform architecture that would not only replace the existing Deskpro architecture but also serve as the basis for a number of other platforms serving other market niches. Introduced in 1991, the new architecture had a highly modular, "open" design that allowed both Compaq and its customers to quickly upgrade with more memory, faster processors, bigger disk drives, and so forth.

FIGURE 3-8

Compaq's Platform Market Grid

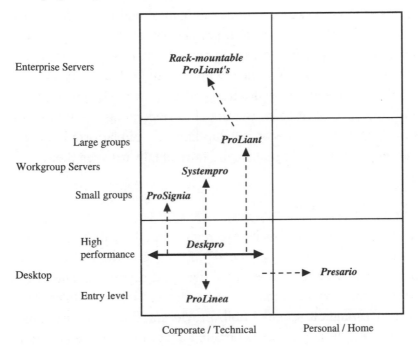

With the rebirth of Deskpro, Compaq aggressively created new platforms that made heavy use of Deskpro platform subsystems. First, certain networking features of the Deskpro were removed to create the Compaq ProLinea platform, targeting the stand-alone market found in small businesses and the home. The Pro-Linea platform was itself improved and leveraged horizontally to create a platform ideally suited for the home market: the Presario line.

Vertical scaling of the Deskpro's subsystems was accomplished at the same time with the goal of creating a new, more powerful server platform for the corporate market: the Compaq ProLiant platform. ProLiant machines could support multiple microprocessors "inside the box." A scaled-down version of the ProLiant platform, branded as the Compaq ProSignia, targeted the fast-growing

market of small workgroups of thirty or fewer computers connected to a server.

Recently Compaq took aim at the highest end of the corporate
market. Using the ProLiant as a key subsystem, the company created a system that allowed rack-mounted versions of the ProLiant
to be stacked together. A sufficient number of ProLiant servers integrated in this manner provides tremendous power with greater flexibility and lower cost than traditional large computer solutions. In
sum, Compaq represents an outstanding case of platform leverage,
both vertically within segments and horizontally between them.

Hon Furniture Company

We need not confine ourselves to high technology to find companies that have used a "beachhead" along the bottom of the platform-market grid to invade other tiers and segments. The office
furniture industry, dominated by Steelcase, Herman Miller, Ha-
worth, Westinghouse, and Knoll, provides a "low-tech" example.
For decades, these producers targeted either the premium or mid-
level market tiers, leaving the low-end market largely uncovered.

Hon had been an also-ran in the office furniture business for a
number of years. During the 1990s, however, Hon made itself into
a formidable competitor by addressing the needs of the lower-tier
market with products based upon low-cost, modular platform architectures and highly efficient manufacturing processes. At the
same time, it developed distribution capabilities for serving that
broad market. Figure 3–9 shows Hon's platform strategy in comparison with those of the traditional market leaders.

Hon's platform strategy translated into strong earnings from
what many would have thought to be a low-margin business. It
used those earnings to expand its beachhead, acquiring a select
group of office furniture companies already entrenched in the mid-
range and premium office furniture niches with well-known
brands. With those acquired brands , Hon broke out of the low-end

FIGURE 3–9

Office Furniture Platform Market Grid

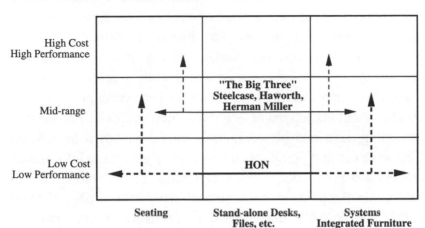

segments and started to penetrate upscale furniture niches. Hon used its low-end capabilities to revitalize the acquired brands with greater modularity and lower-cost manufacturing. The results to date have been impressive. Ten years ago, Hon was number twelve in the domestic market. Today, it is number four.

Making Money in the High End: EMC

It would be naïve to think that establishing a beachhead in low price-performance tiers is the only path to success. Companies that have focused on upper market tiers have likewise enjoyed success with platform-based strategies.

Let us consider EMC Corporation, a leading manufacturer of large-scale storage systems for computers. Started in 1979 by Richard Egan and Roger Marino, the company spent about a decade producing add-in memory products for minicomputers. One of its successes in its early years was a product line of 64KB chip memory boards for Prime and Hewlett Packard minicomputers. During the mid-1980s EMC also began producing disk controller systems for minicomputers. By the close of the decade, the company was approaching $200 million in sales.

The year 1990 marked a point of departure for EMC. It's engineers wheeled out a new product line to the launching pad—Symmetrix. This product family offered large-scale storage systems for IBM mainframes. At that time the mainframe storage market was approximately $5 billion in total revenue, and IBM claimed about 90 percent of it. EMC's then senior vice president of marketing described his company's marketing thrust as follows: "We were the first company to come along and show information officers that not all data was created equal. Some needed fast access rather than 100 percent fault tolerance."[4] The goal of Symmetrix was to offer unparalleled performance in the speed of accessing information, which it would do by integrating EMC's proprietary software technology with commodity components.

Behind the new Symmetrix product family was a robust product platform. The two key pillars of this platform are EMC's ICDA (Integrated Cache Disk Arrays—the storage subsystem) and MOSAIC:2000 (the overall platform architecture). The beauty of the platform architecture was that it allowed for more disks to be flexibly added to an EMC storage system to increase capacity. Users could also swap in different controller boards that would, for example, make the system work with various network protocols. This allowed different types of computers and networks to be easily linked to the same storage system. Customers therefore enjoyed the great convenience of being able to adapt their storage system to new types computers placed onto their network over time.

When EMC first entered the mainframe storage system business with Symmetrix in 1990, its existing competitors (chiefly IBM) were trying to achieve performance largely through specialized hardware components, namely proprietary 14-inch disks called SLEDs (single large expensive disks). EMC's approach was radically different. University research had been exploring the use of RAID technology (redundant arrays of inexpensive disks).[5] EMC's management saw RAID as a great opportunity to beat SLED storage systems in both performance and cost.

First, EMC engineers designed a platform that would use arrays of 5.25-inch disks, which were widely available from suppliers. This reduced materials cost. Second, the engineers coupled the small disks with solid-state memory used as cache in the front end of the storage system. Third—perhaps EMC's greatest point of value added—the engineers developed highly intelligent software, known as caching algorithms, that not only accessed the most recently used data but could also anticipate what data were most likely to be accessed next based on analysis of prior usage. Fourth, EMC also incorporated technology into its platform that allowed components such as disks or controller boards to be swapped in and out of its systems while the machines were still running. These then were the major building blocks: arrays of small disks, cache memory, caching algorithms, and hot-swappable componentry. Their integration resulted in a highly modular and flexible platform architecture—the MOSAIC:2000 referred to above—that allowed EMC's storage systems to be expanded as customers' needs changed.

The modularity of the Symmetrix platform allowed EMC to offer stepup functionality from its entry-level systems in a series of ever more powerful systems. At the time of this writing, the company was selling a series of entry-level mainframe storage products—the 5100s; a series of mid-range systems for mainframes—the 5200s; and high-end mainframe storage systems—the 5500s, which themselves had terabyte storage capacity. Over the past five years EMC's engineers substantially improved the performance of its Symmetrix systems. The company recently announced a 58 percent increase in the access speed of its high-end Symmetrix 5500s.

These systems have been EMC's biggest money-maker. Rather than try to undercut IBM's prices, EMC sold the systems at a 25 percent price premium over IBM's price levels. The distinctive performance of the systems supported that premium. By 1992 sales of the Symmetrix line started to accelerate. The company's share of the mainframe storage systems market had grown to 5 percent on sales of $386 million. Over the next several years, EMC proceeded to turn the industry upside down. By the close of 1994 the company commanded a 40 percent market share. At the close of 1995 its revenues had grown by 39 percent over the prior year to $1.9 billion, with net income of $256 million. The adaptation of mainframes as high-capacity "servers" for the Internet or internal corporate "Intranets" promises continued growth for this product line. As noted by one industry observer, "EMC understood they could leverage their engineering strength in solid-state memory into everyday storage needs by putting [disk] array technology behind it. They could take the commodity 5.25″ disk, combine it with a solid-state control unit, and provide enough cache memory to give customers a product that would boast nearly solid-state data-retrieval speeds—clobbering the electromechanical speed of SLED's."[6]

In 1994 EMC introduced a second product family, the Harmonix line, targeting the AS/400 market. AS/400s are IBM's midrange computers. At the end of 1995 AS/400s retained the second highest dollar installed base in the computing industry. Following the general platform approach, EMC created Harmonix by using its MOSAIC:2000 architecture and adopting many of the key subsystems that had been developed for the Symmetrix line. To that base of technology EMC then added specific software modules and electronics tailored for the AS/400 environment. Within our frameworks, the Harmonix family was a classic platform extension of Symmetrix.

Also in 1994, EMC introduced storage systems that addressed the "open systems" market (computers running nonproprietary operating systems, such as Unix). Once again using the existing general platform architecture and many of the key subsystems from Symmetrix, this new line—called Centriplex—could serve as the central data repository for the RISC-based workstations of IBM, HP, DEC, and Sun Microsystems, among others. Additionally, PCs running Windows NT or OS/2 could also be hooked up to Centriplex. At the time of this writing EMC is also reintegrating the specialized software and electronics of its open systems storage units back into its core Symmetrix products. In other words, EMC intends Symmetrix to be a one-stop source for all the centralized storage needs of the new heterogeneous computing environment.

EMC is a phenomenally successful case of a company that first established a platform beachhead in a high-end market niche, then leveraged its platform into both mid-range niches and entirely new market segments. We show EMC's platform strategy in Figure 3–10. The power of its product platform has led to a decisive victory in what had long been considered the turf of IBM, Amdahl, and Hitachi. These competitors have been hindered in their collective response to EMC by a number of factors: the need to use internally made components, a bias toward the "big" project, and

FIGURE 3–10

EMC's Platform Market Grid

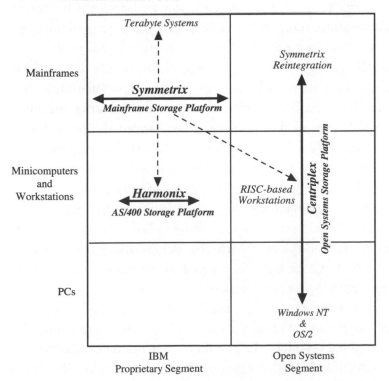

time delays associated with large bureaucracies. One smaller competitor, Storage Tek, has adopted an architectural approach similar to EMC's and is seeking to gain competitive distinctiveness in its own RAID technology. However, EMC is clearly not standing still. It continues to advance the capacity and speed of its products, to improve the underlying building blocks of the platform, and to leverage it into new, emerging market applications on the information superhighway.

More generally, the history of EMC shows that by taking the time to thoughtfully develop robust product platforms—platforms that offer unparalleled value to customers through new technical approaches—entrepreneurs can indeed take on the giants in their respective industries.

RETAKING THE LOW GROUND

Many companies leave the low-cost, low-performance niches of their markets uncovered. If the "sweet spot" for your own business is not yet in the lower tiers, be forewarned that someday some new entrant will figure out how to operate profitably in that region. That is precisely what happened in the traditional office furniture market, which Hon invaded with low-cost, low-performance products for the Spartan-minded office user. It has happened time and time again through industrial history, whether it was Volkswagen introducing the Beetle to fill the uncovered low market need or later, Honda and Toyota. Brother did the same thing in electronics, while IBM and other manufacturers were focusing on higher-end niches. It was also Timex's early claim to fame, followed later by Casio. What threatens mid-range to high-cost tier producers, of course, is that these low-end manufacturers just might scale up their platforms to invade higher tier markets.

To combat this, management needs to investigate how to operate profitably in the low-end of the market. That challenge cannot be met by revisiting products one at a time. New product technologies, materials, manufacturing processes, and even distribution structures may be necessary. These may also require the hiring of new technical talent, and perhaps new management. Both the difficulty and the rewards of retaking the low ground of the market are perhaps best illustrated by the rebirth of the Swiss watchmaking industry.

From the development of church clocks in the late Middle Ages to the invention of quartz technology in 1968, the Swiss have been identified with leadership in precision timekeeping. That long tradition nearly ended in the 1970s when low-priced and reliable watches made by Casio, Seiko, and others poured out of Asia, cutting Swiss market share in Europe and North America from 80 percent to 44 percent. As American consumer electronics producers had done a decade earlier, the Swiss abandoned one market after another to their Asian competitors—first the lower-tier markets, then the middle tiers. And as they retreated to smaller, higher-priced niches, Asian producers consolidated the abandoned markets, gaining economies of scale in the process.

Asian watches forced Swiss manufacturers to retreat by degrees into the higher-priced, lower-volume tiers of the market. By the late 1970s the Swiss had lost practically all of their share of the $75 and under market and were fighting a defensive battle with the much smaller market between $75 and $400. The only market they commanded with authority was at the peak of the market pyramid, as shown in Figure 3–11.

The Swiss firms found themselves sitting on the small peak of the watchmaking mountain, isolated from the broad currents of their industry and unable to achieve anything approaching economies of scale. Clearly, they had to do something dramatic if they hoped to regain leadership in the business they had invented.

The vision for change came from Dr. Ernst Thomke, president of ETA S.A., a subsidiary of Societé Micromécanique et Horlogère (SMH), who advocated development of an inexpensive, reliable, flat plastic quartz watch with top-quality features. Inexpensive? Plastic? These terms were not in the vocabulary of Swiss watchmakers. But several years of continuing losses and several desperate mergers helped build support for Thomke's ideas.

FIGURE 3–11

Global Wrist Watch Market Units Within Price
Performance Tiers

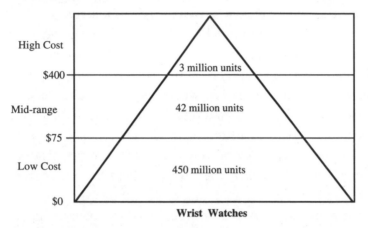

Source: Developed from data in William Taylor, "Message and Muscle:
An Interview with Swatch Titan Nicolas Hayek," *Harvard Business Review,*
March–April 1993, p. 103.

One Swiss executive in particular adopted Thomke's vision and
used it to reshape the face of his industry. Nicolas Hayek took over
SMH, Switzerland's largest watch producer, in the early 1980s. At
the time the firm was losing $124 million on some $1.1 billion in
sales. Like Thomke, Hayek advocated development of a plastic
watch that would be inexpensive and reliable. It would be designed
around a platform produced at low cost using one-third to one-half
the number of parts found in comparable quartz watches.[7] A high-
precision plastic molding process would mount its tiny subcompo-
nents without screws and other fittings.

But Hayek took Thomke's vision one step further. The new
watch—the "Swatch" (Swiss watch)—would incorporate style
features that set it apart from cheap Asian imports. As Hayek
would say later, "the most important element of the Swatch message is the hardest for others to copy. Ultimately, we are not just
offering watches. We are offering our personal culture."[8] The new

watches were designed in styles and colors that set them apart from anything then available. The use of plastic materials facilitated an exciting new approach to industrial design and the use of vivid colors in the housing, face plates, and time hands on watches.

Using the best of contemporary European design, SMH began turning out almost 140 new Swatch models every year: some elegant in their simplicity, others fanciful and striking. By 1992, SMH was producing $286 million in profits on revenues of $2.1 billion. In 1993 it shipped almost 27 million Swatches.

Swatch carried the Swiss watchmaker across both technical and market discontinuities and helped it recapture markets lost earlier to Asian challengers. To the amazement of just about everyone, it bested the Asian watchmakers while producing watches in the world's highest-wage country, where, as Hayek said, "the most junior secretary earns more than the most senior engineer in Thailand or Malaysia."[9]

In addition to bringing a new level of excitement to the traditional watch industry, SMH also sought to leverage its platform technology into new product categories. For example, SMH collaborated with the U.S. firm MobilComm to develop the Swatch Piepser (German for "beeper"), a hybridization of both paging and timing functions in a package no larger than the conventional Swatch watch. This and other recent ventures have served to confound SMH's competitors further: "What will those guys do next?"

SMH's success in regaining large lower-tier markets confirms what can be accomplished when producers think creatively about their platforms and processes.

A PROCESS FOR DEFINING PLATFORM STRATEGY IN YOUR COMPANY

Having presented various approaches to platform strategy, we can now suggest action steps that managers can take to define their own strategy from a product family and platform perspective.

The very first step is to assemble a multidisciplined team composed of engineering, marketing, and manufacturing talent. In our experience, while it is typically not a problem to identify and obtain outstanding technologists to participate in product line renewal, getting marketing experts of similar quality—individuals with insights into customer needs and the skills to validate those insights with in-depth market research—is often difficult and requires the intervention of senior management. The team's efforts may then be guided by the following steps.

Step 1: Segment Markets

The first step is to identify major market segments and the price-performance tiers within them to construct a market segmentation grid of individual market niches similar to those shown earlier in this chapter. Again, major market segments (customer groups) are arrayed horizontally, while price-performance tiers follow the vertical axis. It is important to look forward in time, incorporating emerging segments as well as existing ones. A definition of "the business" that is too narrow will limit the commercial potential of new platform initiatives.

Step 2: Identify Growth Areas

The next step is to identify the growth opportunities in these segments and individual niches. Accomplishing this requires that managers gather five types of data for each market niche: (1) the current sales volume, (2) your own participation rate or market share in the niche, (3) the five-year expected growth rate (anything less than a five-year view into the future is insufficient for planning new platform developments and their derivative products), (4) the leading competitors in each respective niche, and (5) the driving customer needs in each niche. Together, these data should present a clear picture as to where opportunities exist in your markets.

Step 3: Define Current Platforms

The third step is to define your major product platforms and where they "play" on the market segment grid. Defining a product platform for a particular business is not always easy. Different products lines may be based on a single product platform; or a single product line may use numerous platforms. In such cases, platform definition is aided by the use of high-level block diagrams that show the common subsystems and interfaces for a range of derivative products. Once the major subsystems are identified, the extent to which subsystems and manufacturing processes are shared between different platforms within the overall product portfolio should become clearer.

This step will help you determine the extent to which your company is leveraging key subsystems across market segments, or vertical scaling subsystems between tiers of price-performance. Our examples up to this point have been focused largely on manufacturers of consumer products, equipment, and systems. If your company makes software or is a pure services business, however, the definition of platforms for your business may not yet be clear. Chapter 7 will focus on platform definitions and product family management for software products, and Chapter 8 will relate these concepts to information products.

By synthesizing the results of this step with the preceding one, you will see the extent to which your company is focusing its major efforts on high growth versus little or no growth market niches.

Step 4: Analyze Competing Products

The fourth step is to understand how your existing product platforms and their respective derivative products stack up against those of competitors. Within each market niche, you must index the functionality, cost, and quality of competing products relative to your own. The goal here is to identify the major performance and cost drivers that can make your products significantly superior or inferior to those of competitors. In the next chapter we shall address how to perform competitive product benchmarking at a rich level of detail.

Step 5: Consider Future Platform Initiatives

What bold new initiatives could your company pursue in terms of its product platforms? Would a new platform make the company competitive in the lower price-performance tiers of its market segments, as in the Swatch and Hon examples? Or do opportunities exist for applying the concepts of horizontal and vertical scaling?

Take the additional step of envisioning the entry-level products to be derived from new platform initiatives. What would be their key characteristics of performance and price? This is the first cut at a forward-looking product family map. Again, the map you create should look forward at least five years into the future. Figure 3–12 is a useful guide. It shows the initial development of the new platform, an entry-level derivative product from that platform, extensions to the new platform, and their entry-level derivative products. Remember that an extension occurs when a major subsystem of a product platform is substantially changed or replaced either to incorporate new technologies or to address the needs of a new set of customers. Therefore, each market niche within your market segmentation grid that is to be addressed by the new platform may require its own platform extension.

Platform strategy can then drive your platform development. The next chapter shall show us how to turn such platform proposals into reality through a combination of technological and market research and development.

PUTTING "SKIN INTO THE GAME"

We come back to the mindset of new product strategy. Many corporations need to recapture the entrepreneurial essence of their early

FIGURE 3–12

Product Family Planning: Defining Initial Platform Focus, Platform Extensions, and Entry-level Products by Market Niche*

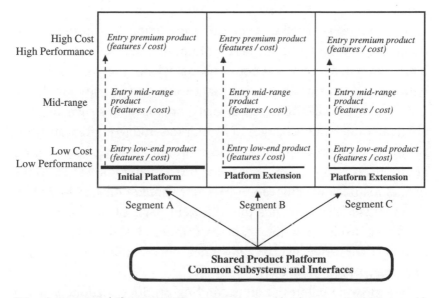

*Hypothetical example for an initial low-end market beachhead strategy. Initial foci at mid-range or high-end market tiers are certainly possible.

years: to be fast-moving, to achieve competitive excellence in technology, and to leverage common assets across individual products.

The mindset that we propose for new product strategy has a simple guiding principle: to obsolete your own products with better ones through continuous product platform renewal. While this may threaten some employees, customers and distributors generally prefer dealing with strong innovators who will be introducing better products tomorrow.

As a corollary idea, management must achieve power in its product platforms through standardization, modularity, and the economic benefits of higher-volume procurement of common subsystem components. It must also design its product platforms to compete profitably in low price-performance market tiers, scaling upward into higher tiers on the foundation of common subsystems and manufacturing processes. Too many firms abandon the lower price-performance tiers of their markets to other companies, even though it is precisely in such tiers that market growth is often the greatest.

This mindset—product renewal, simplifying the business, and competing in the low-cost, high-volume market tiers—may challenge the bureaucracy and conventional wisdom in your company with respect to its products, manufacturing, and distribution. It is a mindset that places renewed priority on the firm's own internal ability to understand changes in its markets and to continuously innovate in both product and manufacturing technology. Relying on acquisitions as a primary source for introducing innovation to the firm is insufficient; innovation can and should come from within. The mindset also demands that different parts of the corporation need to consider how they can work more closely together—designing their respective product lines on common platform and manufacturing technology.

In a growing enterprise an expanding product portfolio is a fact of life. Reconsidering the portfolio from the perspective of platforms, however, provides a unique opportunity to recapture the entrepreneurial spirit of the firm by formulating decisive initiatives that span individual products, markets, and departments. The overriding goal of such initiatives must be to achieve a new level of value cost leadership across the entire portfolio.

That cannot be done without active participation by senior management. Unfortunately, we have observed that the very executives who are responsible for the future of the corporation are typically far removed from new products. They may get excited about a particular product initiative that has caught their fancy, but it is rare to find executives who have put their "skin into the game" with respect to helping to conceive and support the development and market introduction of a whole new generation of products.

Executives have many other responsibilities: They buy other businesses, take care of Wall Street, or approve major capital expenditures to increase the volume of existing products. What easily happens, though, is that the company's customers and the new products they need are left unattended. That in turn hurts earnings, which makes Wall Street a problem, which then forces the reengineering of core businesses and the acquisition of unrelated businesses in markets appearing to offer greater promise. It is a vicious cycle.

Management frameworks, even the best ones, cannot break the cycle. Only executive leadership can. Once management has established a platform strategy best suited for its markets, the next step is to assemble a team to design the new platforms and create derivative products from them. The process for doing this is the topic of the next chapter.

4

Achieving Product Elegance Through Composite Design

C ustomers recognize *elegance* in design when they see or use a product. The product's appearance is pleasing and in keeping with its function. It is easy to use and serves its purpose without complication. If it has user controls, their purposes and operations are readily apparent and self-instructive. Form and function have a seamless unity. In *The Psychology of Everyday Things,* Donald A. Norman explains the difference between poorly designed and well-designed products from the customer's viewpoint:

> Well-designed objects are easy to interpret and understand. They contain visible clues to their operation. Poorly designed objects can be difficult and frustrating to use. They provide no clues—or sometimes false clues. They trap the user and thwart the normal process of interpretation and understanding.[1]

Engineers also recognize design elegance, but at a deeper level, focusing on inner as well as outer qualities: the appropriateness of the materials, the economy of components, and the ease with which they fit and work together. Manufacturing managers, too, know design elegance when they see a design that requires a minimum number of parts and assembly steps. If the product is a piece of software, engineers look for user interfaces that are intuitive, that make simple tasks easy to do as well as allow users to readily perform more difficult tasks.

In sum, well-designed products achieve elegance in both form and function. They are efficacious: They do what they are supposed to do and appear to the user to do so with ease. We see this in many products today, such as the Gillette Sensor razor system, Hewlett Packard's ink jet printers, Braun coffee makers, the Lexus automobile, Quicken personal finance software, and the IBM Thinkpad with its "butterfly" keyboard, to name a few. Products that are efficacious and elegant can be found in every industry.

In commodity product industries, where all products essentially do the same thing, elegance is found in the production process itself. Here, firms achieve advantage by having the highest efficiency in materials yield, which reduces the cost of goods sold. For manufacturers of such products as laundry detergent, toothpaste, or shampoo, materials utilization, and other forms of production optimization are a cornerstone of sustaining profitability.

Elegantly designed products don't simply happen by chance. They are the outcome of a process we call *composite design*. Composite design methodology seeks to optimize product platform architecture through analysis and design of the subsystems that exist in all but the rarest of products. We define composite design as *the identification, analysis on a function and cost basis, selection, and integration of subsystems and interfaces into products that harmonize the form and function of the overall system.*

Earlier chapters have stressed the importance of robust product platforms that are renewed in a timely manner. Product platforms, and their derivatives, that are created with the composite design methodology have the potential for achieving true cost-value leadership.

MAKING A BETTER MOUSE TRAP

The importance of optimizing the form and function of a system and its subsystems and interfaces can be seen in a product as simple as a mouse trap. The Victor mouse trap, the one familiar to most readers, was invented in 1896 and has been in continuous production ever since. Its most recent configuration was patented in 1913 and has become the "icon" of mouse traps. Figure 4–1 shows this "snap trap" as well as the "rat trap," a derivative product based on the same platform architecture. To most, these products appear to be the simplest and most elegant of mechanical

FIGURE 4–1

The Victor Mouse and Rat Traps

mouse traps. They are low-cost, simple to use, disposable, and fairly reliable in their performance.

The Victor mouse trap is produced by one firm in the United States, the Woodstream Corporation, which has automated its manufacture to the point of eliminating practically all labor content. Woodstream is very protective of its proprietary manufacturing processes and allows no outsiders to see them.

This product, like all others, has a hierarchic system that can be broken down into its component subsystems:

Subsystem	Material
base	rectangular wood
spring	spring steel
tripping plate	copper plated steel sheet metal
latch bar	copper plated spring steel wire form
jaw	copper plated spring steel wire form
staples	copper plated wire, 2 sizes
colors	red and black ink
shipping staple	steel wire form

It is obvious that the final form of the wooden base requires a significant number of process steps. The spring requires wire-formed spring manufacturing equipment, as do the other metal parts. The assembly machine must deal with a great deal of complexity, bringing together all of the various components, orienting them, and placing them into the assembly modes. Needless to say, the assembly machine must be a marvel to behold, producing millions and millions of the Victor traps each year.

Despite its market longevity, the Victor trap is not without flaws. The power and energy stored in the Victor trap could cause injury to whoever accidentally trips it—the person setting the trap, an inquisitive child, or a family pet. Further, the bait must be fastened securely to ensure reliable tripping. The tripping plate is latched and held by a very strong spring that requires significant tugging to trip the trap. A careful mouse can nibble away the bait without setting off the trap. Even when the trap is tripped, the nearly 180-degree travel arc of the Victor's jaw can give the agile rodent an opportunity to escape.

It is the identification of these problems—those characteristics of an existing platform architecture that bring displeasure to the user and expose latent needs—that should serve as the goals of new platform design.

In 1991 a clever inventor surpassed the simplicity and effectiveness of the Victor trap with his invention of the Better Mouse Trap, owned and marketed by Intruder, Inc. Figure 4–2 shows both the original Intruder mouse trap and a derivative rodent trap based on the same product platform. The products have only four parts.

FIGURE 4–2

The Intruder™ Mouse and Rodent Traps

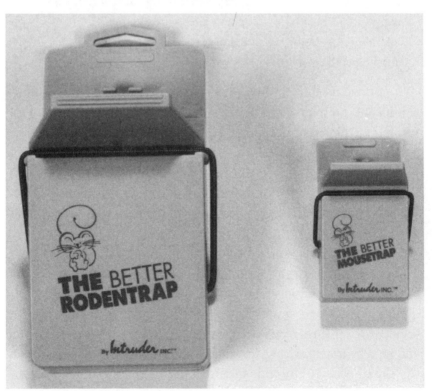

Subsystem	Material
lower jaw	plastic
upper jaw	plastic
trigger/bait plate	plastic
garter spring	steel

Manufacturing of the Better Mouse Trap is simplicity itself. The plastic parts can be made in a single step in a family mold. Only labeling of the upper jaw remains to finish those parts. The garter spring, a purchased part, completes the manufacturing steps. Assembly requires only elemental steps: breaking apart the plastic family mold, printing on the plastic, assembling the parts, and packaging, all of which are done right at the plastic molding machine.

The simplicity of the Better Mouse Trap's design and manufacture does nothing to impair its functionality, which exceeds that of the old Victor design. The Better Mouse Trap's trip plate is so sensitive that simple nibbling of the bait will set it off. Once tripped, the jaw has less than half of the travel arc (70 degrees versus 180 degrees) of the Victor, giving the intended victim less time to escape.

For the squeamish, the Better Mouse Trap has another valuable feature: the upper jaw geometry is such that the user need not handle the mouse corpse. He or she simply depresses the upper jaw and the mouse is released into the garbage container. It can then be reset, often without having to replenish the bait. Its plastic parts can be simply cleaned with water. The Victor user, in contrast, must use significant force to lift the jaw and free the dead mouse, which is often bloody, thus contaminating the trap. Most users decide simply to dispose of the Victor trap once it has killed a mouse. The safety of the Better Mouse Trap is likewise superior. The upper jaw does not kill the mouse with high impact. The mouse is trapped and held in place until it expires from suffocation in less than thirty seconds. The low-impact jaw is harmless to inquisitive children and pets.

So the Better Mouse Trap is the winner over the Victor on a number of scores: safety, simplicity of design, simplicity of manufacturing, reliability, ease of use in arming and baiting, disposal of the mouse corpse, and reuse. In terms of design elegance it is clearly superior. As a product platform it also has superior potential. Because it is made out of plastic, variations in size and color may be simply made to create derivative products such as the rodent trap shown in Figure 4–2. After a hundred years of production, the only derivative we could find for the basic Victor mouse trap was a larger, far more dangerous item called the Rat Trap.

We can surmise that the Better Mouse Trap's inventor looked at the standard Victor snap trap and saw too many materials, too many (or too complex) manufacturing processes, and a set of unpalatable chores for the user. Observing these "unoptimized" factors, he invented a better mouse trap, one that achieves a harmony of form and function through design elegance. In 1995 several million Better Mouse Traps were sold.

Few products are as inherently simple as mouse traps. On the other end of the simplicity–complexity spectrum are such products as an ultrasound imaging machine with more than 30,000 individual components. As one might imagine, the payoff of design elegance increases with the complexity of a product such as this. Nevertheless, some engineers prefer to take an existing product design and make it even *more* complex by increasing the scope and power of particular subsystems or by adding new ones. Effective management of the design process seeks the opposite result. Its guiding principle is: "Simpler is better, and better is more important than new." That principle leads to attractive, easy to use, reasonably priced products.

APPLYING COMPOSITE DESIGN

A company, when seeking to differentiate products from those of competitors by the incorporation of a discontinuity in the platform architecture, can do a better job designing its product platform by using the methodology of composite design. Composite design has six steps:

1. Establish the goals of the system in terms of performance and price, what Deming might call the "aim" of the overall system.[2]
2. Classify and analyze the subsystems of your design and those of its competitors.
3. Measure the design's complexity and those of competitors' products.
4. Index the design and those of direct competitors against standard baselines of function and cost.
5. Build in degrees of freedom to accommodate product line expansion.
6. Integrate manufacturing processes to achieve lowest cost.

Let us now consider each step.

Step 1: Establish the Aim of the Overall System

No journey is successful without first specifying the destination. For product developers, the aim of the overall systems must be clearly defined: current performance at lower cost; better performance at current cost; replacement of mechanical controls with electronic digital or analog controls; and so forth. The aim may also be to create new and better ways to solve a customer's problem, such as replacing photographic film with digital imaging. Whatever the goal, it must be specific, and it must be based upon customer insights.

Critical forms, features, or functions of optimized systems become the "drivers" of design activities. For example, if *size* is the factor of greatest importance in a particular system or subsystem, size becomes the driver of design. Other factors, such as cost, are subordinated to it in a series of tradeoffs. Figure 4–3 classifies some of the critical factors that corporations have considered in optimizing their systems.

Choosing the *right* drivers can make the difference between success and failure. The development of the Dustbuster, another Black & Decker product, provides an illustration. A team of senior engineers realized that people were averse to cleaning up small spills

FIGURE 4–3

Various Design Drivers

Cost	• direct and indirect • transportation	• time and labor • material • capital	
Complexity	• number of subsystems	• parts and components	• processes
Commonality	• similar parts • similar processes	• similar materials	• similar interfaces
Reliability and quality	• performance • service life	• robustness • failure	• safety (fail safe) • modes
Dimensions	• weight	• mass	• volume
Flexibility and variability	• Richness in ability to provide extremes in performance and features without system suboptimization or loss of "elegance" Example: One of the great strengths of the Unix operating system lies in its "shell," where the user has the ability to mix and match any number of program modules (also known as "utilities") to achieve the desired result. This is possible because the universal interface between all modules comprises streams of text characters, so that the output of one module can be the input of any other.*		
Modularity	• Subsystems with elegant interface architecture allow for rich variety within the subfunction without causing disruptions to any other subsystem. Example: The 35mm film cartridge is universal as part of all 35mm camera systems. The film inside the cartridge, however can contain any one of many different films without disrupting other subsystems of the camera.		
Simplicity	• A customer-pleasing level of features and variability with a minimum number of parts and interfaces Example: Swatch, as we described previously, provides an incredible variety of watches based on a product platform of about fifty distinct parts, while many of its competitors models have more than 150 parts.		

*Rod Manis and Marc H. Meyer, *The Unix Shell Programming Language* (Indianapolis: Howard W. Sams & Company, 1986).

because it was too much bother to get the vacuum cleaner out of the closet, unwind the cord, find a receptacle, and plug it in. That aversion led to a design driver, *readiness to serve:* "When the customer is ready to use me, I'm ready to go." The Dustbuster was conceived around this design driver with marvelous simplicity. Its subsystems were a motor, a fan, a switch, a snout, a filter bag, and a battery and charging stand or a cigarette lighter plug for the car version. The Dustbuster remains to this day a truly efficacious product, providing a highly portable, convenient solution for light-duty cleaning where an electrical outlet is inaccessible.

Fly fishing rods provide another example of the importance of design drivers. In this case, it is the use of new materials to allow fishermen to cast farther, either to catch more fish or to impress their neighbors. For decades rod makers used bamboo and other woods. They then shifted to fiberglass, and then to high modulus graphite. What drove their search and adoption of new materials was the quest to make flyrods cast farther. In fact, an engineering professor recently tested the casting capability of generations of flyrods, examining "rod frequency"—the line speed that a rod can generate for the same force in a casting stroke. Figure 4–4 shows the dramatic improvements in the castability of fly rods over the course of an entire century through the use of new materials.

Sony Corporation has thrived on clear design drivers. In 1970 the founder and chairman stated as Sony's objective to be the first company to achieve solid-state circuitry across all its products. Vacuum tubes required too much power and, like lightbulb filaments, burned out after so many hours of use. Solid-state electronics, then, became the driver behind Sony's new product R&D. While the company's initial set of exclusively solid-state products was more expensive than items using vacuum tubes, the disadvantage was remedied as Sony gained experience in manufacturing transistors. Then, having mastered solid-state design, Sony identified its next design driver: "miniaturization." Sony's miniaturization initiatives progressed to the point where humans could no

FIGURE 4–4

Advances in Flyrod Castability

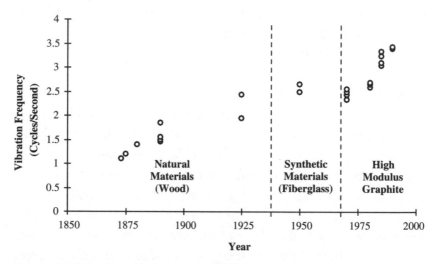

Source: Developed from data in Graig Spolek, "Fly-rod Evolution," *Fly Fisherman Magazine,* December 1995, pp. 12–16.

longer assemble product components reliably. That challenge, in turn, led to the corporation's next driver: automated assembly of miniaturized systems. Today, the company not only uses robotic assembly systems for its own products but sells its manufacturing systems to a diverse range of industries.

A company can easily choose the *wrong* drivers. For example, a power tool rival of Black & Decker, trying to regain some of the market share lost to B&D, adopted "low cost" as its design driver and essentially copied B&D's products. While optimizing low cost, however, the competitor neglected reliability and performance. It used very cheap bearings and other low-quality components in its designs so that tools burned out after just a few hours of heavy use. Product failures were so widespread that the competitor was forced to withdraw entirely from the consumer power tool business!

A company may consciously choose to optimize one subsystem of the new product at the expense of others. For example, the "point and shoot" automatic cameras now in vogue have simplified the user interface to a remarkable degree. These cameras have eliminated the need to focus the lens, to choose the right f-stop and exposure time for light conditions, and to advance the film once a shot has been taken. Simplicity in use, however, has increased the complexity of the camera's other systems. Engineers have had to design an auto-focuser, a light sensor with motorized shutter control, and a motorized film advancer into the product, adding cost and complexity. Thus, based upon user preferences, camera makers have traded off simplicity of use with cost and product complexity.

The lesson in these examples is that you cannot optimize one subsystem and ignore others. Instead, you must consider the system as a whole and be prepared to make tradeoffs.

Earlier chapters have described the "perceived" and "latent" needs of customers. The needs that customers consciously perceive can be uncovered directly through traditional market research and indirectly through their buying choices. Latent needs, those that customers cannot articulate, are more difficult to determine. Nevertheless, uncovering latent needs creates tremendous opportunities for true breakthrough products. Such discovery requires a deeper level of customer insight. As Harvard's Gerald Zaltman once put it, "When needs are not well-articulated or understood by the market itself, you need to develop a deep understanding of customer thinking and behavior."[3]

While a full discussion of how companies can develop that deep understanding is beyond the scope of this book, effective techniques include the use of focus groups, studies of early users of new technologies, and customer surveys that force users to make tradeoffs between features and prices and analysis of those results with conjoint analysis methods. Global platform teams will also have to understand differences in needs of users residing in different regions of the world.

We have observed that multidisciplined teams, if given the charter and breathing room to think laterally and creatively, can often develop a strong set of perceived and latent needs. Those insights must be validated with the types of external market research described above. If management can get the engineers to "buy into" this research, to actively participate in focus groups and survey designs, the platform development will indeed be off to a very good start and headed toward success.

Step 2: Classify and Analyze Subsystems

In this step, a company must break down its products and those of competitors into logical subsystems. The goal of this activity is to identify which products can be built at the lowest cost, which use the fewest parts and types of parts, which are easiest to manufacture, and which provide superior reliability and performance. Tear-down analysis or reverse engineering of competing products, of course, is nothing new. But examining competitors' products in terms of their systems and subsystems tends to be the exception.

We have defined the architecture of a product platform as comprising subsystems and the interfaces between them and the user. The entire platform, and by extension the products based on the platform, must then be viewed as a "system." In the words of W. Edward Deming:

> A system is a network of interdependent components that work together to try to accomplish the aim of the system. . . . A system must be managed. It will not manage itself.[4]

There is a hierarchic structure to the overall system and its component subsystems. If you partition a system, you will typically find that it contains many subsystems, and many of these in turn can be partitioned. For example, for a manufacturer of engine transmissions, the gear box is a system made up of various subsystems: gears, shafts, housings, seals, clutches, lubricants, bearings, and so on. Many of those subsystems can, in turn, be further partitioned. The lowest subsystem is the arbitrary point at which you stop partitioning. In the gearbox hierarchy, bearings may be the lowest subsystem, i.e., the point at which no further partitioning of the system is possible or practical. The manufacturer of the bearings, however, would view the single bearing as another hierarchic system. It's subsystems would be, for example, the outer race, the inner race, the balls or rollers, the seals, and the lubricants.

Figure 4–5 shows the hierarchical nature of systems, illustrated with the example of a simple office chair. System and subsystem analysis is the foundation of composite design in the sense that we attempt to understand the degree of optimization required for each subsystem and its related interfaces to produce an overall optimized system, achieving elegance and value-cost leadership.

An optimized system in this definition is one in which all subsystems, taken as a whole, create the greatest output performance for the least inputs. Indeed, this serves as a good working definition for elegance in design. It is illustrated, for example, by an electric circular saw that delivers superior performance on the job site with the least physical weight, with the fewest component parts, or at the lowest cost.

In one of our own product developments, a marketing person was sent out to purchase three units of each of the most competitive products. The first unit of each competitive product was stress-tested to the point of destruction to determine its reliability and limits. The second unit was torn down for subsystems identification and analysis as suggested above. The third unit of each competing product was put on display in a room adjacent to the engineering department, along with the results of the stress tests and the disassembled parts of the second unit. This created an information-rich environment for designers.

The definition of key subsystems can also prove highly useful in market research. In another one of our product developments (involving an Internet applications software development tool), lead users were presented with the higher level block diagram of the new product platform. They were then asked to suggest their own desired features and capabilities in each of the major subsystems, and to identify existing commercial products that they thought excelled

FIGURE 4-5

Symbolic System Hierarchy Illustrated with a Simple Office Chair

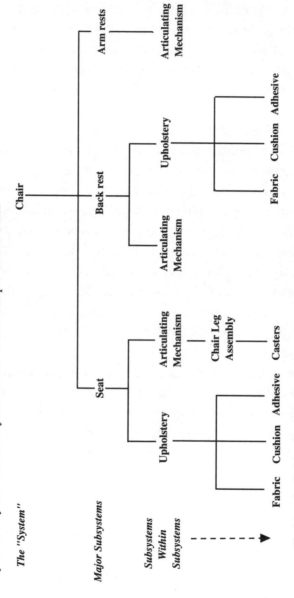

The "System"

Major Subsystems

Subsystems Within Subsystems

The lowest level of the subsystem hierarchy ends with specific materials, components, etc.

in any given area. Successive iterations of the research provided the development team with a ranked list of desired features on a subsystem-by-subsystem basis, as well as a lengthy list of competitive products that could be studied further and perhaps even integrated (through licensing) into the new design. Once again, the key to success was to have marketing and engineering staff working together to conduct and evaluate the lead user research.

Step 3: Measure the Complexity

The superior design demonstrated in the mouse trap example has low complexity in the number of parts and the ease of manufacture. Needless complexity is one design dimension that every product developer must attempt to minimize. But to understand complexity, one needs an objective standard for measuring it. Fortunately, Boothroyd and Dewhurst (of the University of Rhode Island) have developed practical metrics for assessing the complexity of manufactured products.[5]

Boothroyd and Dewhurst calculate complexity using three factors: the number of parts (N_p), the number of types of parts (N_t), and the number of interfaces of each of the parts (N_i). N_p, N_t, and N_i are totaled—i.e., the sum of the N_p, the sum of N_t, and the sum of N_i. These sums are multiplied, and the cube root of the product of this multiplication is calculated to determine the *complexity factor.* Applying this metric to the Victor mouse trap yields:

N_p = 12 parts
N_t = 10 types of parts
N_i = 27 interfaces

12 x 10 x 27 = 3240

The cube root of 3240 is 14.51, which is the Victor trap's complexity factor. Applying the same metric to the Intruder mouse trap yields:

N_p = 5 parts
N_t = 5 types of parts
N_i = 12 interfaces

5 x 5 x 12 = 300

Taking the cube root of 300 gives us a complexity factor of 6.69. Thus, the Intruder is a fraction as complex as the Victor mouse trap. The fewer the *number* of parts, the fewer the number of part *types,* and the fewer the number of *interfaces,* the lower the design complexity.

Measurement of complexity may be applied in the same way by a firm to its competitors' products. Engineers should use this approach to measure complexity in an iterative manner, i.e., each design should be measured for complexity, then redesigned to reduce complexity further. The iterative process should continue until the point is reached where further simplicity cannot be practically achieved. One should be careful not to stop the process too soon, since every reduction in design complexity reduces a host of other costs once production begins.

Mistakes are often the source of wisdom. We recall a consumer product that we helped design where the original architecture contained 31 parts. Subsequent iterations reduced that number to 18 and 11, at which point management insisted that the project move into production. A postmortem review of the project indicated that additional time spent on design could have reduced the part count to 4, thereby saving the company substantial material and assembly costs.

Boothroyd and Dewhurst use similar methods to assess process (manufacturing) complexity. Without going through this calculation, suffice it to say that the Intruder mouse trap scores significantly lower than the Victor mouse trap on this measure. The manufacturing steps the Victor model required on the wood base alone outnumbers *all* the steps of manufacturing the Intruder.

The mouse trap example, although elementary, drives home the point: low levels of complexity in product and process design are tangible measures of elegance. The virtues of reducing complexity, of course, go beyond aesthetics. Reducing complexity almost always reduces direct and indirect costs. Complexity fuels those costs, which grow geometrically if not exponentially. Every additional part requires that it be made or purchased, requiring time, people, and capital. Greater complexity means more purchase orders and more stockroom space. Indeed, we suggest that the complexity of a platform architecture will be mirrored in the firm's organizational complexity.

Step 4: Index Subsystems on Function and Cost

The next task is to rate, or index, present designs against those of your keenest competitors in terms of both functionality and cost. Once you index each individual subsystem of a design, you can then aggregate those indices into an overall index of function and cost for the design as a whole.

We turn your attention to Figure 4–6, which shows a hypothetical indexing for a product platform that you might wish to create in your own business. The platform design has six major subsystems. For each subsystem, you would create indices on various dimensions of function and cost. Function is typically some key aspect of performance that can be clearly measured. Cost can be considered in terms of materials cost, yield, or manufactured cost—whatever makes the most sense for the particular subsystem and your business. You would derive index values for function and cost by actually getting your hands on leading competitors' products, tearing them down, and studying their subsystems in the areas of function, materials, and cost. The best-in-class subsystem within your industry would then be scored as "1.00," and all other competitors' subsystems would be judged relative to it.

From this process you will derive a clear understanding of the best subsystems from across the industry, in terms of both function

FIGURE 4–6

Composite Design: Indexing on Function and Cost

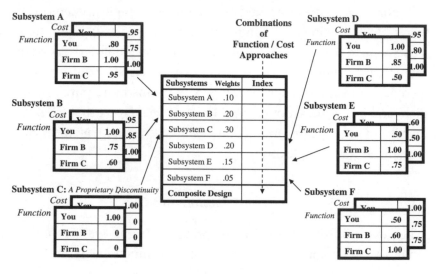

and cost. Your own technology will probably excel in some subsystem areas and be at parity with competitors in others. In fact, *you need not be superior in every single subsystem.* The key is to determine those subsystems within the platform design where you can truly excel and place competitors at a clear disadvantage. In Figure 4–6, for example, Subsystem C is presented as a major new breakthrough—a discontinuity—for which competitors have no immediate response.

Therefore, *not all subsystems need to be optimized to deliver superior performance.* For example, in the 1980s Toyota automobile engines began using a heavy-duty cogged belt system, similar to those used as timing belts, to transmit power from the engine to the alternator, water pump, air conditioning compressor, and other subsystems. Traditionally, lighter and cheaper rubber V-belts had served that purpose. U.S. competitors initially viewed the Toyota innovation as too expensive and overengineered, given its purpose. Closer examination, however, revealed that the heavier cogged Toyota belts required significantly less belt tension than the traditional V-belts to deliver the power transfer function.[6] With greatly lessened belt tension, the remaining components did not have to be so robust and strong, resulting in a system containing much smaller and lighter shafts, pulleys, bearings, mountings, and other related parts. So, while one subsystem—the transfer belt—was more costly, that cost disadvantage was offset by possible improvements in the remaining subsystems in terms of size, cost, and weight.

The next step is to create composite designs. In Figure 4–6, the composite design is represented in the central integration block. Since not all subsystems may be of equal importance in the overall design, you may wish to assign weights to each of the particular subsystems. Those weights can be factored into the calculation of overall function and cost.

The composite designs will have multiple iterations. The first set of them should be a simple computation of the total index scores for function and cost for your own company's present products and those of key competitors. You may find, for example, that for your current designs you are the leader in total function but lag in cost. Or you may be the cost leader but fall short in total function. The goal, of course, is to create a new composite design that will be the combined value-cost leader in the industry.

This is where the fun starts. Using Figure 4–6 as an example, if you were to combine Firm B's Subsystem A and Firm C's Subsystem F with your own Subsystems B, C, D, E, you would have a functionally superior product platform. However, a team member may note that Firm C's Subsystem F may be functionally superior to your own but it is of such marginal importance to the overall composite design that the new manufacturing processes needed to implement it are not worthwhile. Again, *it is not essential to be superior in every single subsystem, but only to be superior in the overall system.* Having created a composite design for function, you would then investigate the cost implications of the design, all the while asking yourself if manufacturing and procurement improvements of a common platform for many derivative products could significantly reduce the cost of any particular subsystem solution.

Obviously, manufacturing and marketing personnel need to be working with engineers to make the process effective.

After numerous iterations on paper, you can measure your new composite design against the function and cost scores of your competitors' current products. Figure 4–7 shows a comparison of Black & Decker's new power tool platform with B&D's own existing product and those of two international competitors. The current cost values for Black & Decker were set as the basis point of

FIGURE 4–7

Power Tool Cost Analysis

B&D's Current Costs Used as Baseline Index

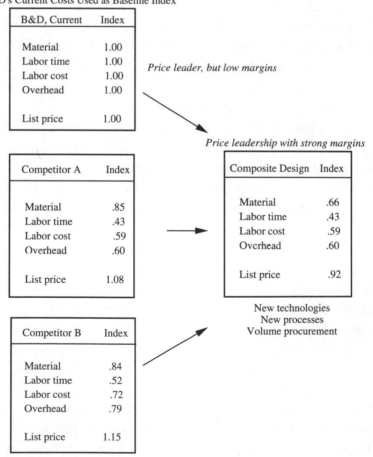

B&D, Current	Index
Material	1.00
Labor time	1.00
Labor cost	1.00
Overhead	1.00
List price	1.00

Price leader, but low margins

Price leadership with strong margins

Competitor A	Index
Material	.85
Labor time	.43
Labor cost	.59
Overhead	.60
List price	1.08

Composite Design	Index
Material	.66
Labor time	.43
Labor cost	.59
Overhead	.60
List price	.92

New technologies
New processes
Volume procurement

Competitor B	Index
Material	.84
Labor time	.52
Labor cost	.72
Overhead	.79
List price	1.15

1.00 for the analysis. You can see in the figure that before the new composite design, Black & Decker sold its product at lower prices but suffered from poor margins. Through the composite design process, the team learned from the analysis of the components and processes used by Competitors A and B. Combining that knowledge with new materials and improved yields, Black & Decker was able to reverse its poor margin position. After the redesign, it could sell this product even further below the prices of Competitors A and B yet achieve a superior gross margin.

We reiterate, the indexing exercise can be invaluable for assessing a company's current product designs relative to those of competitors. It will also focus your attention on what is critically important in a new platform design to make it serve as the basis for distinctive products.

Step 5: Build in Degrees of Freedom

As you begin thinking about your product lines in terms of product platforms and subsystems, the opportunity may arise to single out one or several areas where tremendous leverage can be created by building degrees of freedom into the design. That means a particular subsystem is engineered with room to grow. It is a very simple yet powerful concept.

In the Black & Decker case, the housing of the universal motor was designed to be larger than it had to be for the first derivative products of the product family. As the motors themselves were lengthened to provide more power, the motor housing itself and the manufacturing processes associated with it did not have to be changed. If we turn to computers, the beauty of the original IBM PC was that it came with extra "slots" inside the box. That allowed a host of firms to make printed circuit board-based products that the user could simply add to his or her PC. Similarly, one of the great strengths of the Internet is that one Web page can access virtually an unlimited number of other Web pages. Those links are achieved through a very simple, standardized programming environment. Similarly, many software companies now allow users to add their routines easily to the software that "comes in the box." These examples illustrate that flexibility should be cherished in the development or selection of interfaces between the subsystems of a platform design.

One should not attempt to add extensive degrees of freedom to every single subsystem in a platform architecture, for then the primary result will tend to be a very expensive design in terms of both engineering and manufacturing. However, if you can identify those particular subsystems where providing room to grow leads to great advantage for either your own future developments or those of users, you will have discovered one of the key ingredients of making a truly robust platform.

Step 6: Integrate Manufacturing

Once you have a design that has been improved through several iterations of the "classify-measure-index" methodology of Steps 2, 3, and 4 just described, you should ask "What is the *one best way* to produce it?" This is where having manufacturing personnel on the team can be crucial to the ultimate success of the effort. They understand better than anyone what it takes to build a particular design.

At the same time, manufacturing engineers can also hinder that success if they unduly influence the design to fit the current production operation. Manufacturing companies have tremendous investments in current plant assets, including special-purpose equipment. By training and experience, manufacturing managers are disposed to maximize the use of those assets. It is hard for them not to bring those existing assets into the product development process as a design constraint. However, great products are created only when firms design new products to serve customers, not when they design products to serve their existing equipment.

In finding the "one best way" we encourage product teams to pretend that they are beginning with a clean slate, as if their current manufacturing facilities had been burned to the ground. Obviously, any new entrant to the business would be starting with a clean slate. In many cases a new state of the art plant constructed specifically to produce a new product line will not only lower unit costs dramatically but also act as a barrier to less resolute competitors. If those competitors understand that a new production facility is part of the costs of entering a market, many will stay out entirely. That was the case when Black & Decker built an expensive production facility to make its double-insulated power tools. It was the case too when Gillette developed the process for manufacturing Sensor razor cartridges. In both instances, the cost of the process equipment was so high that competitors were scared off.

SUNBEAM APPLIANCE COMPANY GLOBAL IRON PROJECT

To appreciate the power of the six steps of composite design, let's review the development of a product that used them to great effect: the Sunbeam electric iron.[7]

In the early 1980s the market for steam/dry irons in the United States was practically flat at slightly over 10 million units sold each year. The possibility of bringing excitement to this mature and established product market seemed unlikely. Manufacturers saw it as a zero-sum game in which greater market share could be had only by taking existing business away from competitors by means of price reductions, rebates, and features providing marginal performance improvements, such as Teflon sole plates, "steam and spray," and more steam vents along the sole plate. Once introduced, those features were quickly copied by all manufacturers.

If the iron market was stagnant, it was not for unfavorable demographics. In a study of market data for the period of 1964 to 1982, the Sunbeam Appliance Company discovered that while the annual unit volume for steam/dry irons was essentially unchanged, the number of households in the United States had grown by 60 percent and the population by 30 percent. So why had iron sales not grown in step? Sunbeam concluded that the product simply failed to inspire interest.

For the previous decade, iron makers had been engaged in a great "steam vent hole" race, trying to differentiate their products by increasing the number of steam vents on the iron's sole plate. Consumers, it was thought, correlated more steam vents with better ironing performance. Irons were being manufactured with more than fifty steam vents. Sunbeam, however, understood that this design driver was fallacious, since having more than thirty vents actually decreased the velocity with which steam could penetrate the fabric. Management recognized that it needed a different competitive lever to differentiate its products.

A multidisciplinary team representing marketing, engineering, and manufacturing was assembled to investigate this problem. A free-wheeling brainstorming session followed the precept to "be the product yourself, and determine how you frustrate the user." Several unperceived needs surfaced.

1. Users were often uneasy about whether or not they remembered to shut off the iron. No sooner had they gone to bed, gone shopping, or left on vacation than the thought would pop into their heads, "Did I shut off the iron?" Visions of the house burned to the foundation followed.

2. Each type of fabric—wool, linen, silk, polyester, rayon—required a different heat setting to avoid scorching. But current irons gave no indication as to when the iron temperature had actually heated up or cooled down to the right setting.

Sunbeam's engineers responded to these concerns with two new product features:

1. Automatic shutoff. Motion-sensitive switching was incorporated into the design; it shut off the iron if left motionless in the face-down (ironing) position for thirty seconds or if left motionless in the heel rest position for ten minutes. The iron could be reactivated by moving it.

2. A "ready" indicator. Electronic sensing was designed into the product for each of six different heat settings. A red light in-

dicated that the sole plate had not yet reached the heat setting; a green light told the user that the setting and temperature matched.

Sunbeam patented the automatic shutoff and the "ready" indicator, and introduced them in the Monitor iron at an unprecedented high price level that the marketing and sales groups feared would be rejected by the trade and the buying public. Instead, sales took off. Instead of the 70,000 units forecast by Sunbeam's own staff, almost 185,000 Monitor irons were sold during the year of introduction. The popularity of the iron with dealers spurred orders for other Sunbeam products, more than doubling the company's market share to 20 percent.

The value of Sunbeam's innovations was soon recognized by all competitors and copied in forms that did not violate the two patents. Figure 4–8 illustrates the impact of the design develop-

FIGURE 4–8

U.S. Annual Unit Sales Of Steam/Dry Irons, 1980 to 1994

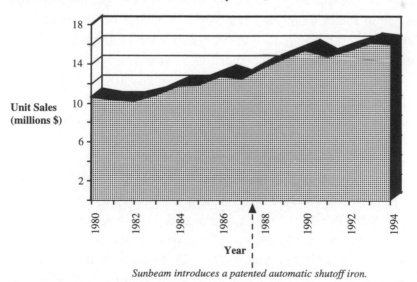

Sunbeam introduces a patented automatic shutoff iron.

Source: Appliance Annual Reports of the United States.

ments on the annual sales volume of irons in the United States. The once moribund market had sprung to life, with sales growing more than 50 percent between 1980 and 1994.

Sunbeam's only serious disappointment in the Monitor was the fact that its success did not extend below the high end of the market. In fact, the effective list price of the Monitor confined it to the premium market tier. That was to be expected, because the Monitor was merely a derivative product, having added two unique features to a product platform that had not been wholly redesigned. The new features added more than $7.50 to unit cost. In the absence of fundamental redesign, the total unit production cost of the Monitor was the highest in the industry.

Going Global

Given the success of the Monitor iron, Sunbeam and its international affiliate, Rowenta, turned their attention to creating a design capable of serving the much larger global market, which then supported iron sales approaching 50 million units a year. The appliance they envisioned would be low-cost and manufactured in high volume in factories around the world. It would be based upon a platform of common parts and subsystems, with adaptations to address the preferences of local markets. It would also meet the product safety and regulatory requirements of many jurisdictions.

Developing a product that fulfilled that vision would require more than adding bells and whistles, as had been the case in the Monitor project. Nothing less than a fundamental redesign of the product architecture would be required. Toward that end, the two companies embarked on the "Global Iron Project," employing the composite design techniques described earlier in this chapter.

The first initiative of the project was to bring together all company engineers, marketers, and executives involved in the iron business in the United States, Canada, Europe, and the United Kingdom. Over the course of a two-day meeting, industry and company research on the iron market was presented and analyzed.

The subsystems of the Monitor and Sunbeam's other irons and their key competitors around the globe were identified and studied. Each iron was torn down with the goal of identifying the best subsystems in terms of cost and functionality. To their disappointment, Sunbeam was determined to be one of the highest-cost producers.

The final act of the conference was to establish a Global Iron Technical Committee and a parallel committee dedicated to market issues. The former would develop a design that would minimize costs and satisfy all regulatory requirements while establishing functional leadership and customer satisfaction. The marketing group would determine the set of features that customers required.

A key assignment of the marketing committee was to determine the set of features that would best satisfy customer preferences in many countries. That would be no small task in that current thinking among marketing managers held that U.S. and European preferences differed greatly. The marketers conducted conjoint analysis within each region to better their understanding of consumer preferences. Selected results of the market research are summarized in Figure 4–9; here, positive values are "good" and the negative values are "bad."[8]

The research uncovered several important surprises. Previously, marketers had perceived the number of steam vents on the sole plate and the location of the iron controls—either on top of the handle (U.S.) or on the back of the sole plate (European)—as key issues of customer preference. They had insisted that those key concerns be addressed on a regional basis. Neither concern, however, was shown to be a design driver. Referring to the line item in Figure 4–9 labeled "Number of Steam Vents," the conjoint utilities values showed that the "great hole race" was important only in the United States; even there, about thirty vents would suffice. Similarly, the "Temperature Control Location" data indicated that U.S. respondents had only a slight preference for a control switch on the handle. That allowed engineers to place the control switch where it was least vulnerable to damage, had the fewest parts, and could interface with U.S. and European manufactured thermostats. The thermostat had to be se-

FIGURE 4–9

Results of Conjoint Analysis for Steam/Dry Irons

	United States	France	Mexico
Price			
$15	0.65	1.51	0.89
$30	0.32	1.18	0.02
$55	-0.40	-2.68	-0.90
Number of steam vents:			
7	-0.99	-0.69	-0.34
15	0.15	0.59	0.72
29	0.29	0.49	0.29
60	0.72	-0.43	-0.65
Temperature control position:			
Body	-0.12	0.27	-0.36
Handle	0.12	-0.27	0.36
Minutes of steam:			
15	-0.31	-0.49	-0.78
30	0.49	0.59	0.83
60	-0.17	-0.10	-0.05

Source: Sunbeam Appliance Company.

cured to the sole plate, so the logical placement for the control knob was directly connected to the thermostat at the saddle of the iron and not at a remote location on the top of the handle.

The market research showed clearly what users *really* cared about and what previous market research had failed to uncover: the steaming time capacity of their irons. Most irons contained a small water tank capable of delivering only seven to ten minutes of steam, requiring users to stop and refill one to three times during each ironing session. As indicated in Figure 4–9 (under "Minutes of Steam"), users in all three regions wanted an iron with *at least* fifteen minutes of steaming capacity, and they greatly preferred thirty minutes. That discovery had an important impact on product design and became a design driver. Sunbeam engineers integrated the water tank into the iron's handle, which added increased capacity for the water and resulted in much longer steaming times.

The market research data also showed that users in all regions strongly preferred a variable temperature control capability ("Temperature Control" in Figure 4–9). This too was designed into the new product platform. These data collectively vindicated the team's discovery of latent needs and gave guidance with respect to perceived needs, such as the desired number of vents on the sole plate or the desired price point for the iron. Using Deming's metaphor, an "aim" of the system was clearly established.

Creating the Composite Design

A team in Sunbeam-U.S. then developed a "paper" composite design. The approach was to break the iron architecture down into its key subsystems and interfaces. For each subsystem, different alternatives were considered in terms of electronics and materials. Similarly, interfaces were closely examined and designed to provide maximum case of assembly. Further adjustments were made to incorporate the most stringent regulatory standards. The team used a bubble chart representing the platform architecture, a simple version of which is shown in Figure 4–10, to help organize its thinking. The chart provided designers with a graphic representation of the alternatives available for the iron's many subsystems. The actual bubble chart used (too large and detailed for inclusion here) contained numerous design alternatives for each major subsystem, be it rendered in materials, electronics, finishes, or manufacturing processes.

The team knew that dramatically reducing materials cost and labor content would be essential if the new product platform was to represent a "low-end, upward scalable" solution. Existing products of Sunbeam and its major competitors (Figure 4–11) were disassembled and analyzed for materials cost and labor content. The team then determined the impact on materials and labor if it could improve those existing designs without changing their basic architecture. Using those determinations as benchmarks, the team proceeded with the design of the new global iron. The result was that

FIGURE 4–10

Bubble Chart of the Global Iron Subsystems

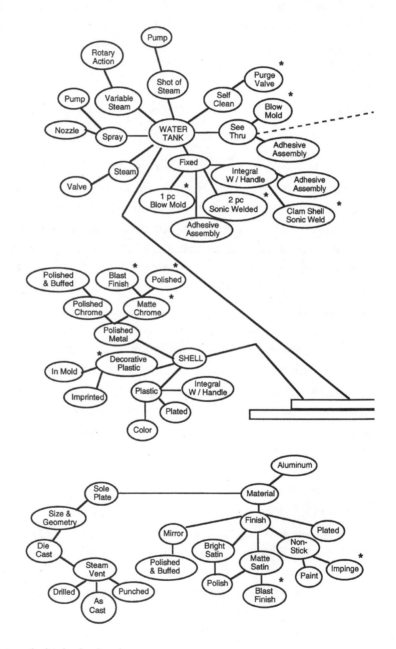

*These features had to be developed.

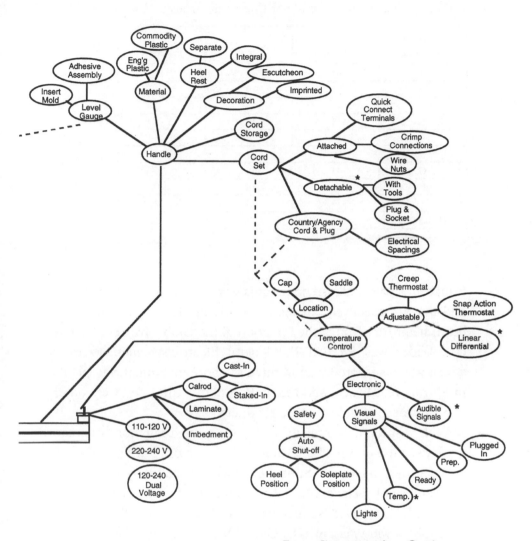

Iron Construction Options
Global Iron Task Force

FIGURE 4–11

Part and Fastener Counts of Major Competing Irons

Competitors' Products	Parts	Fasteners	Type of Fasteners
A	97	18	10
B	74	19	9
C	75	16	7
D	115	20	8
E	147	24	15
F	140	21	10
G	144	30	15
H	103	18	9
I	134	24	12
Global Iron	52	3	2

Sunbeam's part and fastener counts were reduced to only fifty-two and three, respectively. In Figure 4–11, Product A was the Sunbeam steam/dry Iron at the initiation of the Global Iron study. The cost leader was Product B, General Electric's steam/dry iron, which was being produced in three offshore manufacturing plants in Singapore, Mexico, and Brazil. Products C through I were other U.S., European, and Japanese products.[9]

With respect to simplicity and part count reduction, one can readily see the power of this step of the composite design process. The new design reduced Sunbeam's own part count by 46 percent, the number of fasteners by 84 percent, and fastener types by 80 percent. It also moved Sunbeam ahead of the GE unit, the low-cost leader, by a wide margin. The Global Iron design fared even better when compared with competitors C through I.

The reduction in part count and fasteners enabled Sunbeam to drive down its costs of materials and labor. The dramatic nature of those cost reductions is shown in Figure 4–12, which compares Sunbeam's new design with those of other global competitors in the steam/dry iron business based on disassembling and

FIGURE 4–12

Manufacturing Cost Comparisons of Alternative Designs

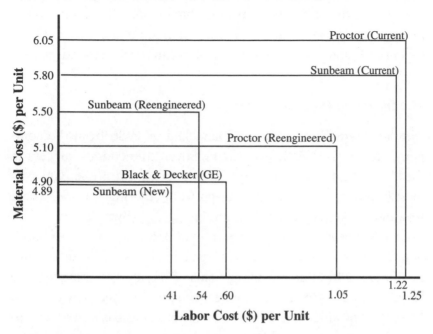

studying their products and the manufacturing processes behind them.

In the figure, Proctor Silex's current product was estimated to have $6.05 of material cost and $1.25 of labor per unit. Sunbeam's current product was not much better. Although incremental redesign of those current products and their manufacturing processes would result in improvements to materials and labor costs, the General Electric product would remain the low-cost leader (at $4.90 material and $0.60 labor per unit). However, comprehensive product and process redesign for the Global Iron put Sunbeam ahead of the pack in terms of both materials and labor costs ($4.85 materials, $0.41 labor).

The new platform had another great advantage. Because it was so modular and its subsystem interfaces so clear, the platform was capable of generating a wide array of derivative steam/dry irons. In other words, it was upwardly scalable. The various derivatives produced from the basic platform were able to meet the specific needs of many market segments, from low end to top of the line, and from region to region, all the while maintaining an overall cost advantage.

The Impact of the Global Iron

The Sunbeam Global Iron was launched in 1986 from the company's redesigned U.S. plant and enjoyed tremendous success in the United States, Canada, and Latin America. Intra-company politics, however, prevented the design from entering Europe, where Rowenta managers insisted on producing their own design.

Still, Sunbeam iron sales went from 800,000 a year to over 3 million. The new product platform became the basis for an entire family of irons sold to all major segments of the market, including the large low-end segment that Sunbeam had never effectively cracked. Derivative products were issued on an ongoing basis. As they appeared, the company's older iron designs were discontinued.

COMPOSITE DESIGN OF MANUFACTURING PROCESSES

Product development engineers cannot harvest the benefits of composite design initiatives without the collaboration of manufacturing and process engineers, working side by side. While the product engineers are going through one design iteration after another—trying to get the function to work and then trying to find the "one best way" to design it to work—the manufacturing engineers must determine the "one best way" to produce the design. Composite design efforts will fall short of their potential if manufacturing insists that the new design be compatible with its current production capabilities. If the manufacturing fraternity is satisfied with simple parity with competitors, then product designers might as well toss in the towel. Composite design calls for the optimized solutions in product, process, and marketing to gain uncontested value and cost leadership. Parity is not acceptable. Composite design will uncover parity wherever it exists: in product design, in process, in marketing, and in distribution. Having found parity,a company can then pursue a superior solution.

We would suggest that the same techniques we have described for product platform design can be productively applied to study manufacturing processes in depth. Manufacturing processes are often viewed as monolithic, nondisturbable, sequential operations. By tearing down those processes and representing them in the form of block diagrams showing the major process subsystems and interfaces between them, you have the beginnings of indexing of your processes against those of other manufacturers. One might examine such factors as materials yield, throughput, tooling cost, capital expenditures, and setup times. One could then begin to consider what elements of the process should be based on proprietary special-purpose equipment as opposed to general-purpose equipment. All these considerations should help produce a more flexible yet cost efficient process.

COMPOSITE DESIGN AND HYBRID PRODUCTS

Products usually originate as single-function products and continue as such for years and sometimes decades, constantly improving in performance, cost, and reliability. For example, the AM radio invented decades ago rambled down its product path as a single-function device. FM radio was invented later and likewise followed a singular product path for many years. Eventually someone saw the benefit of producing the AM/FM radio, which represented a new product path.

The portable tape recorder, another consumer audio product, appeared after World War II. Compact disks (CD) and CD players followed some forty years later. Eventually these single-product technologies were combined into a "hybrid," multifunctional product: a stereo system with AM/FM radio, audio tape, and CD functions. To a great extent, each of the otherwise separate systems benefited from the integration of common subsystems: electronics, speakers, cord sets, dials, power supplies, housings and the like. The result was a new, more dynamic product.

With its introduction of the OfficeJet, Hewlett Packard also demonstrated the hybridization of products. The OfficeJet brought together functions originally found only in separate products: computer printer, fax machine, photocopier, and optical scanner. Those products had a number of subsystems in common. For example, the subsystem that provided computer printing could also serve the printing requirements of the plain-paper fax machine photocopier. By designing around those common systems, HP was able to produce a four-function office machine with a very small "footprint" and an attractive price tag. For home office workers with limited space but multiple requirements, the OfficeJet provided great utility in a small "footprint."

Hybridization occurs when engineers and marketers find opportunities for creating greater utility for the end user while lowering the cost and the size of all the individual free-standing functions. In the Hewlett Packard example, the four functions are contained in a product that is 17 x 16 x 11 inches—significantly smaller than that of the four free-standing products. And at the 1995 retail price of around $600 for the base level machine, its cost was much less than the cost of purchasing a printer, a fax machine, a copier, and a scanner.

Hybridization is not confined to high-tech industries. Consider the flyfishing domain mentioned earlier. The Pak-Vest by Patagonia combines a fishing vest with a backpack for the fisherman wandering far afield. The unit can serve as a standalone fishing vest, a standalone back pack, or a combination of the two joined by the ubiquitous plastic snap buckle found in dozens of other products.

Composite design techniques enhance our ability to create hybrid products without abandoning the elegant subsystems that were essential in the development of single-function products.

STRIVE FOR PRAGMATISM IN THE DESIGN OF
NEW PRODUCT PLATFORMS

Russell Ackoff (formerly of the University of Pennsylvania) observed that corporations that make five-year product plans suffer from trying to predict the technologies that will be available in five years, and then base their new product plans on those predictions. In dynamic industries such predictions are themselves soon obsolete, making the new product plans obsolete. That leads to a never ending cycle of planning and replanning, which in turn yields paralysis. Corporations end up working on more certain things, namely derivative products created from existing platforms and technologies.

Ackoff suggested a more pragmatic approach, which he called "idealized designs." "Such a design or redesign," Ackoff argued, "is a conception of a system that its designers would like to have *right* now, not at some future date. Therefore, the environment in which the system would have to operate need not be forecast; it is the current environment."[10]

The essence of idealized design as applied to products is as follows: Rather than design new products based on technologies that you would like to have five years from today, build a composite design that is the most effective combination of best-in-class subsystems and components available from throughout the world *today*. The new design is the one the designers would choose for their customers if they were free to choose any solution at all, unfettered by the corporation's existing approaches and products. The basic reasoning goes: There are many good solution elements out there in the world, but you need to step outside your office to find it!

An idealized design of a new product platform need not be "perfect," as its developers will continue to learn about new technologies and to incorporate them into successive generations of the platform. Longer-range technology forecasting is important as a continuous process to refresh the firm's inventory of building blocks; it should not be on the critical path for building critically needed product platforms.

In our terms, the "idealized design" of a new platform might be the synthesis of Subsystem X from one of your own product lines, or a ready-to-use piece of technology from the lab; Subsystem Y from another company in your industry; and Subsystem Z from yet another company outside your industry. Since these subsystems already exist, actually creating the new platform is an endeavor that can be achieved in a reasonable amount of time.

Experimentation and learning constitute one of the important emphases of the composite design approach. When a team starts the composite design effort, it will invariably have more questions than answers. These "I don't knows" should be cherished, because the answers to them may be the key drivers behind a truly successful product platform.

A word of caution. Corporations are turning to "standardization" of components to lower procurement costs and production costs. Consider several things first before racing off on a standardization craze. Standardization and product platforms are not synonymous; standardization can be achieved through robust platforms, but robust platforms themselves cannot be achieved solely through standardization. Further, standardization for all components across a product portfolio can lead to rigidity in underlying platforms and inflexibility when it comes to advancing product designs into the future. Standardization by itself can also lead to nothing more than "me-too" products only at parity in the industry. Many PC clone manufacturers, for example, have difficulty differentiating themselves on anything more than price—a path of profitless survival.

An effective approach to standardization is one that is highly selective, carefully choosing elements that should be standardized. First and foremost are the subsystem interfaces (and user interfaces for systems and software). Once robust interfaces are either designed or obtained from the industry at large, and then fixed into place, degrees of freedom emerge for developers to improve particular subsystems or to add entirely new ones.

Second, and equally important, a company must examine its product architecture to identify those particular subsystems which have the potential of unique proprietary technology and production, i.e., to *not be at parity* with the rest of the world. Such key subsystems can drive the entire portfolio and should therefore be standardized across it. Once identified, management can pour resources into those highly leveragable subsystems and make them powerful *assets* of the corporation. This type of standardization is an internal form based on proprietary high-value-added technology.

The other type of standardization is the more conventional external form, where third party components and modules that are available to anybody are integrated with proprietary subsystems to create diverse products. However, if a company concentrates only on this second type of standardization to reduce costs and part count complexity, it will be difficult to achieve sustained competitive advantage. We emphasize once again: *Value, in the form of function that brings utility and pleasure to the user, must also exist with lower cost.*

Composite design, of course, is not the only ingredient for making successful new product platforms. It must be combined with an effective market development plan. That means clearly understanding customer "hot buttons" through focus groups and surveys and translating them into promotional materials and advertisements. It also means priming the firm's distribution channels to handle the new stream of products. It may also mean the development of new distribution channels. Indeed, strong market development must be considered the hidden genie of product development. Without it, even the best of new products will not achieve their full market potential.

5

Organizing for Renewal

The top priority for a business enterprise is to prosper over time. Since responsibility for that job lies squarely on the shoulders of senior management, one would expect that they would organize their companies in ways that assure that product portfolios are kept alive and vibrant. Unfortunately, that is seldom the case, particularly among older established companies. More often, "self-maintenance"—the preservation of the status quo—assumes top priority, absorbing energy and resources that should be directed toward renewal. In the worse cases, the firm can only find growth-fueling innovations outside its formal boundaries, in skunk works projects and in smaller, less bureaucratic companies that it targets for acquisition.

Recognizing the need to generate renewal from within, management theorists have recommended various approaches to organizing business activities: by function, by product, and through matrices.[1] Each of these approaches has found its way into practice, but none has proved to be a universal "magic bullet." Companies have organized and reorganized, but the ideal structure for fostering and commercializing innovation has remained elusive.

During the past decade autonomous cross-functional teams have been widely adopted as an antidote to the vexing problem of portfolio stagnation, often with remarkable success. One of the most memorable was "Team Taurus," which brought together the best and brightest at Ford Motor Company under the leadership of a strong and autonomous team leader, the late Lew Veraldi. Team Taurus created the vehicle platform that brought Ford back from the brink of business failure in the early 1980s and gave the company a new lease on life. Other celebrated cases of team-based product innovation have occurred at IBM, Kodak, and Boeing, to name just a few.

The idea of attacking problems through teams is not new. Over a decade ago, Takeuchi and Nonaka, professors at Hitotsubashi University, reported on the effectiveness of teams in Japanese companies, contrasting them to traditional approaches in product development:

> The traditional sequence or "relay race" approach to product development may conflict with the goals of maximum speed and flexibility. Instead, a holistic or "rugby" approach—where a team tries to go the distance as a unit, passing the ball back and forth—may better serve today's competitive environment. Under the old approach, a product development process moved like a relay race, with one group of functional specialists passing the baton to the next group. The project went sequentially from phase to phase: concept development, feasibility testing, product design, development processes, pilot production, and final production. . . . Under the rugby approach, the product development process emerges from the constant interaction of a hand-picked, multidisciplinary team whose members work closely together from start to finish. Rather than moving in defined, highly structured stages, the process is born out of team members' interplay.[2]

More recently, Katzenbach and Smith, management consultants, have observed that "teams are the primary unit of performance in an increasing numbers of organizations [and] teams naturally integrate performance and learning."[3]

Despite these endorsements, many companies remain burdened

by slow, functionally based bureaucracies that impede break-through technological innovations, new product platforms, and future streams of exciting new products. Even when teams are formed, few are provided with the autonomy required for true success. In other cases the championing executive moves on to other endeavors, or the team's efforts are undermined by corporate committees and procedures and turf-protecting functionaries.

Much has been written during the past few years about the utility of cross-functional teams, and a number of excellent books and articles are available to whoever wishes to study them in detail. The purpose of this chapter is to highlight a few aspects of team-based product line renewal that are often ignored: ownership of the destiny of projects; optimal team staffing; and the importance of collocation.

ORGANIZATIONAL APPROACHES TO RENEWAL

Experience indicates that successful innovation through teams has three ingredients: ownership, empowerment, and constancy. Ownership is control—a charter to make the decisions required by the task. Empowerment provides teams with the time and resources necessary to do the job. Constancy means that ownership and empowerment are granted for the full term of a project, from conceptualization until such time as the concept has either succeeded or failed in the market.

The importance of these three essential ingredients is affirmed in the case of a furniture manufacturer. This seventy-five-year-old company enjoyed several billion dollars in annual sales and had just completed a decade of unprecedented growth. During a lull in its most important annual trade show, the newly hired vice president of R&D was approached by the company chairman, who asked this question: "Well, George, now that you've been with us for a few months, what do you think of our products and the way we do things here? If you could only say only one thing, what would it be?"

George thought for a moment. "Just one thing?" he asked.

"Right," nodded the chairman.

"Nobody owns the product line!"

The Chairman looked confused. "What do you mean? We all own the product line in this company, George."

"Well," George said, "after three months of roaming around the company I cannot find anyone who claims responsibility for either the product line or for any individual product. No one!" Gesturing toward the products showcased behind them, he continued. "This is our most important product line—our biggest generator of sales and profits—and it's ten years old, getting tired, and losing market appeal. And yet I haven't been able to identify any one person who gets out of bed every day, comes to work, and says 'This product line is my responsibility.' "

"You don't understand, George," the chairman smiled. "Everyone thinks about this product line. Each of us is responsible and accountable."

Emboldened by the challenge of getting through to the person at the top, George continued: "Well, sir, in my discussions, I've compiled a list of very simple, straightforward questions about the product line. I haven't found anyone who can answer *any* of them. Maybe you can."

George went through a mental list of questions he had asked repeatedly during his first months with the company:

- Where has the entire product line been in sales and profits over the past ten years? Are year-to-year sales and profits climbing, staying the same, or declining? And what about market share?
- Who decides on R&D, design, marketing, and manufacturing work for this product line?
- Is marketing uncovering the customer needs that will drive the next generation of this product line? And if marketing is, does anyone even listen to them?
- Is engineering aware of new technologies outside of our industry that could improve our choices of materials, components, and so forth?

• Do manufacturing decisions that affect this product line get reviewed by anyone outside the manufacturing department?

"Whenever I ask these questions," George told the chairman, "I only get puzzled looks and one answer: 'I don't know'".

Perhaps your company is like George's, one where growth, complexity, and human carelessness have conspired to obscure clear lines of control and responsibility between individuals and revenue-generating products. It simply follows that when *everybody* is in charge, *nobody* is in charge. The answers to questions like George's can usually be found *somewhere* in the organization, though not in one place. All too often, the only people with a comprehensive set of answers are external management consultants.

The failure of management to invest product line ownership in a single location eventually leads to a business setback—a "wakeup" call that comes after the neglected product line has irreversibly lost its market power. The irony is that most of those setbacks are avoidable. *Every* organization has enlightened and concerned employees who are aware of creeping product obsolescence and the gradual erosion of market share. Many have worthy ideas about how to correct the situation and regain market advantage. But because these individuals don't "own" the product or the product family, they are not empowered to act.

Provide Ownership at Every Level

Within product families, ownership must be provided to teams developing each product platform and its respective derivative products. From an organizational perspective, that means the corporation should "look" like the things it seeks to make. As Morris, a management consultant, and Ferguson, a technological entrepreneur, noted, "Organizational architecture and decision-making" *should* "mirror technical architecture." They describe the "Silicon Valley Model" where teams are formed following "a clean separation between centralized general purpose functions (such as the platform developments we have described in this book) and decentralized or special purpose functions" (such as specific derivative products), so that "individual technologies, components, or products can be switched without the need to redo everything." They go on to add that in these fast-moving firms, "Organizations are very flat, and development groups have simple, clean interfaces to each other determined by architectural boundaries."[4]

Microsoft, for example, has different business units responsible for developing its operating systems software and applications software, and different groups within those business units working on new platform developments within each area. While the company achieves synergy in the marketplace from the two groups, its also achieves strategic flexibility. For example, Microsoft's applications software is developed to run on different operating systems. Frequent communication between teams involved in parallel developments in the two groups helps keep Microsoft's respective developments synchronized.[5]

A platform-based organization resembles James B. Quinn's "spider's web" organization,[6] an adaptation of which is shown in Figure 5–1. In this figure, platform teams are networked to derivative product teams and to one another. As new platforms are brought on line, derivative product teams are formed. Naturally, each team must have a clear charter that, among other things, assigns boundaries for its work and prevents conflicts with other teams. In this way each team is clearly focused. As in the Microsoft example, continuous coordination and communication are required between team leaders to synchronize the activities of platform teams and product teams.

Avoid the Square Peg Syndrome

While it would seem logical for companies to organize in ways that reflect the products or services they are trying to make, it does not always happen. One large manufacturer we know had developed a core business in films and cameras with an organizational structure

FIGURE 5–1

Spider's Web Organization for Product Family Development and Renewal

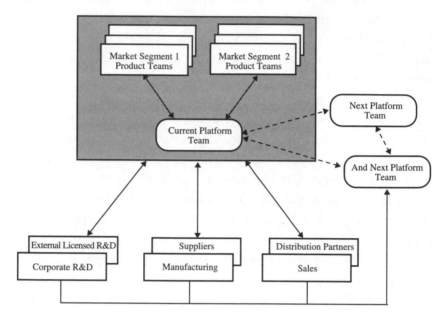

of functional smokestacks (R&D, manufacturing, and distribution). Such an organization was well suited to the company's traditional high-volume commodity products. Facing a decline in that core business, however, senior management started initiatives to create systems that were essentially low-volume, high-value-added products requiring the integration of numerous peripheral technologies, computers, and software. Those initiatives were driven through the existing functional organization. Not surprisingly, few successful systems were ever created. Instead, a new set of peripherals that consume the company's traditional commodity products was produced. Ignoring the market demands for integrated systems, the top functional managers steered systems development toward stand-alone peripherals product development, reflecting the types of engineering, manufacturing, and distribution with which they felt comfortable. The net result was that the company spent vast resources trying to drive a square plug into a round hole.

Avoid Pseudo-Ownership

Perhaps no organizational sin is more demoralizing to teams than what we call "pseudo-ownership." Pseudo-ownership is a condition in which teams believe they have the authority to make critical decisions, when in fact others have reserved that authority for themselves. Pseudo-ownership is typically revealed at the interfaces of the project and the corporate functions that assist it: R&D, design, test and evaluation, marketing, cataloguing, product service, quality control, and purchasing. Each function has its rules and procedures and assumes authority over all decisions within its own jurisdiction. Each serving function seizes temporary control. For example, a team that assumed it had effective ownership of a development project might find that marketing had unilaterally made decisions about pricing and distribution. Such practices are antithetical to the notion of ownership and must be eliminated by senior management.

We return to Takeuchi and Nonaka's analogy of the relay race to suggest a solution to the problem of ownership. But here imagine a relay race in which management handcuffs the baton to the team members. When the baton (project) needs input or service from a specific function, say, pricing, the team visits the pricing group to discuss pricing strategy. The baton is not uncoupled and left in the pricing team area but remains securely attached to the team member. The final decision on pricing is made by the team and not by the pricing function.

Thus, the team moves from function to function, attaching itself by turn to the resources needed for the project. Using this approach, the team can remain small and can move with speed and efficiency through the corporation. The team keeps the involvement of outside functions to a minimum, keeps meetings small, and prevents the jockeying and second guessing that can easily disrupt its progress.

BUILDING TEAMS THAT BUILD PRODUCTS

Staffing Platform Development Teams

Platform and derivative product teams should be small and cross-functional—limited to dedicated individuals who collectively represent a range of functional skills and interests. The selection process must be carefully managed and should avoid people who

- are not busy
- are not critical to the organization
- happen to be available

Chances are that people who fit any of these descriptions will not be the champions of change. As a rule of thumb, if the head of a functional department allows you to recruit one of his or her people without an argument, you have not picked one of the best people.

The best team candidates are people who are attracted by challenge and are not overly risk-averse. They want to excel and make significant contributions to the company and to their own careers. Many times such individuals are frustrated because they are under-utilized and unchallenged, stuck working on old technology and failing businesses. They are the very people who tend to get wooed away by competitors. Why not give them an important new challenge?

The first team member should be an individual with the potential to lead the project from inception to commercialization. Our bias is toward entrepreneurial marketing types who can work comfortably with researchers, engineers, scientists, designers, finance personnel, sales people and—of course—customers. He or she must formulate the "thought architecture" of the project and use it as a vehicle to share the vision, the dream, the potential of the renewal program.

Team member number one works with the top managers to identify and recruit the remaining players, balancing the team with other people from key functions: product design, manufacturing, and marketing development. Once a core platform development team is established, each member must be freed from prior obligations; their attention to the task at hand must be total. They must report directly to the sponsoring executive(s), who monitors the team's work and guides annual salary reviews.

Selecting and recruiting people with the right skills is obviously important. Less obvious is the importance of bringing together people who can share a common vision. A group of individuals who either cannot pursue a common goal or cannot pursue it together is not a team.

The Sponsoring Executive

Cross-functional teams are usually threatened by their own success. Particularly in companies with traditions of powerful functional silos, teams that usurp even a fraction of the decision-making power held by functional executives are bound to ruffle feathers and create adversaries. They are also bound to challenge existing technologies, processes, and market strategies.

Every team must be linked to a senior executive to manage organizational conflicts, someone with both the power and the commitment to provide "air cover" for the team. The role is not without risks for the executive, whose reputation (and perhaps career) may ride on the success of the venture. The executive sponsor must be willing to put his or her own "skin in the game." At the same time the sponsoring executive must avoid the temptation to take responsibility or ownership of the project away from the team. To that point, our advice is this:

• Insist that the team make the important decisions—and take responsibility for the consequences.
• If new people are needed, the team should select them.
• Give direction, participate in problem-solving, and provide "air cover," but only when needed.

• Make his or her support visible to the team members and to other people in the company.

A team's commitment and authority can be anchored with a team charter. A team charter is a document signed by top management stating the objectives and authority of the team. Armed with such a charter, the team can remind itself and others that its purpose is legitimate and authorized by top management. The team charter signed by Sunbeam senior management for the global iron project described in Chapter 4 is shown in Figure 5–2. It was a concise statement of Sunbeam's current situation and where it wanted to be.

FIGURE 5–2

The Sunbeam Global Iron Team Charter

The Global Iron Project's charter is to develop a new steam/dry iron product line that will achieve the following goals:

	Today's Realities	Tomorrow's Desires
Products	Conventional	Global chassis
	Dated design	Modular models
	High cost	Feature/cost leadership
	Long, complex product line	Simpler product line with stepup functions
Market Share	Spotty in various markets	Strong in all selected markets
	Some strong, many weak	Greater than 30% share worldwide
Facilities and Manufacturing	Outdated and outmoded	Flexible and modular
	Fixed high labor content	Absolute minimum labor content
Technology	Pedestrian	State of the art materials and processes

The team is further chartered to determine its own staffing requirements, to prepare and present timelines and budgets to senior management, and to maintain decision-making control over the product line as it moves into production and distribution.

RUNNING THE GAUNTLET

Machiavelli stated a truth about organizational life that remains as potent today as it was in Renaissance Florence: "There is nothing more difficult to carry out, or more doubtful of success, nor more dangerous to handle, than to initiate a new order of things. For the reformer has enemies in all those who profit from the old order."

The order of things is not changed in any fundamental way without upsetting someone's applecart. Teams that set out to renew or replace current products or services are likely to run headlong into either active hostility or disinterest. Managers of aging product lines are unlikely to cooperate. In their thinking, the team's resources would be better spent on their cash cows, even though they may be losing power in the marketplace. "After all," they contend, "we provide most of the profits to this company." And they are often right—for the moment. Others in the organization may simply fail to see the importance of the team's purpose. Both problems underscore the importance of having the team allied to a respected executive of the company.

Even with high-level support, product development involves "running the gauntlet," i.e., passing through barriers and obstacles designed to minimize mistakes and to ensure that every issue is considered. Many products never make it through that passage.

Our gauntlet checklist, shown below, is designed to help executives prepare the team for it's ordeal by fire. Every "no" response in the questionnaire must be considered a serious barrier to success. The sponsor must either eliminate the "no"s or defuse their ability to scuttle or damage the project. If the project is not important enough to command "yes"es, both the executive sponsor and the team may be fooling themselves about the significance or practicality of the task.

1. Is there a powerful senior manager who wants the project and will give it personal backing? Yes _____   No _____

2. Have other top management committed to the project? Have

they assigned a "Champion" of stature and power to lead and manage the endeavor? Yes _____ No _____

3. Is the project viewed as essential to the success of the company? Yes _____ No _____

4. Does (or could) the project have global potential? Yes _____ No _____

5. If successful in its development and implementation, will the project make a significant impact/difference to:
   The product line? Yes _____ No _____
   The end user or customer? Yes _____ No _____
   The company's profits, market share, growth? Yes _____ No _____
   The company's competitors? Yes _____ No _____

6. Are new and previously unapplied technologies accessible that will enrich and expand capabilities or create new features and functions? (Heretofore not available or integrated into our products or those of competitors?) Yes _____ No _____

7. Will a discontinuity and/or a new standard of performance be created by this project? Yes _____ No _____

8. Will this project fulfill unperceived needs of the end users or customers? Yes _____ No _____

9. Can this project be insulated from the bureaucratic quagmire of the corporation and managed on a fast track? Yes _____ No _____

10. Are these critical functions involved and committed from the concept stage to the commercialization of the project?
    R&D   Yes _____ No _____
    Marketing   Yes _____ No _____
    Product Engineering   Yes _____ No _____
    Manufacturing   Yes _____ No _____
    Design/Styling   Yes _____ No _____

When a platform renewal team starts its work, the vast majority of time is spent in collaborative discussion. A specific set of questions can direct and lend purpose to that initial discussion:

1. How do we define our business and market? Are we defining them too narrowly, based strictly on the traditional activities of the company? Are we failing to embrace future possibilities in both the market and the technology? What is the appropriate market segmentation grid (harking back to Chapter 3) for the business?

2. Should we even be in this business? Can we participate in it profitably? Can the market provide the levels of growth and profitability necessary to support a bold initiative and all the hard work that we are about to do? What are the "sweet spots" of the market, i.e., those niches within the broader market that offer the best returns for our labors?

3. Will our existing customers stay with us, given our existing product or service solutions?

4. How do our competitors view us and our products or services: as a "pushover," an "also-ran," or a formidable contender?

5. How are the functions of our products or services being performed around the globe? How many different ways can the customer be served with the equivalent functionality of our own products or services?

6. How are customers not being served by any product, from anywhere around the globe? Of these unfilled needs, which ones might be "must haves" as opposed to "nice to haves" if we could satisfy them? What are the opportunities to bring new levels of excitement to our market?

7. What product or process technologies are the foundations of the desired product set, i.e., the new product platform? In which areas do we have distinctive competence? With respect to the others, which firms or suppliers have such competence? How can we most quickly and effectively evaluate their technologies?

These questions will motivate the team to engage customers, potential partners, and suppliers in its quest for answers. In other words, the team's research should be externally focused. From these basic questions, certain "rules" emerge, which provide further guidance to the effort. The combination of the answers and derived rules become the thought architecture for the team and should be posted prominently within the team room. They become the foundation of the composite design process described in the prior chapter. These questions can also serve as the framework for an initial briefing to senior management.

THE IMPORTANCE OF COLLOCATION

During the height of the German blitz in 1940, 10 Downing Street was declared unsafe, and Prime Minister Winston Churchill, his wife, and his staff moved into a bomb-proofed set of basement rooms of the Board of Trade building overlooking St. James's Park. Known as "No. 10 Annex," those rooms became Churchill's working headquarters and living space for the remainder of the war. Several rooms of the facility were used as map rooms, each dedicated to a particular theater of conflict. Other rooms contained radio and communications equipment. In this warren, Churchill created a nerve center where all intelligence reports, radio intercepts, field reports, and other war-related information were made available to Britain's team of war planners and political leaders.[7] There he and his staff ate, slept, and brought together key people representing British and Allied forces. As plans were laid, everything known to the British about troop strength and locations, war production, the position of German ships and aircraft, and thousands of other details, was available to decision-makers.

Two other key operations—the RAF Fighter Command and the Admiralty's "Room 39"—followed the same model of collocating multidisciplined groups of decision-makers in information-rich environments. There, the loose threads of information, which had little meaning in themselves, could be woven into a coherent picture that all could share. That system was far superior to the one used by the American military establishment at the time. Because of interservice rivalries and lack of coordination, American war planners and diplomats in 1940–41 had no system for effectively bringing together people and information. In fact, one of the shocking lessons of the catastrophe of Pearl Harbor was that the many pieces of information that would have identified the when, where, and how of Japan's surprise attack were known by the State Department and individual military personnel, but were never integrated together into a coherent meaning. According to the late Gordon Prange, a leading authority on the Pacific War, "Pearl Harbor was less a failure of intelligence than a failure to use the excellent data available."[8]

The principles of collocating teams, exposing them to a variety of information, and providing a persistent display of that information are important to business as well. Just bringing team members together into one physical place has been shown to improve communication and information-sharing. There, small bits of knowledge and information that by themselves mean nothing can be pieced together with other bits to form meaningful insights. Team collocation also fosters bonding between individual members and the commitment needed for focused, fast, high-risk projects.

Academic research has measured the communications aspects of collocation. After extensively documenting the specific communications between engineers and engineering managers of a large manufacturer, Thomas Allen of MIT underscored the importance of physical proximity for two people who need to talk to each other.[9] Allen found that if two individuals reporting to different managers were located just 30 feet apart, their probability of communicating dropped to a mere 5 percent! If they had the same boss, that probability was only about 15 percent. Considering that R&D, manufacturing, and sales departments are often located in different buildings (if not in different countries), one can easily imagine the difficulty of achieving the amount and quality of communications required for simultaneous design and renewal of product lines.[10]

Inside the Team Room

Full-time team members must have offices or desks adjacent to one another. They must also have a large, open team room where many types of information can be displayed on flip charts or on notes on the walls. Competitors' products should also be on display, both assembled and disassembled, with notes indicating their suppliers and estimated material and labor costs. Team rooms create the cohesiveness and cross-fertilization essential to team-building, even within large corporations.

Takeuchi and Nonaka described a team room used by Fuji-Xerox in building the FX-3500 medium-size copier (introduced in 1978). Team members from planning, design, production, sales, distribution, and evaluation departments were brought together in one large room. As described by one member of that team:

> When all the team members are located in one large room, someone's information becomes yours, without even trying. You then start thinking in terms of what's best or second best for the group at large and not only about where you stand. If everyone understands the other person's position, then each of us is more willing to give in, or at least to try to talk to each other. Initiatives emerge as a result.[11]

A team room serves not only as a meeting place but as a physical repository for the various questions and answers that a team must deal with over the course of a project. Those should always be highly visible, not stored away in project books or files. At project initiation, we favor calling the team room the "I Don't Know" room. A list of the "I Don't Knows" are prominently posted on one wall and should stay there until they are either converted to "I Knows" or determined to be unimportant. As the answers emerge, they too should be placed on the team room walls. Such answers might include:

- the results of market studies
- the details of all competing products, on a subsystem by subsystem basis
- the platform strategy, as defined in Chapter 3 in terms of a platform-market grid

- engineering designs for key subsystems and interfaces of the new product platform
- manufacturing data and process designs
- engineering and other schedules
- project budget, sales projections, and staffing requirements
- a product family rollout plan
- comments by company executives and visitors
- a special wall section reserved for Post Its of any unresolved question

Circles of Collaboration

Team work, like any other work, requires structure for interactions among team members. Figure 5–3 presents a framework for struc-

FIGURE 5–3

Structuring Teamwork: Circles of Collaboration

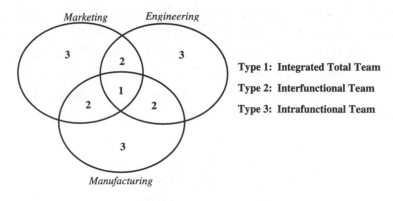

Type 1: Integrated Total Team
Type 2: Interfunctional Team
Type 3: Intrafunctional Team

Integrated Total Team Activities
Setting Direction
Aligning Priorities
Exploratory Market Research
Exploratory Technical Research
Concept Development
Experimentation
Validation:
"It works; we can make it;
we can sell it."

turing team work, depicted as intersecting circles of marketing, engineering, and manufacturing. (A case could be made for representing finance as a fourth circle.)

The core of the figure, where all three circles intersect, represents activities in which all three functions must collaborate. This is the "Integrated Total Team," referred to as Type 1 work in Figure 5–3. Adjacent to the inner core area are three areas where only two of the three circles share the same space. This we identify as Type 2 work in the figure: marketing interacts with product development; manufacturing with marketing; manufacturing with product development. At the periphery of the framework are tasks that each function performs by itself and then brings back to the team for subsequent integration. This is Type 3 work: the type that team members do on their own. There is great efficiency in this structuring of work. Not everybody must to be involved in everything— only in those tasks that require common understanding and subsequent integration. Clearly, an essential task for the team leader is to help the team define those specific activities in a new platform development that are Types 1, 2, or 3.

Vincent Barabba of General Motors has described the areas of overlapping activities (Types 1 and 2 work activities) as areas of "shared organizational knowledge." Organizational knowledge, according to Barabba, is defined as

> the agreed-on, shared portion (the intersection) of what individuals, working on a specific problem, know that is relevant to their collective action. It is established through a dialogue in which each individual brings forward his or her knowledge to the group, which then jointly arrives at shared, relevant organizational knowledge.[12]

It is this sharing of individual understandings within the overlapping areas that enriches the understanding of the team. Those are the areas in which common knowledge is created. And nowhere is this knowledge richer than at the central intersection (Type 1). Type 1 is also the critical area where the term leader and sponsoring executive must assert priorities and focus.

A MULTIDISCIPLINED TEAM AT WORK

Steelcase, the largest U.S. manufacturer of office furniture, provides an interesting case study on how collocated multidisiciplined teams can renew product lines, given proper resources and ownership of their work.

Steelcase had made fluorescent lighting fixtures for its office furniture for many years, but little attention had been paid to this product line or to its platform design and manufacturing processes. Over the years the product line had grown to the point where by 1993 it encompassed four product platforms and a total of 228 style numbers. Not surprisingly, the product line was only marginally profitable, especially in the low-end platforms. Meanwhile, three O.E.M. manufacturers had entered the business and had captured approximately 65 percent of the market with lower-cost designs.

Senior management at Steelcase was on the verge of abandoning the lighting line altogether, convinced that outsourcing might be a viable solution. Before that happened, however, a senior vice president took the initiative to investigate both the market and available product and process technologies that might be used for renewal of the lighting product family. The data convinced him that Steelcase could gain a cost advantage over its competitors if it mounted a dedicated effort to renew the product line. He developed a "thought architecture" for the project that emphasized many of the ideas espoused in this book:

- a robust platform that could be scaled into a variety of derivative products, and which—by virtue of function, features, style, and cost—could revitalize the product line
- the highest degree of modularity and flexibility in platform design, eliminating parts wherever possible
- per unit cost reductions through integrated manufacturing, increased material yield, and high-volume procurement of essential parts and materials direct from manufacturers, not from distributors

- a multidisciplined team with true product ownership from development to commercialization, and through subsequent platform generations

A multidisciplined team of five individuals was recruited to full-time work on the project, one of them the team leader who reported directly to the senior officer. The disciplines represented on the team were marketing, product design, manufacturing, and market development. The team leader was the marketing member. Team members were collocated adjacent to each other and in close proximity to the senior vice president. A project "war room" was provided for the team's exclusive use.

The team was given total responsibility for design, tooling, manufacturing, market research and market development, pricing, advertising and promotion, training, and so forth. Equally important, the team received sufficient financial resources to fulfill those responsibilities. It had, for example, resources to commission a study of the market and the competitive situation. Techniques such as conjoint analysis were rigorously applied in a quest for insights into the features and benefits that customers wanted and were willing to pay for. It had the authority to hire and pay outside experts for help on critical aspects of design and tooling.

The team was determined to create a line of lighting fixtures that could be integrated with office desks and cubicles designed by Steelcase and those of other major manufacturers. Indeed, only a combination of internal and external demand could support the production volumes needed to justify automation and achieve economies in material procurement. Toward that end the team developed a business plan, a capital requisition plan, a pro-forma profit and loss statement, a detailed marketing plan, and other documentation. Indeed, the team viewed itself as a new entrepreneurial company, with Steelcase as its venture capitalist.

Within 367 days of project concept, a new line of lighting fixtures was shipped to initial customers. With production under way, the team was relocated *en masse* to the manufacturing plant, where it continued its intimate linkage to the "new business" it had created. It maintained that control even as other departments within Steelcase became involved in the manufacturing and distribution of the new product line.

As a business, the new lighting line was an early success. Just sixteen months after its first shipment and six months into its first full year of production, the project team reported impressive results:

- Annual unit volume was nearly double that of the older product line.
- Year to date sales were 38 percent ahead of plan, and profits 90 percent ahead.
- Defects were virtually nonexistent, making it possible to eliminate finished goods audits.
- Turnover of manufactured parts inventory was running at over 60 times per year, and purchased goods inventory at over 40 times per year.
- The original 228 styles were reduced to 74.

MULTIDEPARTMENTAL TEAMS

As we have stated, if products are created by organizations it also stands to reason that organization structure should be compatible with the products that the company is trying to make. When products made by separate parts of the organization are integrated together by customers as a "system," management must ensure that the products are themselves compatible and harmoniously combined. To achieve that, platform groups may have to span different organizational entities.

For example, many software firms need to have their various software applications share a common user interface or a common set of procedures for accessing data or communicating over networks. If there is no single group responsible for the design, care, and advancement of those common building blocks, commonality across applications will happen only by serendipity. Similarly, manufacturers of industrial equipment have increasingly turned their sights to provided "systems"—integrated combinations of data acquisition devices, controllers, and computers—to customers. However, most manufacturers remain organized strictly according to existing lines of individual pieces of equipment. With no single group focused on the integration of these various machines, systems integration occurs only downstream and only at considerable expense.

As depicted in Figure 5–4, rather than circles of collaboration, one often finds a circle of noncollaboration within the corporation. This leaves the firm's rear flanks vulnerable to attack by competitors. Major groups are concerned more with protecting their own respective interests than with the activities of competitors and the needs of customers. The ensuing politics can easily disrupt an ini-

FIGURE 5–4

A Circle of Noncollaboration

tiative to build and utilize common subsystems and manufacturing capability between product families. The circle of noncollaboration is one of complexities that confounds management's vision of a better future.

Talking about systems is one thing; making them happen is quite another. Only the corporation's executives can break down the barriers, and to do this they must consider forming multidisciplined platform development groups with individuals drawn from across the corporation.

Chapter 6

Measuring the Performance
of Product Families

U p to this point, we have presented a set of management concepts unified around the theme of product platforms and
families: strategic focus, designing platform architecture, and organizing the development effort. In this chapter we offer practical
tools for assessing platform and product family performance. Traditional measures are seldom useful for this purpose for the simple
reason that they focus on single products and projects.

THE STATE OF MEASUREMENT TODAY

The most broadly used measure for product development is "slip
rate." Slip rate is generally defined as the gap between expected and
actual values as applied to project time and project budget. The appeal of slip rate measures for senior management is obvious: Slip rate
measures project progress relative to plan. Unfortunately, slip rate is
in fact a better measure of the manager's ability to estimate a project's
schedule and budget. Emphasis on slip rates undoubtedly encourages
schedule and budget "padding" by project managers. Further, no one
has proven to our satisfaction that accuracy of schedule prediction is
a meaningful surrogate for technical and commercial performance.

Experience suggests that companies often prosper from late and over-budget projects—projects that would not measure up on the slip rate yardstick. For example, a study of a successful pharmaceutical company showed that the firm experienced overruns on 80 percent of its new product efforts, with an average slip of 1.78 times planned costs and 1.61 times planned schedules. Yet the firm consistently prospered from those late and over-budget products.[1]

Slip rate measures also drive managers away from platform renewal efforts and toward derivative products whose costs and development schedules are more predictable. The product family stepladder framework (represented earlier in Chapter 2) shows that rapid development cycle times are contingent upon what the firm is trying to develop. Projects that contain high levels of technological and market familiarity—the classic derivative product—can and should be pursued rapidly. On the other hand, projects having higher technological and market uncertainty—the hallmarks of new product platforms—require greater patience. Demanding tight schedules for such projects may be self-defeating. We saw this in a study of a large aluminum company, where management was seeking to create industrial products outside its traditional smelting business. Here, tight schedules for new platform efforts led to poor financial outcomes.[2]

The patience required for development of revolutionary products and processes often defies the prescriptions of time-to-market advocates. Yet the rewards for patient and persistent effort often pay off in striking ways. Britain's Pilkington Glass Company's development of process technology for continuous casting is noteworthy in this regard. Plate glass manufacture had involved a number of separate and often laborious steps: mixing and melting ingredient materials in a furnace, casting the molten glass between a set of rollers, annealing the resulting glass in a kiln, and eventually grinding and polishing the cut and hardened product to near-perfect smoothness. During the 1950s Pilkington spent vast sums, and close to a decade, developing the process technology for casting a continuous ribbon of glass onto a bed of molten tin, eliminating the annealing and polishing processes while creating perfectly smooth glass in the bargain. Success in that difficult venture gave Pilkington unassailable cost and quality leadership. However, the traditional metrics of project performance would have marked the float glass platform project as a loser during its development and initial commercialization. In fact, cash flows for the project were negative for the first twelve years, prompting the chairman, Alastair Pilkington, to remark: "If you went to an accountant and said 'I've got a great idea to create a massive negative cash flow for certain, and it may—if it's a great success—break even in its cash flows in 12 years,' you wouldn't find many accountants who'd say 'that's exactly what I want.'"[3]

Some corporations augment slip rate metrics with longer-term measures of performance. Hewlett Packard, for example, introduced a series of innovative measurements for both R&D and manufacturing during the 1980s. One of them was BET, or breakeven time. As defined by HP, BET measured the length of time from the beginning of a project until the cumulative net profit resulting from the sales of new and affected products equaled the cumulative net project investment, using the firm's after-tax cost of capital to discount cash flows.[4] IBM likewise tracks the ratio of sales to development costs for its products.

A number of companies also examine the percentage of revenues from products introduced in the past few years to supplement slip rates and time-to-market measures. Research has shown a strong correlation between industry leadership and a high percentage of revenues generated from recently introduced products. For example, one recent study found that Hewlett Packard gained 60 percent of its annual revenue from products introduced within the prior five-year period; for such companies as Gillette, 3M, Corning, and Johnson & Johnson, the ratio was between 25 percent and 35 percent.[5]

Many other measures of R&D performance have been tried in industry. Some firms count patents applied for and received by their engineers. Others use subjective scoring methods to determine whether teams have met their stated project goals.[6] Despite an abundance of metrics, a survey of some 250 R&D executives by the Industrial Research Institute showed that "measuring and improving R&D productivity and effectiveness" remained their "biggest problem," indeed a remarkable finding given that the creation of exciting new products is the lifeblood of so many corporations.[7]

MEASURES ORIENTED TO THE EVOLVING PRODUCT FAMILY

Fortunately, there are reliable methods for measuring performance from a product family perspective. We developed and have used these measures in a half-dozen large corporations, and many executive participants in our management programs have applied them to their own companies. Case examples used in explaining our metrics, in fact, come from this group of companies. The cases are disguised to respect the sensitive nature of that performance information.

Step 1: Gathering the Necessary Data

No measure of performance can be made, of course, in the absence of relevant data. Gathering data begins with a map of the corporation's product families. The reader will recall the product family map for Hewlett Packard's ink jet printers presented in Chapter 2, showing product platforms, platform extensions, and derivative products. The approach we recommend is to select an initial product family, gather the data related to it, map its evolution, then replicate that process for other product families in the corporation.

To create an accurate product family map, one needs to distinguish among (a) the initial version of a product platform, (b) extensions to the platform, (c) wholly new platforms or product architectures created to replace an existing one, and (d) the specific products associated with each platform generation. We provided definitions of those elements in Chapter 2, and they must be followed rigorously for consistency. High-level engineering diagrams of product architectures that show subsystems and interfaces are most useful in that effort.[8]

Once a product family map is created, the process of associating certain costs and revenues with different elements of the map begins. The types of data required for the analysis include:

- Engineering costs: the amount of money spent on the development of platforms (and platform components) and specific derivative products. If a company does not maintain data on resource allocation to platform developments, a surrogate for the cost of the developments can be derived using costs associated with the first product spun off from a particular version of a given platform. A number of corporations we have worked with differentiate between "product engineering" costs and "manufacturing engineering" costs. It is important not to leave out the latter.
- Development time: the time spent from start to finish in platform and derivative product development. For all practical purposes, platform efforts end when the first platform derivative is released to full-scale production. For derivative products, the development time cycle starts at the point of specific engineering work for the product itself and ends also at the time of release to manufacturing.
- Manufacturing costs: In many businesses, the cost of upgrading the manufacturing facility to handle new products overwhelms engineering expenditures. Therefore, if manufacturing is a significant activity, it makes sense to track and analyze its costs in detail. Those costs may include capital expenditures for new equipment, retooling of facilities, and ramp-up costs associated with bringing new products into production.
- Market development costs: These data may include expenditures on specific promotional campaigns for a new product, channel development expenses, and dealer training programs.

- Sales data: Sales data for each product in a family should be aggregated across its full commercial life cycle. We prefer to use net sales to account for discounts and returns.
- Margins: Sales are one thing, profitability is another. While corporations maintain profitability data for their business units, few link these profits to specific products. In the absence of product-specific P&Ls, some means must be found to assess the profitability of various products. Gross margins for individual products often provide the starting point for such analysis.

A simple spreadsheet or database can be used to keep these data, where the first column or field identifies each platform version of the product family, and the second, the specific derivative products brought to market. Successive columns or fields should contain the engineering, manufacturing, marketing, sales, and margin information for each product. The individual rows or records for each product can then be rolled up into aggregate amounts for platform versions. Since the data represent a stream of products being brought to market over time, all amounts should be adjusted for inflation to bring them to current monetary values. Canceled platform and product efforts should also be included in the data set. Many an observer has noted that corporations learn just as much, if not more, from their failures as from their successes.[9]

Gathering the data may be a matter of simply assembling existing information from larger information systems. On the other hand, the process can be laborious, particularly when responsibility for developing and manufacturing product families is spread around the world. For example, in one firm we spent almost a month poring over the old project notebooks sitting on R&D managers' shelves. More time was required to allocate project costs, with the help of those managers, to specific platforms and products. Though the work was tedious, it provided the company with a handle on the amount it had spent on actually creating its products—something it had never had.

The study team for a product family study of this sort should resemble the platform design teams described in the previous chapter, with representatives from engineering, manufacturing, marketing, and finance. They can facilitate the data collection process and "disaggregate" information to individual platform and derivative projects.

We have yet to work with a corporation that systematically integrates engineering, manufacturing, and marketing information for performance assessment. These data are typically scattered among different organizational units with two unfortunate results: (1) many people see a piece of the picture, but no one sees the whole picture, and (2) few managers see the downstream consequences of their decisions. But shouldn't the engineer who has worked on a new product know its eventual sales and profitability? Shouldn't the manufacturing manager know the commercial consequences of his or her decisions? Clearly they should, and so integration of the corporation's information is essential for assessing performance, just as the integration of the corporation's functions are essential for new product development.

Now let's see what that integration of information can tell us.

Step 2: Understanding the Efficiency of Platforms for Creating Derivative Products

To determine a platform's efficiency, one must answer several questions. The first question is whether a particular platform has provided technical leverage by being a productive base for creating derivative products. We call this *platform efficiency*. If one were to just consider engineering costs, the efficiency measure for a single derivative product can be simply stated as:

$$\text{Platform efficiency} = \frac{\text{Derivative Product Engineering Costs}}{\text{Platform Engineering Cost}}$$

Our use of the term "efficiency" refers to engineering development costs, not manufacturing yields, energy consumption by products, or other types of efficiency. For example, if the average R&D cost of developing a specific derivative product was $250,000 based on a product platform whose engineering cost alone was about $5 million, the platform efficiency for that product would be .05.

This metric can be used to understand the development efficiency for an entire generation of derivative products. All one needs to do is compute the average of the R&D costs of the derivative products for a particular platform version and then divide that amount by that platform version's own development costs. For example, if we examined a set of twenty derivative products created from a single platform over the course of three years, and if the average engineering cost for creating them was $500,000, then the platform efficiency metric for the platform during that period would be .10. In this way, one can see how platform efficiency has improved or declined across multiple generations of a product family. This formula is simply:

$$\frac{\text{Platform}}{\text{efficiency}} = \frac{\text{Average (Derivative Products Engineering Costs)}}{\text{Platform Engineering Costs}}$$

Now let's turn to a product family map abstracted from one of our field studies and apply the measure. The product family map of CONTROLS (a family of industrial measurement systems) is shown in Figure 6–1. As the map shows, CONTROLS has had two distinct platform architectures (that would be clearly supported by their block diagrams, showing the key subsystems and interfaces, if we were to look at them). The first platform was based on analog signal processing and was developed during the late 1970s, and the second platform was based on digital signal processing and first implemented during the late 1980s. The first platform had one platform extension (labeled CONTROLS 1.2) in which the major subsystems of the original design were substantially changed; the second platform had only one version. The specific derivative products based on each platform version are also shown in Figure 6–1, with a total of twelve derivatives. The

FIGURE 6-1

The Controls Product Family Map

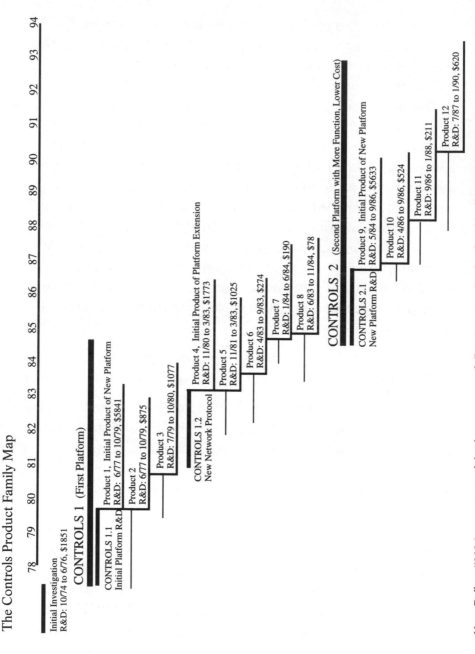

Note: Dollars ('000s) are aggregated development costs of all projects associated with and leading to a given product, adjusted to 1993 dollars. Dates are the start of R&D for earliest of these projects to the commercial release of the resulting product.

154

starting date of the earliest R&D project associated with each product is represented by the beginning of the thin lines leading to each product event on the map. Engineering costs are also shown for each product. Since the company did not keep track of platform costs versus derivative product costs, we used the engineering costs of the first product of each platform version as a surrogate for the engineering costs of that platform version.

Using these engineering cost data, we computed platform efficiencies. The results are in Figure 6–2, which shows the efficiency value for each specific derivative product, as well as the average efficiency value for each of the three generations of the product family. For a company with many derivative products, the average of

FIGURE 6–2

Platform Efficiency for CONTROLS by Product and Platform Version

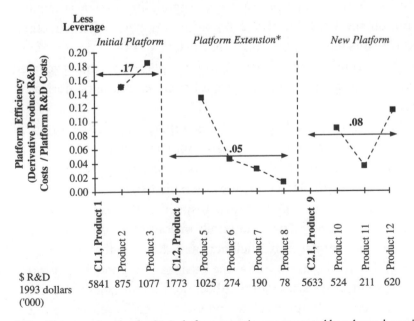

*The efficiency values for the C1.2 platform extension are computed based on a denominator that includes both the platform investments for the initial version and the extension, e.g. C1.1 + C1.

platform efficiency levels wide fluctuations among individual products to reveal the overall trend more clearly.

In Figure 6–2 you can see that the first derivative product of CONTROLS 1.1 was developed for approximately 15 cents on the platform dollar, and the second derivative product, for 18 cents on the platform dollar. The average efficiency of CONTROLS 1.1 was therefore about 17 cents on the platform dollar. The company then took advantage of new component technologies to improve key subsystems in the platform architecture significantly. For the new platform extension (CONTROLS 1.2) you can see that the platform was very successful in terms of efficient product development. The average platform efficiency measure for those products was about 5 cents on the platform dollar.[10]

With the emergence of digital signal processing, the company then "clean sheeted" an entirely new platform design and used this opportunity to reduce materials cost and improve various functions. Here the efficiency results were again impressive, at about 8 cents on the CONTROLS 2.1 platform dollar. Taken together, these results tell a "good story" for the CONTROLS product family. The company was building robust platforms that provided strong leverage in terms of the efficient creation of derivative products.

What is a reasonable platform cost efficiency value? Our study of firms in the electronics industry indicates that platform efficiency values of .10 or less mark the presence of highly leveragable product platforms. However, the desirable benchmark value for a particular company will be industry-specific. We recommend that you study a successful product family in your own company, determine its level of platform efficiency, and then use that as a benchmark for similar groups inside the business. In general, platforms within an industry sector should become more efficient over time, since in general design has become more modular and component technologies better.

The metric, as we have demonstrated it so far, has included only

FIGURE 6–3

Comparing Platform Efficiency for Product Engineering and
Manufacturing Ramp-up and Retooling

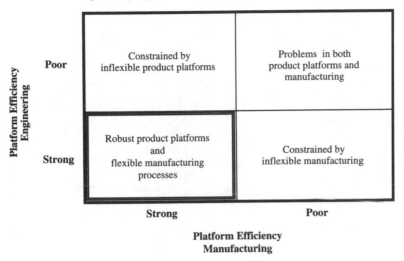

engineering costs. A more comprehensive understanding emerges
if one considers the cost ratios for introducing new products into
full-scale production. Look at Figure 6–3. The least desirable position, sitting in the upper right quadrant of the chart, is when a
company has high costs in both engineering and manufacturing for
new products relative to platform developments. Even if a company
is experiencing high platform efficiency in engineering costs, it
may serve little purpose if poor efficiency is occurring in the manufacturing domain. This position is in the lower right quadrant of
the chart. In both cases, the desired goal should be to move the
company into the "sweet spot" of the chart, where both engineering and manufacturing costs for new products are low relative to
the platform expenditures for product platforms and manufacturing processes.

For example, Figure 6–4 shows the manufacturing platform efficiency over twenty years for a product family of consumables. Over

FIGURE 6–4

CONSUMABLES' Platform Efficiency by Product and Platform Version Calculated with Ramp-up and Retooling Costs Only*

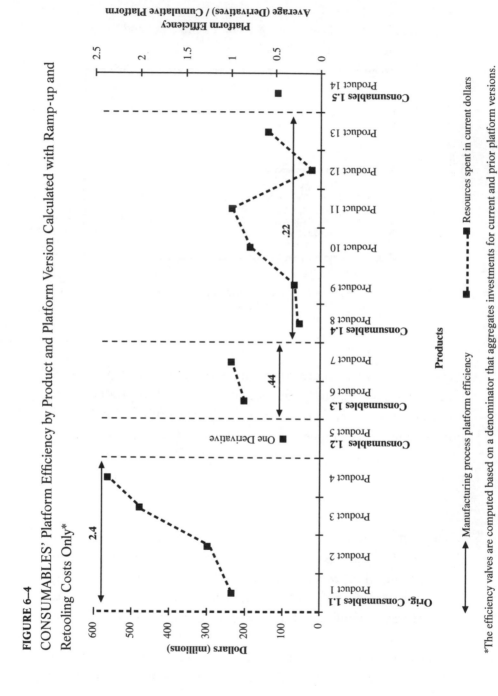

*The efficiency valves are computed based on a denominator that aggregates investments for current and prior platform versions.

158

time, the manufacturing costs for introducing new products into production have been about five times that of the product engineering costs. That is not uncommon in capital-intensive businesses. The ratios in Figure 6–4 were calculated using only the ramp-up and new capital expenditures for retooling the production line, with all amounts normalized to current dollars. There have been five platform generations (the original architecture plus four major enhancements to it). Note that in this case the dashed lines represent actual dollar amounts (rather than efficiency values for single products). We have done this to give the reader a feel for the cost implications of improving the efficiency with which new products are placed into the manufacturing process.

The manufacturing processes in this case have proved difficult to adjust to accommodate new derivative products. Only recently has the efficiency measure come into a range deemed reasonable by management. Management's intention is to revisit the entire manufacturing process to introduce simpler machinery that can be integrated, changed, and added to at lower cost for new product introductions. This will potentially save vast sums in retooling and ramping up the production of new products.

Step 3: Understanding the Time to Market Consequences of Platform Development

We can also use the product family data to understand the dynamics of development time cycles over the course of time. All one needs to do is compute the platform efficiency measure using elapsed engineering time instead of development costs. A strong product platform, while taking relatively longer to create than derivative products, should allow the firm to experience rapid generation of those derivatives.

Using the start and end of R&D for product platforms and derivative products, an elapsed time cycle measure of platform efficiency for any single product can be expressed as:

$$\text{Cycle Time Efficiency} = \frac{\text{Elapsed Time to Develop a Derivative Product}}{\text{Elapsed Time to Develop the Product Platform}}$$

Similarly, an average cycle time efficiency value for a generation of products based on a particular version of a product platform can be computed as:

$$\text{Average Cycle Time Efficiency} = \frac{\text{Average (Elapsed Time to Develop Derivative Products)}}{\text{Elapsed Time to Develop the Product Platform}}$$

Simply plotting the development times for platforms versus those of derivative products based on those platforms can be highly instructive. We can illustrate this with a product family of medical equipment. Figure 6–5 shows the elapsed calendar time in years for the development of two distinct platform versions of this product family. It also shows the average cycle times in years for the derivative products in each generation of the product family.

The cycle time for the initial product platform was about five

FIGURE 6–5

MED's Platform and Derivative Product Cycle Time Efficiency

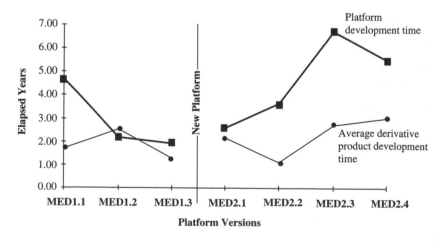

years, and for successive extensions of that platform, about two years. Derivative products were developed on average in about two years. The development of the second product platform was conducted in 2.5 years, which, from discussions with team members, was far too rushed and released too early because of competitive pressures. Subsequent platform extensions to the second platform took longer to complete, and you will notice that the third platform extension took almost seven years to finish. Similarly, development times for derivatives products based on the second platform were longer than those of the first platform. The team was trying to add increasingly complex clinical functionality to the product line and was finding the underlying platform architecture a barrier to rapid development.

Most managers can sense when the underlying architectures of their major product lines are running out of gas. Their responsibility, then, is to fund and sequence new platform development projects to supersede existing platforms. When senior management treats new platform development efforts as if they were derivative product developments, in terms of both time and resources, the tangible results of the new platform efforts will probably be disappointing. Such efforts, where multidisciplined teams must look deeply into technical and marketing alternatives, take time and must be started early. It also stands to reason that if new platform development efforts take longer to complete than derivative product efforts, R&D aimed at platform renewal should be pursued concurrent with derivative product developments on existing platforms. That ensures a continuous stream of products embodying competitive technology.

Step 4: Understanding the Technological Competitive Responsiveness of the Firm

Bringing in an external market perspective can add great value to understanding performance. For product development, we have found it useful to track the degree to which a firm has beaten its competitors to the marketplace with new features or capabilities in its products or services. We call the measure *lead-lag* competitive responsiveness. It readily lends itself to systematic study in the context of the evolving product family.

To perform the analysis, start by constructing a product family map. In addition to marking the various platform versions and derivative products within the family, ask the team members to identify the important new features or capabilities that have appeared over time in the stream of products. Then ask: When did our competitors introduce similar capabilities? Plot the comparative data in the format shown in Figure 6–6.

Figure 6–6 shows the lead-lag competitive response for the CONSUMABLES product family described earlier. The data revealed that while the company started well ahead of the pack, over time the industry became highly competitive and the company lost its position as the innovation leader. That was due largely to the inflexibility of its product platform and the manufacturing processes

FIGURE 6–6

CONSUMABLES Lead-Lag Competitive Response

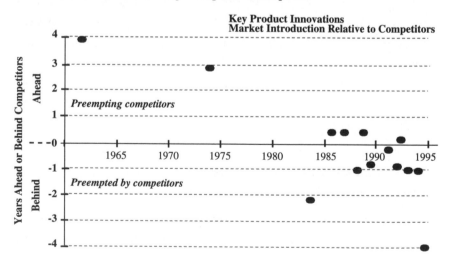

associated with it. Either the company's engineers couldn't innovate fast enough or, when they did, the manufacturing organization impeded rapid deployment.

A word of caution. None of these measures can be viewed in isolation from other metrics. Lead-lag competitive responsiveness is no different. We have witnessed instances in which management was driven by competitive pressures to release new products before they were adequately developed and tested. In such cases, their lead-lag charts appeared good, but, to no one's surprise, the downstream results were poor.

Step 5: Understanding the Commercial Effectiveness of Platforms

We come next to the revenues garnered by products in the marketplace. Great products, introduced in a timely manner, should reap rewards in markets not subject to decline. By factoring in the development costs of platforms and derivative products, one can assess the commercial leverage achieved by product families over time. We call this *platform effectiveness,* a measure of the degree to which derivatives of a product platform produce revenues relative to their cost of development. Platform effectiveness simply compares the resources used to create products with the revenues derived from them, *over the long term.* The cost of development includes the engineering costs, manufacturing engineering costs, market development costs, and expenditures for plant and equipment. Revenues consist of net sales attributable to each derivative product within the family. Platform effectiveness for a single derivative product is represented as follows:

$$\text{Platform effectiveness} = \frac{\text{Net Sales of a Derivative Product}}{\text{Development Costs of a Derivative Product}}$$

And, as with platform efficiency, the effectiveness measure can be aggregated for an entire generation of products, allowing you to compare the performance of successive generations.

$$\frac{\text{Platform}}{\text{effectiveness}} = \frac{\text{Net Sales of Derivative Products of a Platform Version}}{\text{Development Costs of Derivative Products of a}}$$
$$\text{Platform Version} + \text{the Platform Development Costs}$$

For example, if one of Black & Decker's successful drills generated $10 million in sales over its effective commercial life cycle and cost $500,000 to develop, the single product effectiveness measure would be approximately 20. Similarly, if the sales for an entire generation of power tools amounted to $1 billion, and the platform development costs (including new plant and equipment) were about $20 million and derivative product costs about $10 million, then the platform effectiveness measure would be about 33 for that generation of products. A higher value for platform effectiveness is obviously *better.* This is the opposite of the platform efficiency metric, where more efficient creation of derivative products results in lower numbers.

To illustrate the single product effectiveness measure, we turn to another product family of measurement systems, which we shall call MONITOR. This family comprises measurement devices that gather industrial process information in real time, identify emergency events, and forward them onto information systems. The product platform took three and a half years to develop, and from it five derivative products were created. In total, the start of R&D for this platform to the end of its commercial cycle spanned a period of about ten years.

The sales department of the division allocated annual sales revenues to each specific product within the MONITOR product family, as did the engineering department for engineering costs. All dollar amounts were adjusted to their present value. While the two departments had systematically maintained their respective data over the years, no one had ever considered combining them so that product developers could see the tangible rewards of their labors.

FIGURE 6–7

MONITOR's Platform Efficiency and Effectiveness on a Product by Product Basis

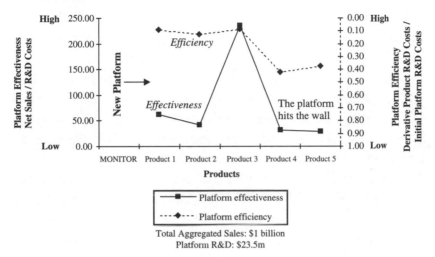

Total Aggregated Sales: $1 billion
Platform R&D: $23.5m

In this particular case, manufacturing ramp-up and retooling costs proved impossible to gather and therefore were not included as part of development costs.

For this analysis, we combined the computed values of platform effectiveness with those of platform efficiency to suggest that these two measures are related. Figure 6–7 shows the two metrics plotted from the products of the MONITOR product family. To facilitate comparison between platform efficiency and effectiveness, we have plotted the efficiency scale in reverse value order, so that high efficiency values (low numbers) are at the top of the axis.

Let's start with the efficiency measure. The platform efficiency measure shows high levels of efficiency for the first three derivative products based on the MONITOR product platform. Each of those products was developed for about 10 cents on the original platform dollar (using the right-hand axis). For the fourth derivative product the metric spikes upward (less efficient) to 42 cents on the platform dollar. The fifth product experienced a similar lack of platform efficiency, costing about 36 cents on the platform dollar. In other words, the team was finding it increasingly difficult to add new features and capabilities to the existing product platform.

The platform effectiveness measures for the MONITOR product family show that this difficulty translated into declining commercial performance. Platform effectiveness indicates the commercial leverage of engineering investments into products as a ratio of total product sales to product development costs. You can see (referring to the left-hand axis) that the commercial leverage from the MONITOR product line grew strongly from the Product 1 to Product 3, which itself returned $259 for every $1 spent on development! The fourth and fifth derivative products experienced a decline in sales relative to development costs.[11] Customers began to demand a combination of greater flexibility and lower cost. The MONITOR product platform had difficulty accommodating those needs. Meanwhile, competitors had been redesigning their product platforms, driving toward more flexible, lower-cost designs. Those efforts began to eat into MONITOR's dominant position. As one R&D manager put it, the platform had "hit the wall." It had to be renewed.

Many factors can lead to declining effectiveness. For example, a market either in explosive growth or in free fall will greatly impact the metric. However, it is important for a firm to realize that it can shape markets and create new levels of demand. That cannot be done if a product platform has outlived its utility, in terms of either function or cost.

What should platform effectiveness be for your company's product lines? Reason again suggests that platform effectiveness values will vary from industry to industry. In electronics and systems companies, we found that a 30:1 ratio of sales to development costs indicates very successful product lines. We have also encountered several product families addressing mass markets where the ratio exceeded 500:1 for certain "big hit" products. Once again, the most pragmatic way to establish a benchmark for platform effectiveness in your own company is through internal study, observing those values associated with your most successful product families.

Step 6: Understanding Profit Potential

Our last measure targets the profitability of derivative products by examining gross margins, product by product, within a product family. We call this measure the CPR, an internal cost price ratio. The cost price ratio is computed on a per unit basis as:

$$\text{Cost Price Ratio (CPR)} = \frac{\text{Cost of goods (material + labor + fixed and variable overhead)}}{\text{Net sales (Gross sales less transportation, returns, and discounts)}}$$

From individual product CPRs, one can easily derive averages to summarize overall profit position for a product line.

To demonstrate this measure, we shall revisit the fluorescent lighting case described in Chapter 5. You will recall that the company's offerings were in four price-performance segments: low cost, "standard," premium, deluxe. For those segments, the company had created four distinct product platforms, each with a unique platform architecture as evidenced by a quick look at the respective block diagrams of the designs. From those four platforms, 228 unique derivative products were created. The vast majority were simple style changes that added nothing to the mechanical functionality of the respective platforms. Each platform also had its own bench-assembly process with no real automation.

Figure 6–8, the internal cost price ratio analysis of the existing product line, shows that the company was not making a lot of money on its lighting fixtures, especially in the low-end platforms. In the figure, the old product platforms are arrayed according to their market segments, and major models within them. You can see

FIGURE 6–8

Internal Cost Price Ratio Analysis for the Old Line of Lighting Fixtures

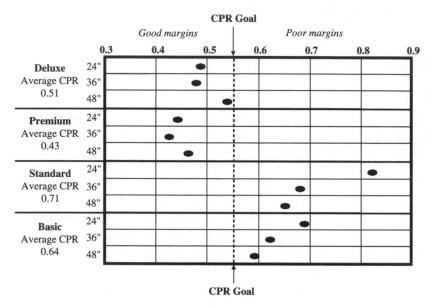

Points are average CPR for all models within market segment and fixture length. Cost Price Ratio = Cost of Goods Sold/Net Sales.

that the old line was profitable in the deluxe (average CPR of .51) and premium segments (average CPR of .43), but only marginally profitable in the low-cost (average CPR .71) and standard segments (CPR .64). That was unfortunate, because many more low-cost and standard models were being purchased by customers than the higher-end models.

As told in Chapter 5, a new product platform was designed to serve all the market segments. It was first targeted at the previously unprofitable low end of the market and then scaled upward into the high-end segments. The standardization of key subsystems and components allowed economies to be achieved in procurement and manufacturing. This was pervasive across the entire product family.

FIGURE 6–9

Internal Cost Price Ratio Analysis for the Redesigned Line of Lighting
Fixtures

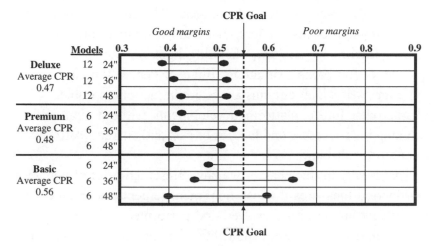

Bars indicate range of CPR for all models within market segment and fixture length. Cost
Price Ratio = Cost of Goods Sold/Net Sales.

The CPR for the new line were also dramatically improved, as
shown in Figure 6–9. The company was finally able to make money
in all market segments.[12] Rich in features and achieving economies
through standardization in mechanical function and design, the
manufacturer had created a far more profitable and exciting line of
products.

Looking Forward by Understanding Lessons from the Past

What is so often lost in the way corporations measure their performance is the principle of continuity. The entire focus of accoun-
tancy seems to be on single periods. Each year is treated separately.
History gets chopped off at the knees, and the corporation's ability
to systematically learn from that history is largely forgone. Perhaps
that is the greatest misuse of today's common measures and statis-

tics for firm performance. By its very nature, new product development spans multiple periods.

What worked or did not work yesterday may not apply to today's situation. As noted by Henry Kissinger, "The study of history offers no manual of instructions that can be applied automatically; history teaches by analogy, shedding light on the likely consequences of comparable situations. But each generation must determine for itself which circumstances are in fact comparable."[13] Yet to approach future platform developments without first understanding the successes and failures of past and current platforms is to proceed half-blind.

That is why in this chapter we have presented a set of coherent multiperiod measures that can help management understand how its product families have evolved and performed over time. Being historical, these measures can facilitate a richer degree of learning. Clear measures, based on objective data, can also be important internal communications vehicles. We have yet to work in a corporation where cadres of forward-thinking individuals were not pressing forward with creative ideas to renew the existing business. Yet often their arguments fall on deaf ears. The analysis techniques presented here can strengthen their arguments and serve as an impetus for change.

We are often asked if the measures can be explicitly applied to future product planning. Can one, for example, establish goals for platform efficiency, effectiveness, and profitability for new platform efforts based on past measurements? The answer is yes, but be very careful in doing so.

Many of the measures—platform efficiency, time cycle efficiency, lead-lag competitive responsiveness, and the cost price ratio—can provide benchmark values that can be directly applied either to new product plans or to products that are completed and just introduced to the market. However, levels of platform efficiency achieved in a successful product line five years ago may well be obsoleted by breakthroughs in product and process technology.

In those cases, such benchmarks become marks for teams to beat. Use of the platform effectiveness measure as a benchmark is even more speculative, simply because new products normally take time to achieve momentum in the market. However, if commercial life cycles for products are relatively short in your business, you will probably have a handle on the sales coming from new products within a few years and can therefore apply the measure to set three-to-five-year platform effectiveness objectives with a reasonable degree of confidence.

7

Product Family and Platform Concepts for Software

You can look at and touch a power tool or an ink jet printer, take it apart, and come to understand the platform architecture and manufacturing processes behind the product. This is more difficult to do with a piece of software, arguably even harder to do for an online publication, and seemingly impossible for a service such as insurance. Yet we believe that the management of businesses making nonphysical or intangible products cannot ignore the concepts of product families, product platforms, production processes, and the derivative products based on them. Well-designed software platform architectures, like those of physical products, provide great benefits for developers and users.

The key, of course, is to understand what a platform means for nonphysical products, and then how best to manage it to keep products and services fresh and vital for customers. That meaning and its management implications are the point of this chapter and the next.

THE LAYERS OF COMPUTING TECHNOLOGY

Software products are built on four layers of technology that, when interconnected, deliver computer capability to the end user. A simple layered model of computer technology is shown in Figure 7–1.

FIGURE 7–1

A Layered Model of Software Technology

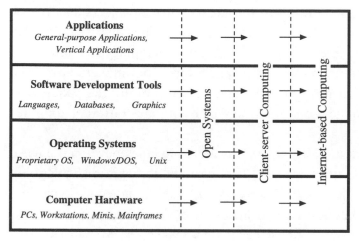

At the bottom of the figure lie the various forms of general purpose computer hardware, ranging from palmtop computers to supercomputers. There are, of course, special-purpose computers like the "black boxes" used in airplanes or routers that allow communication between different types of computers.

All computers, large or small, general-purpose or special-purpose, require operating systems. Those form the next layer. Operating systems do a number of things: They stage and execute tasks in the computer's processor(s), read and write information to storage devices or networks, manage files on disks, display information on the computer monitor, and read keystrokes and mouse clicks.

Over time, proprietary operating systems have given way to what is generally known as open systems, transformed by the technologies of client server computing and networked operating systems. Today, the client server paradigm is itself being transformed by the Internet, largely in terms of degree and scale. With each paradigm shift, the rules of software development have changed, forcing software companies to reinvent their products.

Sitting above the operating system are the many tools used to create end-user applications. Those tools include programming languages and libraries of specific routines or objects that may be assembled to make completed programs. They also include database management systems, tools for developing user interfaces or graphics or multimedia applications. Tool makers have tried to make their tools modular and flexible, so that the people who develop applications programs can combine different tools together.

Using these tools, other software companies have then created applications programs, the final layer of software technology. In general, applications software products are designed to do particular jobs. They are either general-purpose software products, like word processors, spreadsheets, or bookkeeping systems, or special-purpose software tailored to specific industrial, medical, scientific, engineering, or administrative requirements.

In software, the definition of what is included at any given layer of technology has tended to expand over time. For example, Novell gained prominence by adding networking to PC operating systems to facilitate local area networking. Now Microsoft has included that capability as a standard feature of its Windows NT operating system for PCs. One can observe the same type of expansion in each of the layers of computer technology. The migration toward hybrid or multifunction products is common, and predictable, across the entire software industry. If a technical breakthrough proves useful, software developers quickly incorporate it into the next generation of their own products. Breakthroughs become part of commonly used technology.

TRADITIONAL THINKING ABOUT SOFTWARE PLATFORMS

People in the software business use the term "platform" in an idiosyncratic way. During the 1970s and 1980s a "platform" referred specifically to the type of computer that the software was made to run on. For example, Lotus Development Corporation initially targeted the Intel-based personal computer as the "platform" for its spreadsheet product, and the Macintosh computer and Unix workstations as successive platforms. Other spreadsheet companies targeted minicomputers or mainframes as their "platforms."

During the latter part of the 1980s, the computer industry was transformed by the ascendance of Microsoft in the PC arena and open systems in workstations, minicomputers, and even mainframes. Microsoft's operating systems swept across the universe of Intel-based computer manufacturers and became the *de facto* standard for PCs. The Unix operating system also became popular for minicomputers and workstations, replacing proprietary operating systems. The emergence of those standards allowed software companies to make a single product, or a family of products, operational across a broad range of hardware. A PC software company, for example, could develop a product with the confidence that it would be marketable to all PC users, whether their hardware was manufactured by Compaq, Dell, IBM, Hewlett Packard, or any other PC equipment maker.

Software producers and their customers were thus freed from the particular designs of hardware manufacturers. That hardware independence coincided with a new use of the word "platform." Software developers began to think of "platforms" as the particular operating systems upon which their products functioned, be it Windows, the Macintosh operating system, or one of the popular versions of Unix. For companies that had been making software for proprietary computing environments, the rules had fundamentally changed.

The emergence of networking capabilities for sharing programs, data, and output devices between computers reinforced an operating systems focus on the definition of the software platform. In the PC environment, distributed file systems and resource sharing were provided as "add-ons" to DOS/Windows by such companies as Novell, while in the Unix environment such capabilities became part of the base operating system. Later, Windows NT also provided distributed file systems and resource sharing as part of the base operating system.

Thus began the great surge toward implementing client server computing in software to take advantage of networked environments. Once again, for makers of older style software, the rules had changed, and for a time chaos ensued.[1] Implementing client server capabilities meant redeveloping software to use new tools, incorporating new communications and database technology to deliver new functionality to end users. That has been an expensive, difficult process, but the capital investment has been justified by the benefits derived from integrating information and using it to make better and faster decisions.

Today we are faced with another paradigm shift: the Internet. It is similar in design to client server computing, but the degree of distributed computing and its impact on how people use computers is greater by an order of magnitude. "Servers" on the World Wide Web, the computers that dish out data and programs, have potentially tens of millions of people as users. The degree of openness and linkage between users that is now required by the new wave of Internet software products is nothing short of remarkable. As with prior paradigm shifts, makers of software are confronted by a new challenge. In many cases, they must "clean sheet" the design of their software products. Industry leaders have been challenged by new entrants unfettered by older technology.

A large part of the software industry and software users, however, still view the operating system environment as "the platform." Externalities are important, because they are part of the total environment in which a particular system must function. However, an externally focused platform definition does not suffice for a software company wishing to manage the architecture of its own products. In short, management needs an internal definition of a software product platform.

THE ARCHITECTURE OF SOFTWARE PRODUCTS

Every software product—be it an operating system, a programming tool, or an end-user application—has an internal product architecture.[2] As with physical products, this architecture can be structured in a way that creates a robust platform architecture from which derivative products can be efficiently developed.

Consider a very simple example, the screen saver. Screen saver software was developed to serve a clear customer need: to avoid monitor damage from phosphorus burnout, which occurs when programs are left running unattended for long periods. Using programming languages and graphics design tools, software developers created programs to detect user inactivity after a specified period of time. These programs interact with the operating system to replace whatever is on the screen with a moving image, thereby avoiding phosphorus burn out. The original screen returns as soon as the user touches the keyboard or clicks the mouse.

Screen savers are now delivered with libraries of different images—swimming fish, bursting fireworks, and even flying toasters! Each image is a distinct module employed by the generic software *engine* in a similar way. The user picks the image he or she likes, effectively creating a derivative product. Some screen savers offer programming interfaces for creating customized screen saver images. This simple example reflects the general software platform architecture that many developers are trying to achieve. The platform is the *engine,* and derivative products are created by developing add-in modules that can be seamlessly plugged into the engine.

A software product family—which in the screen saver example is the engine and the collective set of images developed for use with it—can provide great choice and variety to the user. This variety is achieved by providing users with customized modules that can be incorporated into the software engine at *no additional integration cost.* This approach is presented in Figure 7–2. The software platform is the design and implementation of the engine, a core set of

FIGURE 7–2

Generalized Architecture of a Software Product Platform

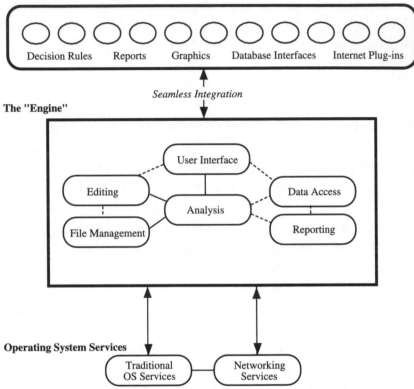

programs that propel the entire system. Modules are developed and plugged into the engine to provide variety, either as new versions of existing products or as entirely new derivative products. Thus each new derivative product represents either a viable upgrade or a new product purchase for the customer.

Like physical product platforms, the underlying engine of a software product family designed in the manner described here will also incorporate major subsystems. These key subsystems, shown in Figure 7–2, are:

- to add and enter information (the "Editing" Subsystem), where information is broadly defined to include data, pictures, and other types of multimedia content
- to store and distribute information, either on disks or to other computers on networks ("File Management")
- to analyze information provided by the user and maintained in the system, be it through decision-making algorithms or any other method of analysis ("Analysis")
- to query subsets of information and analyze them ("Data Access" and "Decision Making")
- to generate either hard copy or electronic reports ("Reporting")
- working with all of these subsystems is a common user interface—how the software looks and feels to the user—be it for using menus, displaying information, getting on-line help, or indicating and handling errors ("User Interface").

Just as in physical products, the integration of software subsystems is greatly facilitated if the internal interfaces between modules are clearly defined and use industry standard mechanisms where they exist. In this way, one module may pass data in a certain format to any other module.

Derivative products—comprising add-in modules that are attached or plugged into the underlying software engine—might be a specific set of analysis modules or reports tailored to a certain type of business; interfaces for exchanging data between the basic software "engine" and other external information systems; or modules that read and write information to particular communications networks and/or storage devices. Add-in modules represent incremental development efforts that address specific user needs.[3,4]

The power of the platform approach for software is similar to that of physical products: A software developer can provide a family of products without starting from ground zero to create every single one. R&D efforts to migrate the software to a new operating system or networking environment, or to use a new set of software development tools, can also be focused at the platform level and then populated automatically across the entire product family. In most cases, a company's improvements to its software platform are released as new versions of an existing product, i.e., version 1.0 to 2.0 to 3.0, and so forth. In other instances, however, platform improvements can open new markets for the same basic technology.

A platform strategy for software can also have compelling benefits to end users. What the end user tends to see and use most are the add-in modules described above. If those add-in modules are clearly separated from the underlying software engine, they can be carried forward across generations of the product platform, often without radical revision. End users can thus be shielded to a significant extent from changes in the underlying technology from year to year. To achieve that, however, software developers must carefully consider the design and implementation of the interfaces within their software products.

The Power of Interfaces

The interfaces in the software platform design are the key enablers, the source of its power. In general, there are three essential types of interfaces. The first are the internal program interfaces within the engine itself, the mechanisms by which the key subsystems of the engine work together. The clearer the internal interfaces of a software platform, the easier it will be to replace existing subsystems periodically with improved versions over time, thereby enhancing the overall functionality of the product line.

The second basic type of interface includes those between the system and the user or between the system and other information systems. The former comes under the rubric of "the user interface," and the latter deals primarily with mechanisms to facilitate the sharing of data between different systems. Clarity and compliance with industry standards are essential in developing successful external interfaces. Consequently, most software companies make sure that their products conform with user interfaces of the popular operating systems. Incorporating those standard interface designs makes it possible for users to learn new software products quickly. When standards do not exist, leading companies attempt to create them through participation in industry groups; they then work the emerging standard to their own advantage.

The early success of Netscape (an Internet software company) is illustrative of the importance of getting external interfaces right. Netscape essentially "gave away" its Internet desktop browser. Because of the browser's utility, millions of users adopted it as their preferred vehicle for surfing the Internet. That made Netscape's browser a *de facto* industry standard, to the chagrin of competitors. Once masses of Internet users adopted its product, Netscape turned to selling a growing family of backend Web site server development and management tools to its user base, including an add-on product "suite" that extends the capabilities of its Internet browser.

The third type of interface exists between the platform and the add-in modules attached to it, as in the screen saver example. When such interfaces are well designed and clearly documented, they provide significant leverage for the producer firm. First, the firm itself can focus its resources on new applications features—utilizing, rather than reinventing, underlying platform capabilities. Developers external to the firm can do the same, using the basic platform to serve their own particular needs and markets. Once again, Netscape bears out this concept. Netscape developed and marketed a "Plug-in Applications Programming Language" that allowed other firms to add functionality to the Netscape Navigator browser. This opened the floodgates to software developers seeking to leverage the Netscape platform to their own advantage. A multitude of software companies began developing "plug-ins" for Netscape's browser.

Enforcing the use of standard interfaces, both with the software platform and between its plug-in modules, entails certain costs. The interfaces themselves must be researched and developed, and there are overhead costs associated with adhering to interface standards. To appreciate those costs, consider two different software platform architectures, shown in Figure 7–3. The first has two key subsystems: one to edit data and the other to query files that retrieve data. Both subsystems handle their own file access

FIGURE 7–3

A Comparison of Two Software Designs

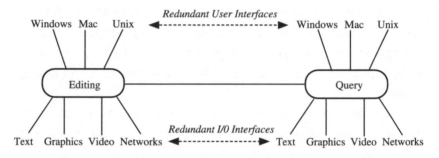

Design "A"
Proliferation of Interfaces

Design "B"
Single, Common Interfaces

and user interface functions. The second platform design separates out the data access and user interface, placing them in separate subsystems.

In the first design, the developers of both the editing and the query subsystems write their own procedures for accessing data from the computer disk and presenting information to and interacting with the user. In fact, developers might well argue that each subsystem, *by itself,* will work faster if it performs its own file management and user interface procedures.

However, new file formats and data types (graphics, video, etc.)—even a new standard user interface—are likely to emerge over time. The software company must move quickly to incorporate these in its platform design, or the software will become obsolete. Thus, in the first design, each subsystem development team must modify its own programs if the platform subsystems are to be upgraded. Since data and file management is not their primary specialty, the respective teams will implement the new data access features differently, being stronger in some aspects and weaker in others. In the second design, a single subsystem that contains a single, common implementation of the new data access features can be used by the two other subsystems. The proliferation of interfaces for accessing different types of data are thereby minimized. Over time, this makes evolving the overall system to take advantage of new technologies far more effective and manageable.

Achieving modularity while minimizing the number of interfaces between subsystems is the essence of elegance in software design. In this, the product developer faces a dilemma: Optimizing each subsystem and its interfaces may result in suboptimization of the entire system. Indeed, trying to optimize each subsystem in a software platform will usually result in suboptimization of the entire system. It is the optimization of the overall system that matters most, and this requires the flexibility to advance the underlying software engine with successive generations of industry technology. If the number of unique interfaces between subsystems, and between subsystems and add-in modules, is allowed to proliferate, attempts to enhance the product family through derivatives and platform extensions will be difficult and time-consuming. Every attempt to substitute a revised subsystem or a new add-in module will create a need to alter the myriad specific interfaces between new and old elements. One change creates a ripple effect from a particular subsystem to all others. In software, the ripple effects emanating from one particular subsystem to all others can be devastating.

To avoid that, each subsystem and add-in module should be task-specific. Further, interaction with any particular subsystem must be done through a single channel, commonly used by all other subsystems. That provides the opportunity for any given subsystem to be neutral in terms of its impact on the overall system as the subsystem is improved or replaced over time.

The foregoing discussion underscores an important axiom of design: Managing internal and external interfaces is as important as building new functionality into major subsystem or add-in modules. This axiom is not unique to software. Designers in other industries must recognize the importance of subsystem interfaces and of conforming to industry standards in external interfaces. However, the extreme rate of change in the software industry raises the stakes for interface issues. Adhering to a limited set of robust interfaces becomes one of the essential rules and tools for long-term success in software development.

APPLICATIONS OF THE MODEL:
THE VISIO SOFTWARE PRODUCT FAMILY

Visio Corporation, a software company that makes a highly acclaimed drawing and diagramming programs for personal computers, provides an excellent example of a firm that has mastered software product platforms. The company was founded in 1990 and shipped its first product in 1992. Since then Visio has received numerous industry awards for its product excellence and sales rate.[5] These accomplishments were achieved in the face of intense competition from the many drawing programs made for business and technical markets. Visio's modular and flexible software product architecture has played a key role in its success.

From the beginning, the founders had a clear vision: to create a major software industry platform into which both the company itself and then other companies or end users could easily incorporate "add-in" objects or shapes needed to draw charts, diagrams, and the like. In the words of Ted Johnson, vice president of product development at Visio:

> Visio was designed to address the drawing and diagramming needs of a wide range of users from general business users to highly skilled technical professionals. The product's extensible architecture enables companies to develop custom solutions, extend the product's basic "shrink-wrapped" functionality, or incorporate the product into mission-critical applications for specific departments and workgroups.

Figure 7–4 is a screen shot of the product as it might be used for creating a simple flowchart. Computer users will have little trouble seeing how the product is used. On the left side of the screen are objects from a library of shapes specifically designed for creating flowcharts. Visio calls its shape libraries "stencils." Visio shapes are more than graphic designs; many carry a certain "intelligence" that makes their use more convenient. For example, the software can automatically adjust connections between different shapes when something is moved or rescaled on a chart. The company calls these SmartShapes.

Figure 7–5 is another screen shot. In this case, the product is using a library of shapes customized for creating computer networking diagrams. By comparing the two figures, you can see that the same platform is being used for two different sets of "add-in" modules, each comprising shapes for two respective market niches.

FIGURE 7–4

Visio Screen Shot, Flowcharts

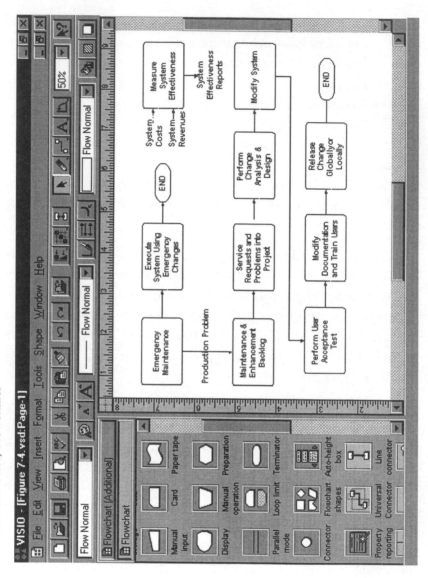

Source: Reproduced with permission of Visio Corporation.

186

FIGURE 7–5

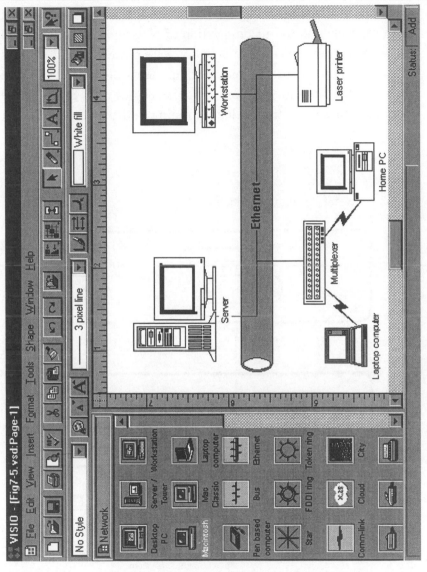

Source: Reproduced with permission of Visio Corporation.

187

Visio's architectural approach is clearly similar to the screen saver example and to our description of Netscape's software cited earlier. Visio's representation of its software product architecture is shown in Figure 7–6. The major components of the platform are shown at the bottom: the core graphics engine, the SmartShape management subsystem for incorporating and then manipulating

FIGURE 7–6

Visio's Software Product Architecture

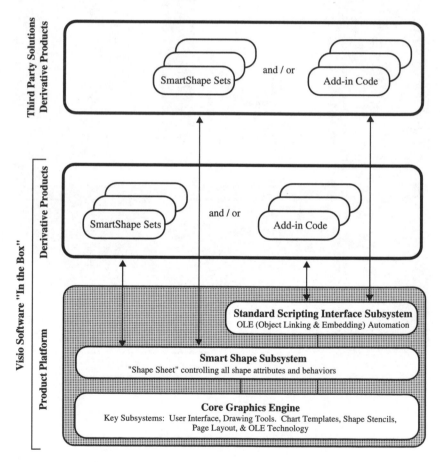

Source: Reproduced with permission of Visio Corporation.

graphic objects, and an applications programming interface that provides a standard scripting language to allow developers to create their own Visio plug-in programs.

The power of Visio's platform approach lies not only in its elegance but in the many add-ins offered through the Visio product family. Those add-ins make it possible for the company to address the needs of different user markets. There are two types of add-ins: SmartShape libraries of graphic objects and add-in programs or code. One can think of the add-in programs as automated guides to help users in the creation and presentation of charts. In the Windows software business, people tend to call such programs "wizards."

The middle of Figure 7–6 shows Visio's shape libraries and plug-in programs. Those add-ins fall within one of Visio's two basic market segments: the general business market and the technical or engineering market, as well as other vertical market applications. A partial listing of Visio's product family is:

- advanced flowcharts
- advanced network diagrams for telecommunications users
- advanced electrical engineering for circuit board layout, logic diagrams, and timing diagrams
- market analysis and presentation charts
- advanced software diagrams
- advanced space planning
- chemistry charts to represent cloning, mutations, experiment designs
- chemical manufacturing diagrams
- petroleum manufacturing diagrams
- biotechnology and medicine charting
- mechanical engineering plans
- accident reporting for property insurance
- landscape design and home planning

Each of these "add-ins" contains hundreds of unique shapes. The software architecture is carried forward into pricing. In the spring of 1996 the base engine product (with more than a thousand SmartShapes) retailed at about $150 for the business version and $300 for the technical drawing version (with more than three thousand SmartShapes). Additional plug-in libraries, such as those listed above, retailed for between $29 and $99. Users can also go to Visio's World Wide Web (www.visio.com) site to browse and download new shapes and program modules developed by other users.

Lastly, at the top of Figure 7–6 are shapes and plug-in programs developed by other companies using Visio's software development tools. Using those tools, developers have created customized applications based on the Visio platform—usually other modules that interact with the Visio platform to create graphics for unique purposes.

Visio's management of its technology indicates how a software developer using elegant interfaces and add-in modules can leverage a single platform. The wealth of value-added functionality provided by the add-in modules also creates the impression for the buying public of richness and diversity in a company's product offerings. "If I buy this basic product and spend the time to learn how to use it, it is a good investment because I can use the product for so many different things." For incremental sums, a user can upgrade what she or he has to serve new perceived needs. That translates into productivity for the end user, just as much as it does for the software developer.

MANAGING THE EVOLUTION OF A SOFTWARE PRODUCTS FAMILY

Earlier discussion of physical products made the point that a firm's R&D resources should leverage existing platforms through derivative product development even as it renews existing platforms with better designs and more powerful component technologies. That approach applies equally to the management of software product families.

In software, however, prototypes often become initial products, which themselves often serve as platforms for future products. That may occur because programmers or their managers consider each piece of software a personal creation that ought not to be scrapped or because data processing budgets are so tight that starting with a blank page is unacceptable. Among entrepreneurial software firms, for whom competitive advantage is fleeting and time-sensitive, the race to produce the next great product reinforces the reuse of code, even when that code is arguably not worth reusing. Whatever the case, software firms often weigh themselves down with cumbersome old code.

At Visio Corporation we saw a very different approach. One set of marketers and engineers has been constantly building new add-in modules for the current version of the product platform or engine. Concurrently, other teams have worked to renew the core platform and to embrace technological change occurring in the broader industry.

If a software company pursues a product platform approach correctly, then its entire product family can be upgraded to a new computing environment without having to substantially reprogram all the various add-in modules that were developed for an older platform. The only way that such a smooth migration can be accomplished is to develop and sustain clear, robust interfaces between the underlying engine and the add-in modules.

For example, Microsoft's introduction of a 32-bit, multitasking architecture for its Windows operating system forced Visio to renew its basic engine so that its various derivative products can enjoy the benefits of greater memory access and parallel execution with other programs. Since Visio had been looking forward to a 32-bit architecture and was an early recipient of Microsoft's new technology, the changes necessary to its major subsystems within the core graphics engine were performed rapidly. Further, because of clear, robust interfaces, Visio's SmartShape sets and add-in code from prior versions remained operational and useful without change.

Managing a software platform's transition from one technological environment to the next is one of the greatest challenges for software developers. When done well, the migration is largely transparent to users, and the product family continues to grow as applications developers exploit the more powerful capabilities incorporated into a new platform.

We generalize this model of managing product family evolution for software in Figure 7–7, which is our earlier software architecture picture recast in terms of time and activities. The focus here is on applications software, not on software tools or operating systems. The bottom part of the figure shows the underlying layers of core technologies for software-based systems. The top part shows the two basic elements on which the applications developers must work directly: (1) the engine or platform elements of the software family, comprising the services shared by all derivative products (such as user interface functions, database access and administration, and report generation functions), and (2) derivative products, which, as we have suggested, are best structured as add-in modules targeting specific uses.

Starting the Product Family: Understand the Needs of Lead Users

When development work begins (T0 in Figure 7–7), the primary goal of the development team is to understand the needs of lead users and, from that understanding, to design the initial product platform from which successive products will be derived. To build the software platform, the team must also understand the computing infrastructure within which the final product must be integrated or used. It must consider alternatives and make choices. External discovery is a critically important process, because new generations of software tools, operating systems, and hardware

FIGURE 7-7

Managing the Evolution of a Software Product Family

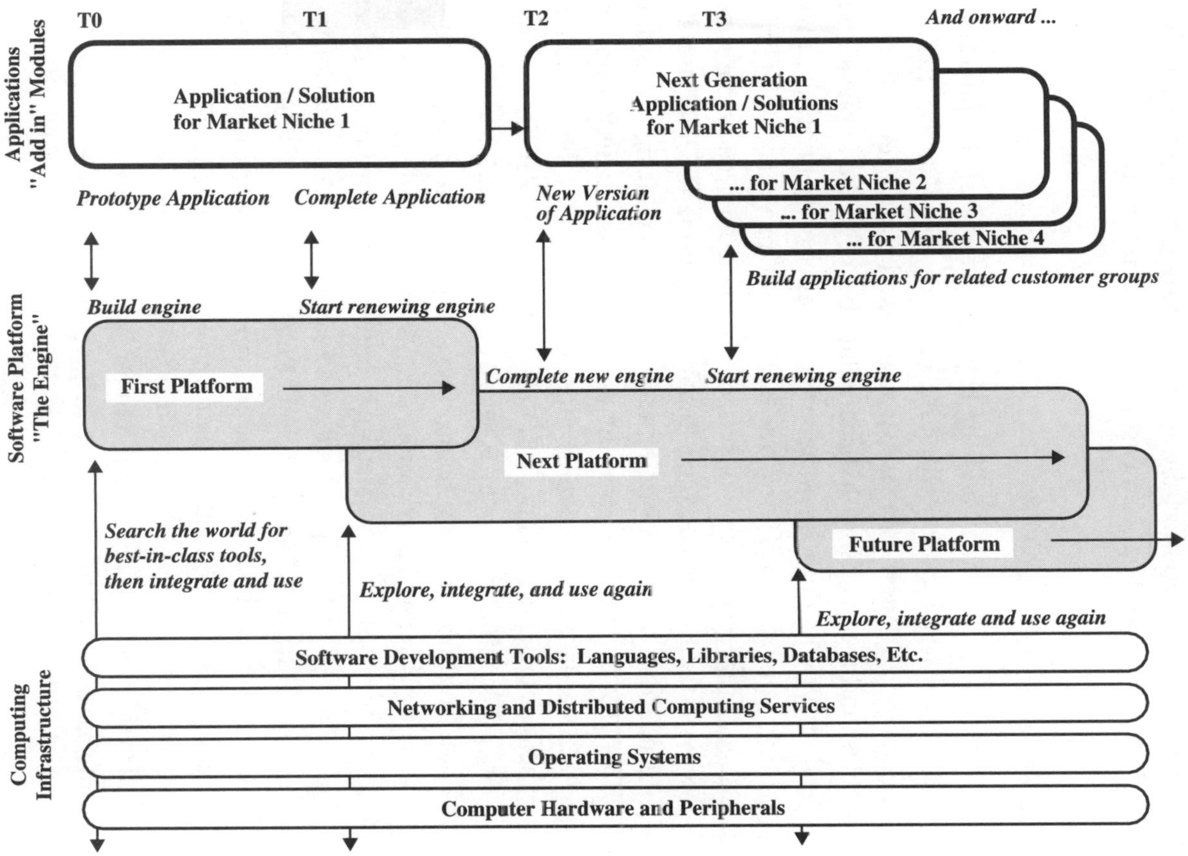

tend to have a wonderful way of resolving problems or roadblocks confronting a team or at least making them less troublesome.

Design Key Subsystems

The team must then build the key subsystems of the platform. In the figure, we have labeled those key subsystems as the user interface, the common database structure, and report generation modules, and mechanisms that share data between the application and other systems in the user's computing environment. There may be others; in the case of Visio, the editing and manipulation of graphic shapes represent a key subsystem. As the team creates the subsystems, it is also prototyping initial applications for lead users and using those prototypes to improve the platform design. It is during this prototyping stage that the team uncovers the limitations of its initial designs or of the tools chosen to implement them. Eventually the platform takes shape, and the team can complete its first working application.

At this point many teams focus entirely on completing and launching the first application, often straining under the imperative to bring revenues into a fledging venture. A first product is released (at time T1 in the figure), either to an internal customer or to the market. Problems are reported. Bugs are fixed. Other problems arise in the fixing, and those too are addressed. Engineering resources are consumed in putting out fires. Eventually, the first product begins to stabilize. Market development and full-fledged distribution then become the main preoccupations. All the while, the list of "wouldn't it be nice to have this particular feature" in the product begins to grow.

Begin the Process of Platform Renewal

At this juncture management faces a critical decision: Should the incremental features be added to the existing product? Or should the team pause to reconsider the overall design and subsystems of the platform? Attention to the survival of the product family demands that at least several engineers begin addressing weaknesses in the existing software platform, even as the first working application is being finished. In fact, no software product or family of products is ever finished; none has all the features needed by users, and none fully resolves the many little annoyances they encounter. Thus, if management waits for an initial application to be finished before embarking on substantial improvement of the underlying platform, the latter may never happen!

Learning from its mistakes, a small platform renewal team can explore new software development tools, advances being offered by operating systems vendors, and even those planned by manufacturers of hardware and peripheral devices. It can then quickly begin creating a new platform architecture, carrying forward some subsystems from the initial design and also replacing others with complete rewrites. If the team does its work correctly, it may be possible to create a new platform that makes many of the problems and bugs associated with the first working application disappear with later versions. With the new platform completed (at time T2 in the figure), it can reimplement the first working application and introduce it as a new version to the market.

Armed with a renewed platform, the company can spin off derivative products for new or related markets—just as Visio advanced from business markets to technical drawing markets. That is where the product family begins to emerge (at time T3 in the figure), and the effort to replace or renew the second platform begins.

APPLICATIONS OF THE EVOLUTIONARY MODEL: A PRODUCT FAMILY OF EXPERT SYSTEMS

The approach we have described above for managing the evolution of product families has been used by a number of highly successful applications development firms—even those making the most complex and specialized of software products. For our example we turn to a family of expert systems developed by Lincoln National

Risk Management (LNRM), a subsidiary of Lincoln National Reinsurance Company.[6]

LNRM develops and sells knowledge-based systems for underwriting new life insurance policies. Life insurance underwriting is the process whereby an insurance company examines the health, age, and lifestyle particulars of a policy applicant, the statistical probabilities of death, and other data, and then decides either to enter into a policy agreement with the applicant or to reject the application. Traditionally, that has been an expensive and labor-intensive process, utilizing both clerical and highly trained professionals. Further, the entire process typically takes insurers four to six week from the day the individual fills out the insurance application form to when the underwriting decision is made.

For life insurance companies that process hundreds of thousands of new applications each year, software capable of automating the underwriting process has the potential to save millions of dollars in labor expense and eliminate weeks of processing time for the typical policy. Improving the underwriting with computers can also reduce improper pricing and thereby improve the ratio of claims paid out to premiums taken in—known as the "loss ratio." LNRM recognized that potential and successfully developed expert systems to handle the process more effectively and at a substantially lower cost. For some user companies, portions of LNRM's software reside in the insurance agent's laptop computer, so that new applications can be approved on the spot through communications with the agent's company (contingent on a successful personal history and blood work checks).

Providing this capability through software required a massive effort by LNRM. To handle the underwriting process, an expert system must

1. Identify the problems or issues that exist in any given case (such as a family history of heart disease)
2. Determine what information is needed to resolve those problems

3. Order and receive that information from a variety of industry data bases
4. Either make the underwriting decision automatically for "simple cases" or guide human underwriters through decision models that speed them to informed judgments

LNRM has developed a product family of expert systems that address the underwriting of life insurance, individual health insurance, and insurance claims adjudication. The product family is based on an underlying software engine. The key subsystems of the engine include a "knowledge base" processing subsystem, a relational database structure for holding client data and insurance pricing schedules, and the case loads and progress of underwriters. The engine also has subsystems for the user interface, reports, and data exchange with third-party data vendors who provide medical examinations and personal history information needed for underwriting.

LRNM's various derivative products are based on distinct knowledge bases—algorithms and decision rules—that are shared and combined within specific products. In the medical domain, for example, the firm has created hundreds of "plug-in" knowledge bases covering everything from respiratory ailments to cancer to cardiovascular disease. To appreciate the complexity involved in this endeavor, one need only consider the many factors that contribute to premature death—family history, medical conditions, risky jobs and hobbies, drinking and driving, and criminal associations—and then consider what it would take to computerize the decision-making requirements for assessing the risk for any given individual seeking a certain amount of life insurance.

When LNRM's development team started its work in 1987, it did so with an expert system prototype for underwriting a single medical condition, asthma. That prototype had been created by the parent company's medical director and an in-house programmer. Senior management saw the potential of this simple prototype for fundamentally changing underwriting practices in its industry, and

FIGURE 7–8

The Evolution of an Underwriting Systems Product Family 1988

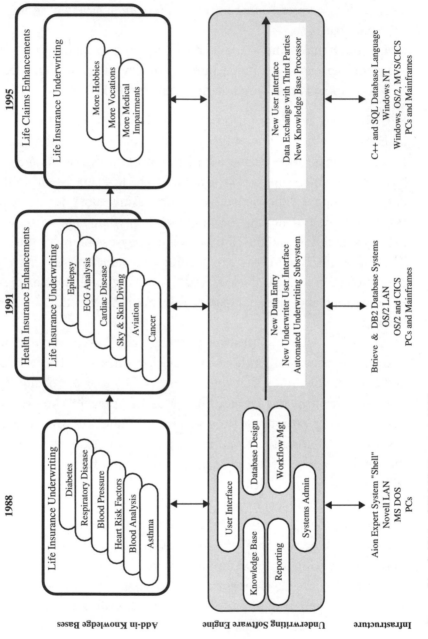

Source: Lincoln National Risk Management, 1996.

198

funded a team to create a product of larger capabilities. A collocated development team was assembled with personnel representing different functional areas: the medical director, senior underwriters, programmers, and, later, a salesperson. This, as many of the other successful cases described in this book, was a case of team working as a "company within a company." The product family that evolved from its efforts is shown in Figure 7–8.

From the first prototype, the team defined its first product and the platform that would support it, as shown in the figure under the 1988 time period. The team then began hunting for a number of best-in-class components: development tools for knowledge-based systems, a database management system, and communications technologies. It struck deals with vendors of those components and integrated them, using the first asthma prototype as the test bed. As pairs of underwriters and programmers began building medical knowledge bases for asthma and a selected set of related health impairments, a "core technology team" worked at developing and stabilizing all major platform subsystems: a basic design of the knowledge bases, the information databases, the user interface, reporting, and systems administration. That platform was then used to develop the company's first life underwriting system.

With that initial success under its belt, the core LNRM team revisited each of its software tool choices. The underlying software engine was redesigned to use OS/2 on PCs, a relational database, and to be functional on mainframes running MVS/CICS. That work was finished around 1991. More recently a new platform has been completed. Here, the underwriting engine was redesigned to also work in the Windows environment. It was also rewritten in an object oriented language—C++—to facilitate greater sharing of underwriting knowledge bases.

Over the years management has consistently directed its programmers away from developing new software development tools. Rather, they have been directed toward finding best-in-class tools developed by other software companies. Those tools have then been integrated to enhance the product line. Each new platform effort was carefully planned and staged in sequence. Renewal has been treated as a necessity, the *ante* paid to be a long-term player. According to Russell Suever, who manages all the technology development and service activities of LNRM:

> Our expert systems are production systems that are used by thousands of people around the clock. We have found that a new generation of the expert system platform takes several years to develop. It makes no sense for us to pretend otherwise. We have to know what is coming down the road in terms of technology, and we must start our next generation systems early enough to keep our customers satisfied.
>
> Even though we may substantially change our underlying platform software, the plug-in underwriting knowledge bases—the parts of our system that users see and which are our greatest value added—must be carried forward from one generation of the expert system to the next. We have tried to make the migration from one operating system to the next, or from one database system to the next, largely transparent to the end user. From our clients' perspective, our product platforms provide a clear upgrade strategy.

The platform perspective has also been carried forward into project planning and staffing: LNRM has its platform teams and knowledge-base plug-in development teams. That has had clear benefits for the company and its customers. First, higher-risk projects have been decoupled from more time-driven enhancements. Platform developers have been supplied with the necessary time to experiment and think things through. On the other hand, the applications developers working on new risk management knowledge bases have been able to complete more specific tasks without being held back by planned platform improvements. This approach has helped LNRM release new elements of the product family consistently and frequently.

THE FUTURE OF SOFTWARE DEVELOPMENT

All software development entities are confronted by rapid change in computer technologies. Software development has gone through three major epochs since the early days of the computing industry and is currently in the throes of a fourth. The first was a period dominated by proprietary closed systems; the second was one of open systems; and the third, the emergence of client server computing as a standard feature in networked environments. Transitions between each of these periods have been marked by both chaos and fundamental change in the types of software required by users. Today the Internet and a host of emerging technologies associated with it are sweeping across industry and forcing software developers to rethink the architecture of their products and the functionality that they must provide.

During the epoch of closed systems, applications, tools, and even operating systems level code were all combined into one messy entity, yielding hard-to-change and largely unintegratable islands of computing. Many businesses continue to run their operations on those old software systems. Indeed, many managers who discover that they can share information between the popular software products used on their home computers are amazed to find that exactly the opposite situation prevails back at the office. When they request an integration of sales, manufacturing, and engineering information, they are told that "our systems are too complex," or "sales data and manufacturing data are kept on different systems, and they aren't compatible."

Those excuses have already grown thin for many executives, who realize that business decisions cannot be made good without information from across the corporation and from around the world.

The Internet and a host of associated technologies are now sweeping the industry and forcing software developers to rethink the architecture of their products and the functionality they must provide. In today's environment the platform approach to software development is the best approach for keeping pace. Software products are simply too complex to develop on a piecemeal basis. It is far more efficient to develop underlying platforms and to launch derivative applications from them. The firm can then renew its software product platforms while it is creating derivative products from existing platforms.

Common interfaces, rather than myriad unique interfaces, are essential for maintaining a fast pace of renewal. That is all the more important at a time when alliances between software companies are becoming commonplace. For those alliances to work well, their products must also work together. Achieving that with some degree of elegance requires a high degree of clarity and robustness in the interfaces between a company's software and systems to be combined with it. Indeed, design and development of software products boils down to questions about how firms can best manage the interfaces within their software architectures.

The product family concept as we have applied it here to software—the underlying platform, modular add-ins, and robust, common interfaces linking them together and to the user—provides a powerful differentiation between new generations of software products and those embodied in legacy systems of the past. These ideas should not only guide the developers of new systems but also help corporate and individual consumers better consider which particular package or system will best suit their needs not only today but in the future.

Twenty years from now we will probably look back at the acceleration of the Internet during the 1990s as a revolutionary period in the development of both the global information society and the methods by which information systems and products are developed. Over the past ten years companies have used the Internet as a two-way information conduit to the outside world and have created World Wide Web servers for dishing out information to existing and prospective customers. Now the Internet is reaching inside the corporation in the form of "Intranets," internal servers within various departments that utilize the same protocols and provide the same ease of use and administration as the larger external Internet. Typically, those Intranets run on private networks inside the corporation and its branch offices, surrounded by "firewalls" to prevent external access. One market research firm stated that 1995 sales of Intranet technology accounted for 43 percent of the $1.1 billion market of Web servers, and that within a few years spending for internal corporate use of Internet technology will exceed that for external applications.[7]

Software development will change to exploit this new infrastructure. Let us speculate: Rather than a single software development entity making a single "system," hundreds of firms will be contributing smaller, Internet-compatible "applets" that may be seamlessly combined by integrators and users within a distributed computing environment.[8] The software firm of the future will have the potential of seeing its program modules used in hundreds of different applications, many of which it will not control. Instead, the design, development, and integration of software will be controlled in aggregate by masses of developers with shared interests. Waves of software innovation will move through time in the same way that a leaderless swarm of bees navigates from one nest to another. "Beta" test sites will be replaced by thousands of users downloading programs through the Internet and combining them in ways and for purposes that few program developers will have anticipated.

Is this wild speculation? We believe not. One need only consider current events surrounding the Internet and the emergence of electronic communities to realize that the "swarm" has already taken flight.[9] Equally significant is that users are already demanding far more than word processors, spreadsheets, and database management systems to run on their computers; they want to inform and entertain themselves through exciting new "content." That leads us to the next chapter, the design and development of on-line information products.

8

Electronic Information Products

Information products have existed since the development of written language. The clay tablets of the Sumerians and papyrus scrolls of the Egyptians provided information on ancient commerce and theology. Medieval "copyists" preserved and disseminated the knowledge of classical times in laboriously inscribed books. The technology of printing created an explosion of information in sixteenth-century Europe. Books, pamphlets, and broadsides suddenly became available and affordable to the masses, facilitating, in the opinion of many historians, the political and religious revolutions that swept the continent for the next three centuries.

Modern digital technologies are creating yet another information revolution, a true sea change in how we capture, store, and transmit information. New businesses and industries are emerging to provide information products to both consumers and corporations. How those products can be developed and marketed is a new and important challenge to many businesses.

Our focus in this chapter is confined to information products provided through on-line services and on the Internet, in particular the World Wide Web (WWW). Like software, these information products represent a burgeoning area of new product development.[1]

The Internet is a loosely coupled collection of tens of thousands of computers communicating worldwide through industry standard protocols. The Internet is associated with a number of computer hardware and software products. On the hardware side, we find high-speed modems for telephone lines and cable, multimedia "cards," and such peripherals as joysticks. Software development has grown apace with the Internet to include:

- "browsers," such as the Netscape Navigator or Microsoft's Internet Explorer, which allow users to navigate the Internet and display information
- search engines that help users find what they want on the Internet, searching by topic, category, or company name
- authoring and server management tools that facilitate the creation and publishing of Web sites, with security to facilitate consumer purchases over the Internet
- actual content, such as on-line magazines or cyber-worlds, even three-dimensional ones, where people can meet, browse, and interact

Our concern here is not with software tools *per se,* but with the content developed with them and packaged as information products. You will see that the application of the platform concept is quite different for information products relative to software.

The year 1995 was a watershed year for the Internet. For the first time, more PCs were purchased than television sets. More electronic mail messages were sent (95 billion) than postal messages (85 billion). And, the seven major regional U.S. phone companies handled more data traffic than voice traffic.[2] According to a 1995 study released on the Web by CommerceNet/ Nielson, 37 million people in North America had access to services through the Internet of whom about 24 million used the Internet on a weekly basis.[3] Between August of 1995 and March of 1996, the number of individuals having access to the Internet grew by an impressive 50 percent.

Thus we have our "information superhighway." However, many observers (ourselves included) believe that for the most part we are still driving fairly old cars on it. The vast majority of Web sites present static information in a manner that can hardly be called exciting. The information superhighway needs content: exciting, compelling information products and services that consumers will use time and time again, and through such usage will make the Internet a significant revenue-generating medium for content providers.

ACCESS AND CONTENT

To understand the evolution of the Internet industry, one must differentiate between the providers of *access* to the Internet and the creators of its *content*. The on-line service providers, such as America Online and CompuServe, offer access in return for membership and usage fees. Once connected, users can access the information products of the on-line provider, news groups, or the World Wide Web. Until now this has been a growing business, but intense competition has put a lid on membership and usage fees. Further, companies such as AT&T and MCI now offer users direct access to the Internet, in effect helping them to bypass the traditional on-line service providers. Indeed, more and more users are expected to seek direct Internet access in the years ahead.

The content side of the Internet business includes the traditional on-line access providers as well as other firms. The access providers are now preoccupied with creating new content for their members. Microsoft's joint venture with NBC to create on-line, multimedia news content for the Microsoft Network is illustrative. Other companies act as distributors, charging users directly for access to and usage of on-line magazines and other forms of entertainment, and databases that cover specific industry, product, scientific, and government fields.

The shift toward content must invariably change the basic business model of companies providing products and services on the Internet. To date, most on-line content providers have made their money by charging user access fees and advertising fees to vendors who want their banners displayed on Web pages with links to their own Web sites. Forrester Research estimates that only $80 million will have been spent advertising directly on the Web in 1996. However, explosive growth is expected over the next several years, reaching $4.8 billion by the year 2000. As content becomes the differentiating factor, the business model will change toward one in which advertising revenues are complemented by fees for specific services and on-line events. Purchase of physical goods will increase. Internet-based TV-style programming, virtual industry events (such as trade shows), and on-line shopping malls will become more common over the coming decade. Interactivity of this new media will be a differentiating factor over traditional broadcast media.

The evolution of television from the major networks to cable channels provides an analogy for these changes to the Internet. For decades the major networks attracted viewers with free programming, then sold those viewers to advertisers. Cable entrepreneurs turned that business on its head. Their specialized programming for niche channels provided an opportunity to charge users a monthly fee and one-time fees for special events such as boxing matches. That may well occur in the on-line business. Today both major on-line access companies and pure content providers charge corporations for advertising on their Web pages. As in traditional media, the more users they attract (i.e., the number of "hits" on a Web page), the more they can charge. We speculate that this practice will evolve, like cable, to a user-paid arrangement. As it does, the market research side of information products development will become even more important. Product developers will have to identify quickly and then rapidly develop exciting new applications.

SURF'S UP

If the reader has not yet experienced the Internet or the World Wide Web, we encourage you to do a little "surfing," and experience these information products for yourself. The only way to appreciate the new technology, the nature of on-line product development, and its potential for your own business is to use the technology itself.

Visit some Web sites yourself, or have a computer-literate employee act as your tour guide. If this is your first time on the Internet, fear not; it is simple and our tour will take only a few minutes. The sites suggested below are representative of several major classes of on-line information products.

- *Consumer purchasing.* The L.L. Bean home page (at http://www.llbean.com) provides an excellent example of an on-line product catalog. L.L. Bean has added value to its page by allowing users to view pictures and descriptions of all the National Parks, with links to the tourism Web pages of each state in which the parks are located. At the time of this writing, L.L. Bean did not allow direct purchases over the Internet, because the mechanisms for ensuring the confidentiality of credit card numbers were not sufficient. Many other companies, however, allow users to purchase goods directly through the Internet with their credit cards.

- *Science.* Take a look at digitized color photographs taken by the Hubble Space telescope in the Public directory at http://www.stsci.edu. If you have children, this can be a wonderful site to visit on a rainy weekend afternoon. From here you can also surf over to the Visible Human Project (http://www.nlm.nih.gov) to learn about this effort to create a complete, anatomically detailed, three-dimensional mapping of the human body.

- *Entertainment.* To appreciate the merging of Hollywood and Silicon Valley, visit "The Spot," a soap opera–type episode updated daily with new intrigues (http://www.thespot.com). "The Spot" grew from 10,000 "hits" a week in June 1995 to more than 500,000 hits a week by May 1996. NBC's recent acquisition of TV rights to "The Spot" indicates that new forms of Internet content can be leveraged into the TV broadcast world. In the years ahead, the merging of the World Wide Web, cable, and broadcast television will provide fertile ground for new content development combining the visual excitement of TV programming with the interactivity of Internet programming.

• *Government Information.* Are you doing business abroad? Then visit the International Trade Administration's Web site at http://www.ita.doc.gov for a wealth of information on the economies, needs, and import/export regulations of foreign markets. If patent issues are important, take a side trip to the United States Patent Office site (http://www.uspto.gov) to view patents and trademarks associated with your own particular business.

• *Take your pick.* To appreciate the diversity of content being provided on the Internet, scan the topic indices maintained by the Yahoo! Internet search engine (http://www.yahoo.com).

Not a week passes in which new information products or service are launched on the Web. Almost anything goes. Internet content development has reached a frenzied pace and has become today's "Wild Wild West" of creativity and commercial initiative.

INFORMATION PRODUCT FAMILIES, PLATFORMS, AND DERIVATIVES

Developing on-line information products to exploit fast-emerging opportunities requires a clear platform strategy.[4] But what is the nature of information platforms? We have found that they have two essential parts: (1) information content and (2) computer-based manufacturing processes for acquiring, refining, and distributing it to target users. The content component is a *repository* containing raw information that can be sliced and diced in various ways to create specific products. The manufacturing component is essentially a *refinery* that, like a petroleum refinery, acquires source data, cleans and harmonizes it, does the slicing and dicing required to

FIGURE 8–1

The Information Products Platform

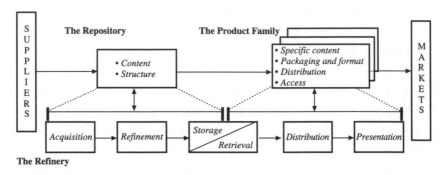

make specific derivative products. The relationships among the information repository, the refinery, and resulting derivative products is shown in Figure 8–1.

The Information Repository

Information databases, broadly defined, have both content and a structure for storing and maintaining that content. For Internet-based information products companies, the principal content has been text (articles or stories) and bit-mapped pictures. Any of the Web sites listed above exemplify this. Companies are also expanding the types of information maintained in their repositories. For example, video and sound clips are now found with increasing frequency on popular Web sites. Animation, or moving objects, within three-dimensional virtual worlds are also coming into style. In other words, the repositories are becoming increasingly multimedia and diverse.

Information types must be subdivided into identifiable, retrievable pieces. A magazine, for example, might be considered a unit of information; so, too, however, might be individual articles in that magazine or, at the lowest level of granularity, single words within articles. A determination must be made as to the lowest divisible unit of information that will be stored, retrieved, and manipulated. For an on-line shopping service, the individual products being sold are the basic information unit.

The appropriate information unit is situationally determined. McGraw-Hill's Primis service provides a useful example. McGraw-Hill has developed a substantial repository of books, articles, and cases. Through an on-line service, a college professor can browse and select just those book chapters, articles, and cases most suitable for students taking a particular course. Based on the professor's choices, Primis compiles a composite, course-specific set of reading materials, then prints and delivers the appropriate number of copies to the university bookstore. Professors no longer have to worry about finding the perfect text or obtaining copyright permissions for photocopying various articles. In a matter of just a few days, they can receive a bound set of materials uniquely designed for a particular course. The information units that matter in this example are chapters, articles, and cases, indexed by topic and author to help the professor search the repository.

A finer level of information unit granularity is found in the repository of business financial statements maintained by Mead Data System's Nexis. Here the footnotes accompanying the financial statements are defined as information units, allowing the user to select particular financial statements for analysis on the basis of key attributes of those footnotes. Thus, part of the design process for creating an information repository is determining which information units are meaningful and appropriate for the given domain.

The repository is the foundation on which the firm creates its families of information products. A well-designed repository makes it possible to mine the most value from its content for a given level of cost. The greater the scope, depth, and complexity of the platform structure, the greater the flexibility for deriving a variety of products. The greater complexity of the repository structure, however, the greater the cost and effort to maintain it. Because repositories for on-line products are stored on computers, the costs are largely in the areas of software programming and systems maintenance.

CorpTech provides an example of how the ability to slice and dice information in the repository is associated with the potential for rapidly and efficiently creating new products for new market niches. CorpTech is an information products company that creates both printed and on-line directories of high-tech companies. Its repository contains data on the management, products, and financial performance of the listed firms. Those detailed data are gathered by telephone surveys of about 40,000 firms. In addition to indexing the firms by industry and location, the CorpTech database has a variety of product and technology categories. Figure 8–2 shows the evolution of CorpTech's repository and its derivative products. Those products are used by many types of customers: sales forces, advertising departments, or university students doing job searches. The size and richness of the repository is CorpTech's primary competitive asset.

For CorpTech and other information products companies, renewal of the repository has two basic dimensions: data acquisition and database restructuring. The acquisition of dynamically changing source data is virtually continuous. On-line news services, for example, must obtain late-breaking stories. For CorpTech, information on quarterly performance and product introductions of high-tech firms must be regularly updated. The other dimension of repository renewal—rethinking and restructuring the way information units are maintained—is periodic and driven by changing customer requirements. Over time, a company may find that its customers want new types of information or need different combinations of information. Each need may require a change in the repository structure. The rethinking of the repository design is directly analogous to the way successful physical product manufacturers described in this book—Black & Decker, Hewlett Packard, Compaq, or EMC—have renewed their own respective product platforms.

FIGURE 8–2

CorpTech's Product Platform and Derivative Products

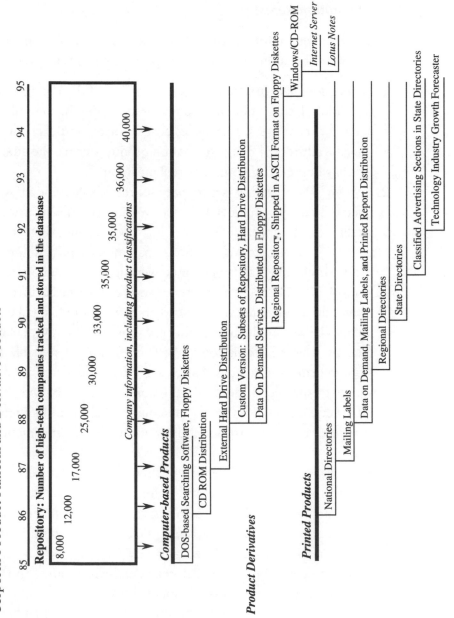

213

The Information Refinery

We described the information refinery as the "manufacturing" process for information products. This process has five steps:

1. *Acquisition.* The first step is the acquisition of data or raw information. Issues of quality, scope, breadth, depth, credibility, accuracy, timeliness, relevance, cost, control, and exclusivity must be addressed. For information products firms, the adage "garbage in–garbage out" has real meaning.

2. *Refining.* Data refining is a primary source of value-added. Refinement can be physical (e.g., conversion of data from one medium to another) or logical (e.g., labeling, indexing, integrating, or restructuring relationships among data). Refining includes "cleaning" data and/or converting it to a standard format. Meta-analyses on repositories may also be performed to glean further meaning from the combination of individual elements. Refining adds value to the repository in two ways: (1) by creating usable information and (2) by making it possible to store information in ways that enable efficient generation of a variety of specific products. That second value-adding process often requires the conversion of acquired data from its native structure to a more meaningful or useful set of information units.

3. *Storage and retrieval.* These steps represent a bridge between the upstream acquisition and refinement, which feed the repository, and the downstream stages of product generation. Storage can be as simple as placing sheets of printed information in labeled binders. In today's environment, however, it usually means computerized storage employing some form of database or knowledge management software.

4. *Distribution.* Like any other product, information must have a medium of distribution to the end user. It may take various forms, including the printed page, fax, delivery on compact disk, electronic computer mail, radio or television transmis-

sion, or multimedia information delivered through Web sites.

5. *Presentation.* A fundamental characteristic of information products is that the value of information, and therefore the value-added in producing information products, is pervasively influenced by the context of its use. Ensuring ease of use and sufficient functionality is part and parcel of the information product itself. There are hundreds of thousands of Web sites, for example, but those considered "the best" are far better than others in terms of their ease of use, creative design, and general appeal. In fact, many information products companies compete as much on the quality of the interface, i.c., their information ergonomics, as on information content.

A Refinery at Work

To illustrate the refinery concept, consider Individual, Inc., a repackager of news information. (You can visit the company's Web site at http://www.individual.com.) Individual, Inc., creates customized news stories for thousands of customers based on each customer's unique preferences and needs. It provides the stories through various electronic media. The company's selling proposition is that "less information—as long as it is the right information—is more."

Individual's information repository on any given day contains about twenty thousand news stories indexed and stored in a computerized database. The news stories (the raw material) are electronically acquired from about four hundred suppliers through computer and telecommunications networks. That raw content is reformatted into a common structure for further processing. Story content is then matched to customers' keyword profiles stored in a database separate from, but complementary to, the information repository. Matching is done with a software search engine that matches customer profiles to streams of incoming text.

Industry and market templates have enhanced the refining process. Templates currently exist for electronics, computers, health care, biotechnology, telecommunications, finance, energy, and government, among others. Each template contains terminology and company names deemed useful for finding stories relevant to particular readers.

New customers reveal their particular interests through a detailed information request form, where they specify their industry affiliation and particular information interests. As customers receive information, they provide feedback that helps the company to improve its industry templates and to refine its understanding of customer interests.

After extracting the appropriate stories from the repository, Individual's refinery formats news stories into one of several derivative product designs for distribution via fax, electronic mail, the World Wide Web, or Lotus Notes, at the customer's option. For site licensed customers, Individual's daily repository of news stories can be transmitted electronically in whole to the customers' computer.

The design of the company's refinery infrastructure resembles a human organization, with its allocation of different functions to groups operating under a hierarchical control structure (Figure 8–3). At the front end of the process, work is allocated to PCs based on volume and type of source input, be it file transfer or electronic mail. Dozens of PCs operate to gather those data, and more can be added as the number of information suppliers increases. In the middle section of the process, workstations filter news stories. Here too, additional workstations can be added to handle increased volume. At the back end of the process, clusters of PCs distribute the final product through fax, e-mail, Web server, Notes, and direct computer linkages. As the business grows, more clusters can be added in a modular fashion. In other words, the design of the refinery is scalable.

FIGURE 8–3

Individual, Inc.'s Information Refinery

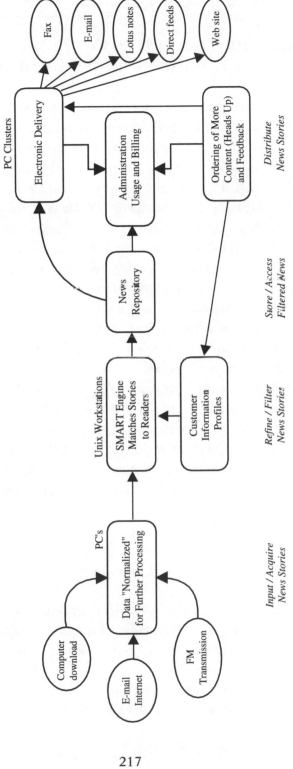

CREATING THE PRODUCT FAMILY:
ZIFF DAVIS INTERACTIVE MEDIA DEVELOPMENT

Armed with these platform concepts, we can now consider how a well-managed repository and refinery can create a rich family of information products. To illustrate, we turn to a major on-line content provider, Ziff Davis Interactive Media Development (ZDIMD). ZDIMD's parent company, Ziff Davis Publishing, publishes *PC Magazine, PC Computing, PC Week, Computer Shopper, MacWeek, Mac User, Windows Sources, and Interactive Week,* among other well-known computer magazines, and licenses or syndicates editorial content to fifty-five other publications distributed in more than one hundred countries.

ZDIMD was started over a decade ago when Ziff Davis management recognized the potential of the Internet and on-line services to undermine its traditional "hard copy" businesses. Instead of resisting the technology, management decided to master it and to mine its commercial potential. ZDNet, ZDIMD's service, has risen to become the world's largest special interest publisher of electronic content on buying, using, supporting, and understanding computers. Like other major players in the industry, ZDIMD has made money from membership, usage fees, and advertising shared with on-line services providers. The company also achieves substantial advertising revenues from graphical banners for advertisers on its own Web site. While those advertisers have tended to be computer hardware, software, and services providers, ZDNet is finding that it can branch out into other consumer areas, such as automobiles.

ZDNet provides a family of on-line information products and services. Users access ZDNet either through the major on-line service providers, such as CompuServe, Prodigy, America Online, and the Microsoft Network, or directly through the World Wide Web. (Readers with Internet access should visit the ZDNet Web site at http://www.zdnet.com.) At the time of this writing, more than 250,000 people used ZDNet on CompuServe alone. In fact, the ZDNet Web site was receiving more than 30 million hits every month! The company's own tracking systems showed that it had more than 625,000 unique users every month. The demographic profile of the users parallels that of the parent company's magazine readers: PC users who are upscale, sophisticated early adopters of new technology, and have high disposable incomes.

Figure 8–4 is a screen image of the ZDNet home page. Take a moment to study the home page, because it reflects the rich variety of information and services that on-line publishers seek to provide on the Web. The basic page layout provides a guide to the company's product family. At the top of the figure are various "buttons," starting with "What's New." On the left side of the page are buttons that link to "Today's News," a massive shareware library, computer product information, and other sets of information. In the middle of the page are highlighted "feature" articles drawn from Ziff Davis's hard copy publications, and to the right of those are additional news stories and product reviews. Additionally, you can observe that at the bottom right of the figure are special ZDNet "resources," where users can search through posted job positions from across the computer industry, look at upcoming trade shows (Ziff Davis's parent company, Softbank, owns numerous industry trade shows), or get a personalized list of news stories drawn from around the world. Throughout the successive pages of this Web site are various advertising banners, which ZDIMD creates and displays for a large number of companies. ZDNet also provides direct links to those advertisers' own Web sites so that users can gather specific product information.

Behind many of the buttons on this home page are a series of successive Web pages. On each successive Web page, one will typically find a combination of services and advertising banners—paid advertisements. ZDIMD establishes its advertisement fees by using computers to track the number of accesses to any given Web page; the more "hits," the higher the fee. One might question whether

FIGURE 8–4

ZDNet Home Page

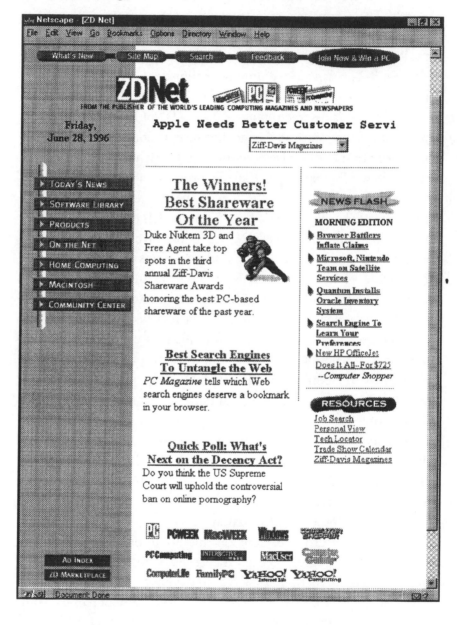

these on-line publications draw revenue away from their traditional hard copy brethren. Ziff Davis's experience has been the opposite. The two media forms have proved synergistic.

A substantial amount of ZDNet's content, then, is drawn from the parent company's various magazines. At the time of this writing, the company drew upon a foundation of more than 200,000 individual magazine articles, computer benchmarks, and software reviews. These are key information units of the repository. Within ZDNet's information refinery, those data are gathered in electronic form. They must be translated into a common format, "cleaned," and otherwise manipulated so that they can be stored within a single multimedia database. Each article, for example, is provided with certain index information indicating companies referred to in the article, industry groups, and specific products or services discussed. Topics and commonly used keywords are also "tagged." Error messages associated with each piece of content are also created and indexed. All text, pictures, sound, and video must also be formatted for appropriate display on the Internet. Many incoming sets of information must be divided into finer levels of detail and stored accordingly. Lastly, everything must be checked for computer viruses. To accomplish those many tasks, ZDIMD had to develop its own proprietary "manipulation language," called ZML. Figure 8–5 shows this stage of the refinery.

Once all that information has been refined and placed into ZDIMD's repository, derivative products can be made. One set of derivative products comprises on-line versions of Ziff Davis's computer magazines. Those are the buttons on the bottom of the home page, or the featured news stories in the center of the page. However, if all ZDNet did was simply to make it possible to read existing magazines from a computer monitor, there would not be a substantial amount of value-added.

To add value, the company has developed new services based on its understanding of what its users need and will appreciate. For example, consider the "Search" button at the top of the home page

FIGURE 8–5

ZDI's Information Refinery

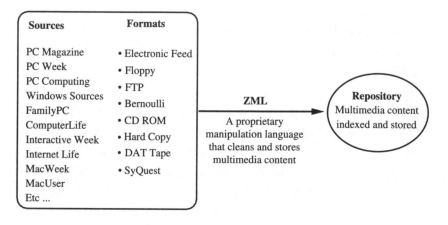

(Figure 8–4). Here users can employ ZDNet's customized search engine to obtain articles and product reviews from across the parent company's numerous magazines. Figure 8–6 indicates how ZDNet applies the refinery laterally across several different traditional products to create product variety for customers. Common information units are labeled on the left side of the figure, abbreviated to include published articles, lab tests of hardware and software products, benchmarks, and advertiser indices. Across the top of the figure are some of the many products in ZDNet's magazine portfolio. On the righthand side are two hypothetical customers, who, having entered their keyword search strings, proceed to get information from across the entire repository. Between the two users in the figure are the major conduits through which access has been provided, be it ZDNet on the World Wide Web, America Online, or whatever.

A robust repository and refinery allows information products companies to acheive mass customization for users through software interfaces that allow the user to enter queries and view the results rapidly. Note how similar this approach is to the platform

FIGURE 8–6

Achieving Mass Customization from the ZDI Repository

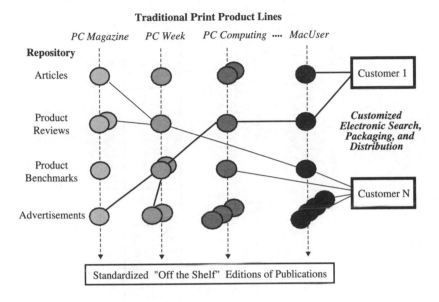

approaches used by Black & Decker, Hewlett Packard, EMC, or any of the other companies profiled in this book. For those physical product manufacturers, a major platform subsystem may be the universal motor, the ink print cartridge, or the small, inexpensive disk—all of which have been used and combined in different variations to create specific derivative products. For an information products company like ZDIMD, the main platform subsystems are articles and databases, used and combined in different ways to provide the user with a product tailored to his or her needs. That underscores the power and the universality of the platform approach.

Other derivative products can also be seen by looking at the lower-right region of the ZDIMD's home page (Figure 8–4). One is "Personal View," accessed through a button in the Resources section at the bottom right of the home page. Personal View is a news reader service that is similar to that provided by Individual,

FIGURE 8–7

ZDI's Product Family and Platforms

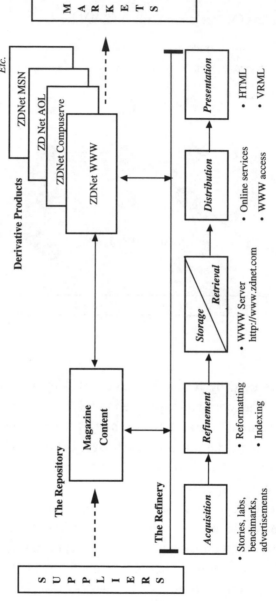

224

Inc., as described above. Users can select from a broad range of topics in developing their unique news interest profile. ZDNet receives tens of thousands of news stories daily from electronic sources, then matches those against each user's interest profile. When users enter Personal View, they automatically receive a list of news stories that address their interests, followed by specific story content. From a product development perspective, ZDNet had to augment its repository structure with a new information unit—the news story—and enhance its acquisition, refining, and user presentation processes to deliver the service successfully.

Job Search, another Resource button, contains postings that ZDNet maintains as distinct information units in its repository. Users can browse through the various jobs offered and submit their applications electronically. Another useful service is the the "Software Library," accessed on the left side of the home page. ZDIMD has compiled a library of more than five thousand shareware software programs that it has scrutinized and qualified. Users can download those programs to their own computers.

The key point here is that many of these products and services are derived from a single information repository. The repository itself is continuously updated and refined by a carefully developed and automated refinery. ZDIMD's platform strategy is brought together in Figure 8–7.

DISCOVERING AND EXPLOITING EMERGING MARKETS

While most of this discussion on information products has focused on technology, one cannot overstate the importance of marketing. As for other companies in the Internet business, the challenge facing ZDIMD's management is to identify and develop or license new content complementary to its brand.

For product developers, the questions are: Who will use the Internet in the future and what information will they seek? The answers to those questions will drive the design and development of new on-line products. A great advantage goes to the enterprises that foresee emerging market needs and, armed with a robust platform, exploit them. Firms that lack skill or energy in market research may never create products in time to create market franchises. One information products entrepreneur described the marketing dynamics of the Internet content business as follows:

> It is a market of a thousand niches served by tens of thousands of firms, each offering dozens if not hundreds of different products. In the information business, the company that recognizes a market need first, and delivers a product soon thereafter, can establish a franchise that dominates the niche. Since information gets old, customers will tend to continuously repurchase information from the franchise holder. The pace of action is so fast that there is rarely sufficient time to perform thorough market research for new products. A company just has to go for it, all the time seeking to take its information assets into the new uses. Once you have the information, the marginal cost of adding another customer or creating a new product can be very, very small. The opportunities for leverage are indeed substantial.[5]

The ability to effectively segment highly dynamic markets and prioritize niches is a key success factor for those participating in this industry. There are no certainties in the process: Market growth rates are highly unstable, and new competitors emerge daily. However, having worked with a number of entrepreneurs in this fast-paced industry, we have observed criteria useful for prioritizing emerging niche applications:

- The potential of the information product or service to be dynamic, and to create a "buzz" of excitement in the marketplace. Such excitement can lead to explosive growth. This can come only from the creative minds of the concept developers. Serious players in this industry have top-notch "creative directors" who design exciting, compelling content.
- A significant number of potential users for the new information

product. Market estimates in information products are largely derived from user populations of related products or services, or from populations that exist in the physical domain. It is interesting to note that a number of on-line service providers experience their greatest audiences after 7:30 P.M., putting them in direct competition with broadcast television and cable programming.

- The availability of content and the difficulty and cost of developing it and integrating into the firm's repository and refinery processes.
- The availability of software development tools to create the user interface, and of the capacity of the existing Internet infrastructure to download the intended information at a reasonable rate. The tools issue remains problematic for new areas such as secure Internet shopping and the creation of 3D cyber worlds. The bandwidth issue remains problematical. Advances in telecommunications infrastructure are still stymied by the explosive growth of new Internet users and the volumes of multimedia content. This throughput problem, however, will drive innovation forward to solve the problem.
- The ability of the firm to maintain dynamism in the content, because frequent changes are required to keep products fresh and vital to users.
- The presence of significant reciprocal linking opportunities, i.e., opportunities to link and co-market with on-line partners, thereby creating synergy in the eyes of the user (e.g., Microsoft's joint venture with NBC).

Content providers continuously seek opportunities to create and strengthen their brand images in the on-line world. A flexible repository and a highly automated refinery contribute to that goal by making the incremental cost of creating new products unusually low, especially when compared with physical products. Creation of a new information product, for example, may simply be a matter of a different type of data sort or statistical analysis on the computer. It may be a new "episode" in the emerging genre of Internet TV-style soaps or gaming. Development in this environment is fast, a matter of months if not weeks or even days. Further leverage is achieved by the fact that single purchases are the exception if the content "grabs" the customer. Once a customer perceives the information or entertainment as having value, repeat purchases are the rule.

We have observed similar leverage in many of the physical product cases described throughout this book. A consumer, having bought a Black & Decker drill, feels compelled to complete his home workshop with a sander, the hedge trimmer, and the circular saw. The user of an HP ink jet printer keeps on consuming disposable printer cartridges. Information and entertainment can be equally addictive.

The on-line information products business is justifiably described as "a brave new world." However, for us it bears important similarities with the business of making and marketing physical products. Both must be renewed through the integration of new technologies and market understanding, and both benefit from the power of thoughtful platform strategy that provides the opportunity to create a rich array of products—developed at incremental cost and tailored to specific customer needs.

9

Bridging to the Future

So, have we hooked you? Does the notion of the product family—of common building blocks, product platforms, and derivative products—make sense to you? More important, can you see how it can improve your business?

If the answers to those questions are yes, then the architectures and manufacturing processes behind your product line must be renewed. That can happen only if senior management directly participates in the articulation of a multiyear product line strategy based on the creation and renewal of robust product platforms. That brings us to the focus of this final chapter: the processes used by corporations and the role of executives in planning and managing the development of new products.

PROCESSES FOR MANAGING NEW BUSINESS
AND PRODUCT DEVELOPMENT

In American industry, the preferred process for planning and controlling product development is the "stage-gate" or phase review system. This system is often depicted as a development funnel (Figure 9–1). A large number of new product concepts enter the front end of the funnel, and those deemed unpromising are termi-

FIGURE 9–1

The Development Funnel

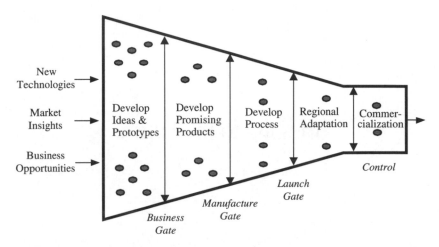

Projects that should be sharing technology compete.
Manufacturing is "downstream," and a "gate" to product innovaton.
Single project focus — at the expense of families and platforms.

nated before downstream investments are made. Only the most worthy few pass through to production and market launch.

Each project in the funnel must pass through gates at successive stages of development: market opportunity identification; concept development; design; prototype; manufacturing development; launch and ongoing support.[1] Each gate is a trial by fire in which product teams must justify their work to management review committees and make a case for continued funding. Projects that survive one gate proceed to the next, where they meet another set of inquisitors.

The stage-gate process inevitably pits one project against another in the contest for limited resources. Product champions quickly understand that they are in a zero-sum game and that additional resources for their projects must inevitably be taken from someone else's plate. It is not a process that encourages collaboration. Projects that should be sharing core technologies, market insights, and product platforms are placed in competition. Sharing of resources, capabilities, and business opportunities occurs only by convenience or chance. Such an approach to managing and controlling new product development is therefore incompatible with our notion of building product families from robust common platforms and technology.

The stage-gate system also gives effective veto power to manufacturing. As one of the gates on the path to commercialization, manufacturing has the power to shape the physical properties of new products. To get manufacturing's approval, product teams are inclined to develop what the factory can build. In effect, manufacturing becomes the customer whom product developers must please. That encourages incrementalism at the expense of real innovation and renewal, and it relegates industry leaders to secondary status over time. To achieve the simultaneous design for manufacturing of new product platforms that we described in Chapter 1, management may indeed have to bulldoze existing manufacturing processes into the parking lot!

Despite the time and money spent by industry creating and implementing product development processes, our experience indicates that many managers and employees are befuddled by the details. Figure 9–2 is how one senior manager sketched his company's new product development process as he understood it. As the figure indicates, the process was highly detailed in terms of checklists and procedures. It was also highly ineffective. The products that emerged from this process had little in common, and development cycle times were often too long. Different parts of the organization simply ignored points in the process where interaction was supposed to occur.

Like great products, management processes should be elegant in their simplicity and effectiveness, with every element serving an important purpose. Overly complex processes are unmanageable, cumbersome, and inflexible; they force people to spend more time

FIGURE 9–2
One Company's New Product Development Process

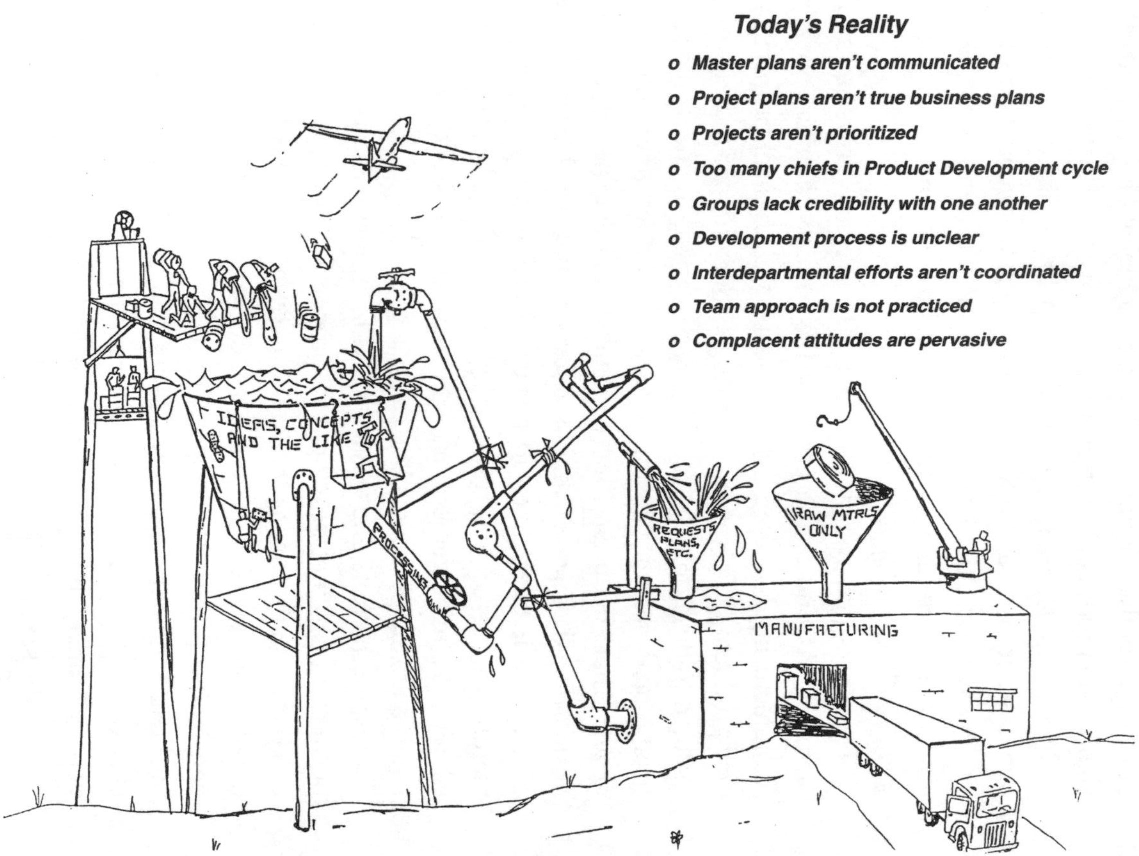

Today's Reality
o Master plans aren't communicated
o Project plans aren't true business plans
o Projects aren't prioritized
o Too many chiefs in Product Development cycle
o Groups lack credibility with one another
o Development process is unclear
o Interdepartmental efforts aren't coordinated
o Team approach is not practiced
o Complacent attitudes are pervasive
IDEAS, CONCEPTS AND THE LINE
PROCESSING
REQUESTS PLANS, ETC.
RAW MTRLS ONLY
MANUFACTURING

doing paper work and making presentations than designing and building products. That results in long cycle times and added costs. One manufacturer that studied the overhead imposed by its existing development process of checklists and frequent stage-gate reviews discovered that it added eighteen months to the new product cycle time! Not surprisingly, the real innovations in this company came from "guerrilla" campaigns operating entirely outside the system. We observed another corporation with a similar stage-review process that recently was forced to cancel work on a platform project running into the tens of millions of dollars. The reason: Competitors were at the point of releasing second-generation products by the time this company had reached manufacturing ramp-up for its first generation.

Even companies that recognize the dysfunctional nature of process complexity sometimes blunder into new processes that are equally bad. One such company we visited, enthralled with the reengineering mania, had done away with its formal departmental structure and formed process teams led by coaches. Unfortunately, the flowchart of activities to be followed by these teams ran across ten pages. The teams were thrashing in their new process as cycle times, inventories, and morale worsened.

It is no surprise, then, that employees who jump ship to smaller and less bureaucratic firms experience a sense of delight and liberation in having broken free of "the process."

For large organizations, processes are instruments intended to bring order out of chaos. Too much order and control, however, discourages innovation and renewal. A certain level of creative chaos is needed to move any organization, large or small, beyond its current technology and habits. That is one of the lessons we have learned from entrepreneurial startups. These enterprises are almost devoid of management process, yet they provide the economy with many of its innovations. Overcontrol by senior management simply grinds down that creative chaos and undermines the initiative and speed of development teams.

A PRODUCT FAMILY DEVELOPMENT PROCESS

A simpler, more elegant approach to product development is represented in the concepts presented in earlier chapters, and those can be applied to your current business. If your corporation uses a single product management control process loaded with procedures and checklists, consider trimming it and front-loading it with a multiyear, multiproduct planning process. To get started, identify a product line in need of renewal, preferably one that addresses a market with a lot of upside potential. Next, form a multidisciplined team of individuals open to change and give it three months to evaluate the future of the product line.

The first activities of the team should be to understand the product line from a product family and platform perspective. The analysis is guided by three basic questions:

- *What are the product platforms in the existing business?* Have the team create block diagrams of the various platform architectures and manufacturing workflows. From those they can determine the degree of commonality across these product platforms and the manufacturing processes associated with them.
- *What stream of products is derived from these platforms?* Create a product family map similar to that developed for HP's ink jet printers in Chapter 2. Then, using the platform-market grids presented in Chapter 3, have the team determine the extent to which 'common platforms are being leveraged across markets. Also, have the team determine the extent to which platforms are being applied to emerging market opportunities.
- *Are the company's derivative products being developed efficiently?* Use the performance measures presented in Chapter 6 to determine efficiency of derivative products. If they are costing more to engineer and manufacture than they should, what are the underlying causes of that inefficiency? Have the team compute other measures presented in Chapter 6, including the platform effectiveness, the cost-price ratio, and the lead-lag responsiveness relative to competitors.

The answers to these questions will establish a common understanding for the need and direction of product line renewal. Planning the future evolution of the product family then follows five key steps:

1. defining a new platform strategy
2. determining the core platform building blocks of the new platform
3. building a composite design of the product platform and assembling the required building blocks
4. developing a rollout plan for derivative products and platform enhancements

FIGURE 9–3

The Power Tower: An Integrative Model of Product and Process Innovation

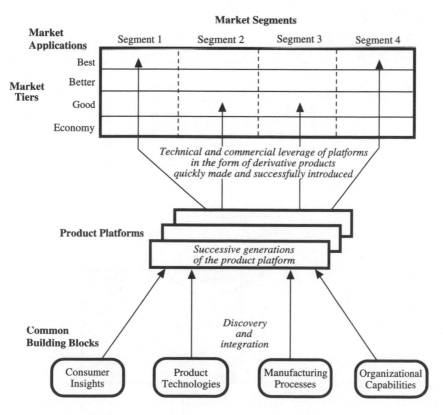

5. organizing and empowering the team that will implement the platform and its derivative products

The power tower framework presented in Chapter 2 and reproduced in Figure 9–3 is the "thinking tool" that guides the entire effort.

1. Defining Platform Strategy

The team must define its platform strategy. Whether it is a high-end or low-end focus should be determined by the growth opportunities in the market. Using a platform-market grid similar to Figure 9–4 as a guide, the team must gather information, market niche by market niche, regarding the current size, the growth rate, the firm's own percentage share, and leading companies compet-

FIGURE 9–4

Understanding the Market

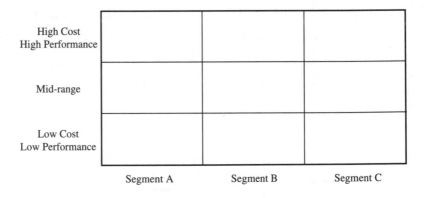

FIGURE 9–5

Defining Initial Platform Focus, Platform Extensions, and Entry-level Products by Market Niche

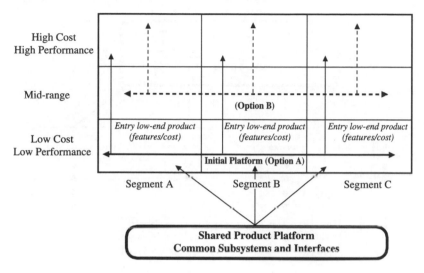

ing in each market niche. The team should then discuss the compelling product or service solutions for each particular niche in terms of both function and cost.

From that understanding, the team can then propose alternative platform strategies on this grid, all the while being mindful of the need to leverage a common platform within and across market segments. Figure 9–5 is a guide for representing alternative platform strategies simply.

2. Determining the Core Platform Building Blocks

Next, the team must identify the building blocks behind the new desired product platform(s). As you will recall, we group the building blocks into four categories: market insights, product technologies, manufacturing processes and technologies, and organizational capabilities (with a focus on distribution channels and information

FIGURE 9–6

Identifying the Platform Building Blocks

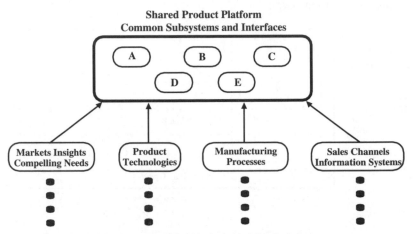

List the core building blocks behind the platform.
Distinguish between those that are internally owned,
or that are externally available, or that must be developed.

systems). Figure 9–6 shows a general planning guide for performing this activity.

Some of the building blocks will be available to the firm internally; others must be obtained from external suppliers or partners. Those building blocks at the unique disposal of the firm—what Prahalad and Hamel (from the University of Michigan and the London School of Business, respectively) call the core competencies of the corporation[2]—are the crown jewels. Other building blocks may not exist in the firm or among suppliers and therefore must be developed by your company or a subcontractor. For purposes of clarity, the team may wish to use different colors to distinguish between internal building blocks, external ones, and those that need to be newly developed.

Platform building blocks must be evaluated objectively:

• What are the market insights, core product technologies, manufacturing technologies, and distribution structures currently controlled by the corporation? Are any of them exclusive to the firm?

- Measured objectively, are these competencies superior to, equal to, or below parity with those of other firms?[3]
- Does the company bring anything new to the market, or is it simply an integrator of commonly available technology, and therefore a producer of "me-too" products?

The answers to these questions will determine the best approach to dealing with the new platform design. Some of its building blocks may come from corporate R&D. Others may exist only outside the firm with companies from whom technology should be licensed or otherwise obtained.

3. Building a Composite Design of the Product Platform and Assembling the Building Blocks

The techniques of composite design were presented in detail in Chapter 4. The goal is to create product platforms and manufacturing processes that are elegant in their simplicity, form, and function, and that support efficient development of derivative products.

Composite design begins with an understanding of user needs, in particular the latent needs to which no existing products are responding. In addition to understanding the market, the team must have a thorough knowledge of the company's own products, those of the most competent rivals, and the best available materials and technologies for rendering those obsolete. Recall what we said in Chapter 4 about the difference between latent needs and perceived needs, and the importance of understanding latent needs for creating a truly exciting, powerful product platform. To gain such an understanding, each team member must *be the product* and consider how he or she frustrates the user. Those insights must then be validated through good market research. We prefer to use conjoint analysis on surveys comprising respondents from various market segments. Without those data, the team will rely on old perceptions and will probably create pedestrian designs. Strong marketing personnel are therefore an essential ingredient for platform development teams.

Next, the team must study the existing designs of its own products and those of competitors. While this analysis takes some time, it is the only way a team can be sure that it will reach beyond parity relative to competitors. The team can measure the complexity of competing platforms and index major subsystems of both competitors' products and their own against standard baselines of function and cost. From those activities, the team will observe the best-in-class subsystems from across industry. Those can serve as key elements of a new platform. Charts that the team can use to guide its composite design are provided in Chapter 4.

The new platform's performance standards and the price range of the platform's derivative products should be based on a foundation of market and technical knowledge, with particular attention given to interfaces—both among internal subsystems and between subsystems and the user. Those subsystems and interfaces give power to platforms. New materials and componentry, along with design for visual appeal and user functionality, must also be considered as the team works its way through the technical details. All the while, the team must ensure that the platform has the flexibility to accommodate stepup functions and applications to different market segments.

Best-in-class manufacturing processes must be integrated with platform design. The objective here is to drive the labor content and assembly steps out of the manufacturing process, making the platform one that can be made anywhere, even in high-labor-cost markets. The use of subcontractors for certain aspects of manufacture must also be considered at this point.

These composite design steps, of course, will have to be adapted for businesses dealing with such nonphysical products as software or electronic information products. There, subsystem interfaces and external interfaces are often based on industry standards, far more so than the majority of traditional physical products. Industrial design for software and on-line information products is largely the ergonomic elegance of the user interface as opposed to traditional packaging. The manufacturing of such products can also be very different. For example, teams may have to create the software engines and add-in modules described in Chapter 7, or the repositories and refineries described in Chapter 8, so that computers perform the "manufacturing" and the Internet can handle the distribution.

4. Developing the Roll-Out Plan For Derivative Products

Armed with its platform strategy and platform designs, the team can then develop a roll-out plan for the derivative products that will populate the product family. This may take the form of a forward-looking product family map, as shown in Figure 9–7. Here, entry

FIGURE 9–7

The Product Family Roll-out Plan

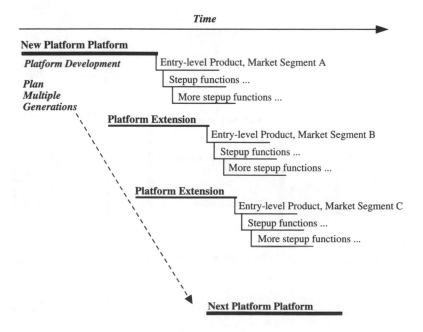

level products and stepup functions for each market segment are specified. Platform enhancements should also be planned. Once you have identified a platform's subsystems, improvements on a subsystem-by-subsystem basis can be staged across successive generations of the product line.

As an integrative step, the team should create a new power tower for the business, where the building blocks, platforms, and derivative products come together in a simple visual form for the benefit of top management.

5. Organizing the Implementation Team

Armed with a product family plan, management must then organize and empower a platform implementation team. The team itself should be designed as a composite team encompassing the essential skills required to create a robust platform. Figure 9–8 is a planning

FIGURE 9–8

The Composite Platform Team

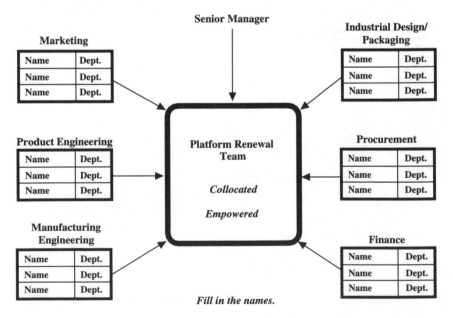

Fill in the names.

guide suited to manufacturing businesses. It can be easily adapted to software and on-line information product companies. As you fill in the names, you need not be confined to any particular business unit or to the company itself in searching for the best candidates. Subcontractors, suppliers, and even customers should be considered.

The team should then be prepared to present to senior management a multiproduct, multimarket, multiyear plan for funding. In turn, senior management must itself be prepared to fund worthy initiatives on a multiyear basis, shielding team members as best as possible from the vicissitudes of the stock market and the firm's own quarterly results.

Such resource allocation will probably mean that management will fund fewer individual projects, focusing its investments on the creation and renewal of product lines of central importance to the corporation. That strategic focus will work to the benefit of the organization and its customers. Teams must also be encouraged to set clear targets for platform and derivative product functionality and then stick to them. That will help spare the organization the pain, expense, and opportunity cost associated with muddling about in the fuzzy front end of product development.

UNDERSTANDING THE LIMITATIONS OF PAST PRACTICES AND MOVING FORWARD

Any company can change the way it designs products and does business. Many cases presented in this book—ranging from mouse traps, to power tools, to computer printers, to irons, to software, to Internet services—confirm that fact. Platform thinking and methodology have helped companies succeed in each of those product areas.

Consider one last case. Unlike mouse traps or irons, which have a small number of parts, this one shows how principles described in this book were successfully applied to what is one of the most complex product development projects in the world: the creation of a new jet passenger plane.

In the early 1990s a group of managers and engineers at Boeing recognized that the company had a proliferation of platform architectures—the result of developing new airplanes one design at a time over a period of years. A decisive platform strategy cutting across product lines simply did not exist. The team recognized in this a tremendous opportunity not only to build a new airplane but to change the way the company did business. Top management listened, agreed, and formed a platform team under the leadership of a senior executive. Boeing also invited some of its key customers to become full-time design participants. That alone was a significant departure from past practice.

Under its motto "Working Together," the platform team determined that there were four essential building blocks to its business: aircraft technologies, design technologies, manufacturing processes, and distribution and service processes. Further, it concluded that Boeing needed only fourteen key competencies to run its business, and only a few of those related directly to aircraft hardware. Others had to do with the entertainment technology provided to passengers; navigational technologies for pilots; and service capabilities unique to the requirements of commercial airlines. The fourteen competencies, it was decided, had to become the focus of the team and of top management.

The team also studied the many processes then used in running the business—sixty in all, and more than a thousand information systems behind those processes, which were supported by three thousand employees. The "new business" envisioned by the team would run those systems with fewer than half that number.

The team then created a new platform design for what would become the Boeing 777. Its principle of design was very similar to those advocated here: namely, that a major portion of each airplane should be standard and designed around the same subsystems. The remaining portions would be options, either designed in advance (as stepup functions) or unique to specific customer needs.

Prior to the 777, Boeing planes used few common parts. As a

rule of thumb, the number of parts was directly related to the size of the aircraft. The bigger and heavier the plane, the greater the number of unique parts. The 777 reversed that tradition. The 777 design provided more options and flexibility for customers while using significantly fewer unique parts and more common parts. For example:

- *Doors.* A typical aircraft passenger entry door has 1,400 parts, most being unique. In the seven doors on the 777, 95 percent of the parts are common to all doors.
- *Overhead bins.* In the past, overhead bins were unique to each airplane. The 777 has only three standard bin geometries. They are usable with any class of seating by simply changing the hinge points.
- *Seating.* Reconfiguring the seating in previous aircraft required a week of work. Thanks to the 777's new modular "interfaces" between the seats and the aircraft structure, seating can be re-configured overnight.
- *Galleys and restrooms.* Previous aircraft galleys and restrooms could not be relocated without extensive plumbing, electrical, and structural changes. In contrast, the 777 design provides predetermined zones for galleys and restrooms, which can be easily relocated without changes to the electrical wiring, plumbing, or the aircraft structure.

Using this approach, the platform team planned a product family that will eventually include:

- the baseline 777-200A
- a longer-range 777-200B
- a larger capacity 777-300A
- a larger and longer-range 777-300B
- a very long range, smaller-capacity 777-100

The platform team also formulated ten commandments of aircraft design and manufacture for Boeing—a "thought architecture" that has guided the 250 separate development teams organized to implement the many subsystems, processes, and derivative products that have grown out of the initial 777 venture. Boeing's ten commandments are:

1. Engineering and Manufacturing commit to work together to develop a more producible, more error-free design.
2. Engineering will define systems and structure concurrently—before release.
3. Engineering will define more accurate details and assemblies using product definition—before release.
4. Engineering will make sure all the parts are defined and fit together using digital preassembly—before release.
5. Manufacturing will accomplish sufficient planning and tool design to provide valid producibility knowledge to Engineering Design—before release.
6. Engineering will incorporate Manufacturing's producibility knowledge into the design to the maximum possible degree.
7. Manufacturing will sign Engineering data sets verifying their producibility—before release.
8. Manufacturing will assign a manager to team with each Chief Engineer.
9. Material, Customer Service, and Finance will also identify a manager to team with each Chief Engineer, as appropriate.
10. These Design Build management leaders will organize and plan their activities to accomplish the above.

Today, this approach is being institutionalized throughout the company. The goal is to be sure every new airplane has high levels of standardization with options and stepup functions engineered, tested, and ready to be installed, as well as flexible interfaces to accommodate unique customer requirements. Buying an airplane will closely resemble the process of acquiring a new automobile—customers will select a basic model and then add options meeting their specific tastes and budgets.

Boeing's success underscores the power of product platforms and should provide encouragement to dedicated managers and employees that even the largest organizations with the most complex products can change dramatically for the better.

LEADERSHIP: VISION WITH VIGOR

Senior management can either ignore or respond to initiatives like the one described above. Responding means funding platform teams, supporting their work, and creating linkages between them and other parts of the organization. Responding also means giving platform and derivative products projects sufficient time and independence to complete their work, sparing them continuous reappraisal by management committees. Once the product family plan meets with senior management approval, the entire stream of products identified as part of first generation of the platform should also be approved in principle. That is not to say that late or over-budget platforms or derivative products are above the scrutiny of management. Markets may also change suddenly, requiring changes to the product family plan. However, every single derivative product should not have to rejustify its existence on a periodic basis. The focus of management discussion and approval should be on the platform itself, the efforts to renew it, and the roll-out plan of its derivative products. Spending valuable time on individual derivative products only deflects executive attention from the underlying foundations of the business.

ASKING FOR THE ORDER

In some cases only strong leadership by top management will effect change. For a company to be able to bring a discontinuity to the industry—whether through product technology, manufacturing process, or distribution—the CEO may have to introduce a discontinuity in the way employees think about today's problems and

tomorrow's desires. Executives must "ask for the order." Otherwise nothing will change. We observed this in the cases described
in this book. The president of Black & Decker stated that the company could not achieve sustained market advantage unless double
insulation could be introduced across the entire product portfolio
at no increase in cost to the end user. That caused a sea change in
the way the company's designers approached their product platforms and manufacturing processes. In the HP case, management
challenged engineers to achieve color printing below $500. At
EMC, top management challenged engineers to create a storage
system based on redundant arrays of inexpensive disks that would
outperform existing systems. At Visio Corporation, the founder
started the business with the mission of creating a robust, flexible
software platform for graphics and drawing that could seamlessly
integrate with other software. At Lincoln National Reinsurance
Company, a steering committee of senior managers decided that
the company had to be a leader in using computer technology to
manage risk in the context of underwriting. Ziff Davis executives
challenged employees to create an on-line service to provide new
media relative to its traditional hard copy publications.

In each of these cases, the senior executives asked for the order.
And as everyone knows, *when it becomes important to the boss, it
becomes important to us.* Each executive must of course define
what "the order" needs to be. Then, he or she must become personally involved.

Great product companies usually have leaders who truly love
their companies' products, understand how they work, and enjoy
being around the people who create them. During a recent interview on National Public Radio, Bill Gates described his enthusiasm
for the products created by his company and noted that he spends
most of his time with Microsoft product developers. "Products are
what I like. It's where I can make the greatest contribution."
Gillette's CEO, Alfred Zeien, by his own reckoning, spends 30–35
percent of his work time on the development of new products.[4]
Like Gates or Zeien, executives can help create the company's

product and technology road maps and can then remove the internal obstacles that might prevent their realization.

Research, as well as our own experience, has shown that many senior executives do not participate directly in the critical phases of new product development. Typically, they get involved only when decisions on major capital expenditures are on the table—too late in the game to make a difference. Delegating that responsibility to corporate planners also will not suffice; most corporate staffers are too detached from the marketplace and the laboratory to understand the latent needs of users or the potential and pitfalls of product and process technologies. To the detached executive or staffer, R&D is a mysterious "black box" that consumes resources and sometimes produces remarkable results. They do not understand what type of development is achievable or what might be compelling to customers.

If your corporation is led by an executive team whose primary focus is on products and customers you are indeed fortunate. If it is not, you must determine what you can do to change the thought architecture used to manage the business.

We began the book with the metaphor of an arch spanning a *chasm of uncertainty*. We suggested that all companies eventually face discontinuities (the chasm) that threaten their position in market. Lulled into complacency by past success, or comforted by the panorama seen through the rearview mirror, many corporate leaders drive their organizations into the chasm.

Our arch suggests a better way: bridging the chasm with the conceptual building blocks offered in this book—platform strategies, composite design, platform teams, and product family-based performance metrics (Figure 9–9). These can help any product-driven company in bridging the difficult transition from the present to the future.

Arch-building requires the care and feeding of the marketing, engineering, manufacturing, and other talent of the enterprise. In some cases that may be as straightforward as cleaning out the cre-

FIGURE 9-9

An Arch Bridging the Chasm

Labels in figure:

TOMORROW'S DESIRES
- UNCONTESTED VALUE/COST LEADERSHIP
- ROBUST PRODUCT FAMILIES
- PROSPEROUS SURVIVAL

TODAY'S REALITIES
- AGING PRODUCT LINES
- UNCLEAR VISION OF THE FUTURE
- UNMANAGEABLE COMPLEXITY OF PRODUCTS AND ORGANIZATION

CHASM OF UNCERTAINTY
- TECHNOLOGICAL CHANGE
- NEW TENACIOUS COMPETITORS
- ORGANIZATIONAL UPHEAVAL

ARCHITECTURE / THOUGHT

Arch stones:
Expanded Markets
Streams of Derivative Products
New Platforms
New Technologies
Top Management Vision & Involvement
Performance Measures
Collocated Platform Teams
Composite Design
Platform Strategy

TORTUROUS PATH OF PRODUCT DEVELOPMENT

BY-PASS

CEO   MKT   R&D   MFG   R&D   MFG   MKT

250

ativity-sapping bureaucracies that develop over time. When HP began losing its way in the late 1980s, the two founders, William Hewlett and David Packard, returned from retirement to active management roles. Their mission was to remove the central planning and review committees that had grown up as internal impediments to the company's innovators. They broke up the central bureaucracy, tossed out the procedures manuals, and allowed the company to return to the culture that had nurtured past success. According to current CEO, Lou Platt, "The most important aspect of management in this company is cultural control. Get that right and the rest follows."[5]

All this, of course, points to the central importance of top management in establishing the tone and direction of the enterprise. By being involved in platform strategy and development, and by supporting efforts to undertake such initiatives, the executive nurtures the robustness of the corporation. The company's Board of Directors must themselves also be brought on board. They must understand and contribute to the corporation's arch-building and must consider new business and product initiatives in the context of achieving growth through continuous platform renewal. For that, the CEO is the best teacher.

How CEOs can best encourage the product development effort is, no doubt, situationally determined. There are no magic pills and no instant cures in the medicine bag of corporate leadership. Nevertheless, management must facilitate the development of the building blocks of the future—the technologies, processes, materials, and services that will drive the company's platforms and products forward in time.

It all starts with executives asking for the order and, even before that, knowing what order to ask for. If John Kennedy had not asked for the order—to put a man on the moon by the end of the 1960s—would it ever have happened? Probably not. So we suspect it will be, or not be, with your own enterprise.

Notes

Preface

1. James Utterback, *Mastering the Dynamics of Innovation* (Boston: Harvard Business School Press, 1994).

Chapter 1. The Power of Product Platforms

1. The story of Black & Decker's program was first described in Alvin Lehnerd, "Revitalizing the Manufacture and Design of Mature Global Products," in B. Guile and H. Brooks, eds., *Technology and Global Industries* (Washington, DC: National Academy Press, 1987), pp. 49–64.
2. Black & Decker demonstrated the explosive latent market demand for low-priced power tools, even before the Double Insulation Program, when it placed a number of the older $25 drills on retailers' shelves at a special price of $9.99. They flew off the shelves.
3. The Public Broadcasting System produced a wonderful tape on the making of the DC3 for its *Nova* series, titled "The Plane that Changed the World."
4. See "The Architecture of Complexity," Proceedings of the American Philosophical Society, vol. 106, no. 6, December 1962.

Chapter 2. Managing Product Platforms

1. We are grateful to Ron Benton of Hewlett Packard for his assistance in developing this section. Information is also drawn from David

Packard, *The HP Way* (New York: HarperBusiness, 1995), pp. 117–21.

2. This stands for the group that designed the standard: the Personal Computer Manufacturers Communications Interface Association.

3. Further discussion of the impact of common product architectures on development speed can be found in Kim Clark and Takahiro Fujimoto, *New Product Development Performance* (Boston: Harvard Business School Press, 1991), and Preston Smith and Donald Reinertsen, *Developing Products in Half the Time* (New York: Van Nostrand Reinhold, 1991).

4. We have found that the subsystems and interfaces of a product architecture, as well as changes to them, can be identified by simply asking seasoned engineers for high-level block diagrams of their major product architectures. We find this the most concrete method for identifying different generations of a product platform. Other methods for classifying the evolution of a product family have also been proposed by Stephen Wheelwright and Kim Clark in *Revolutionizing New Product Development* (New York: Free Press, 1992), which looks at degrees of product and process change, and by Marc H. Meyer and Edward Roberts, in "Focusing New Product Strategy for Corporate Growth," *Sloan Management Review,* 29, no. 4 (Summer 1988): 7–16, where we applied a method to track levels of change in core technologies, customer groups, product uses, and distribution channels to assess the strategic focus of technology-based firms.

5. Susan Sanderson and Mustafa Uzumeri, *Innovation Imperitive* (Burr Ridge, IL: Irwin Professional Publishing, 1996).

6. Urban and Hauser's text on performing market research for the design of new products is a helpful reference source for specific market research methods and tools. See Glen Urban and John Hauser, *The Design and Marketing of New Products* (Englewood Cliffs, NJ: Prentice Hall, 1980), in particular chapters 7 and 8.

7. Thomas J. Allen, *Managing the Flow of Technology* (Cambridge, MA: MIT Press), 1977.

8. Abernathy and Wayne demonstrated this principle through the stagnation of the Model T automobile, which was caused by the high-volume but inflexible mass production system implemented by Henry Ford. W. Abernathy and K. Wayne, "The Limits to the Learning Curve," *Harvard Business Review,* September–October 1974, pp. 109–119.

Chapter 3. Platform Strategy

1. Oscar Suris, "Ford Planning Overhaul Again of Products," *Wall Street Journal,* March 19, 1996, p. A4.

2. A. T. Cross has augmented its traditional Century pen product line with a premium brand (the Townsend, whose retail price exceeds $350), and a lower-priced brand (the Solo, $12.50). Most recently, the company has introduced a more stylish, contemporary design called the Metropolis to target younger customers (with a price range of $30 to $120).

3. Figures derived from Compaq Computer Corporation Annual Reports and press releases.

4. Harold Ano, quoted in Teri Prior, "EMC: Donnybrook Champs," *Upside Magazine,* September 1994, pp. 36–51.

5. R. H. Katz, G. A. Gibson, and D. A. Patterson, "Disk System Architectures for High Performance Computing," *Proceedings of the IEEE,* 77 (December 1989): 1942–58.

6. Carl Greiner, the Meta Group (Stamford, CT), quoted in Prior, "EMC: Donnybrook Champs."

7. As stated in Swatch's Internet home page, its watches have on average about 50 individual components, while the industry average is approximately 150.

8. William Taylor, "Message and Muscle: An Interview with Swatch Titan Nicolas Hayek," *Harvard Business Review,* March–April 1993, p. 103.

9. *Ibid.,* p. 99.

Chapter 4. Achieving Product Elegance Through Composite Design

1. Donald A. Norman, *The Psychology of Everyday Things* (New York: Basic Books, 1988), p. 2.

2. W. Edward Deming, *The New Economics* (Cambridge: Massachusetts Institute of Technology Center for Advanced Engineering Study, 1993).

3. Gerald Zaltman and Robin A. Higie, "Seeing the Voice of the Customer," Report no. 93-114 (Cambridge, MA: Marketing Science Institute, September 1993), p. 7.

4. Deming, *New Economics,* pp. 50–51.

5. G. Boothroyd and P. Dewhurst, *Product Design for Assembly* (Wakefield, RI: Boothroyd & Dewhurst, Inc., 1987).

6. Belt tension in V-belt power transmission applications is required to keep the V-belt faces in intimate contact with the V-pulleys, wedging the belt as deeply in the pulley grove to provide surface friction and avoid slipping. The energy transmission factors are tension, surface area of belt to pulley, strength of belt, and belt flexibility. If the belt or pulley is wet or has been contaminated by lubricants, the belt slips and squeals. The friction of the belt to pulley causes heat in the belt, causing it to age, to lose its flexibility and elasticity, and subsequently to

stretch. When the belt tension relaxes the belt starts slipping, heat is generated, the V-belt surfaces glaze and harden, and the power transmission capability is reduced. In the case of the cogged belt the contact of belt to pulley is obtained by the meshing of the formed teeth on the belt to the formed teeth on the pulleys. Minimum tension is required, simply enough tension to hold the belt intimate with the pulleys being driven.

7. Some data for this section are contained in "The Global Iron Proposal," Harvard Business School Case 9-688-082. Alvin Lehnerd was Executive Vice President, Allegheny International Appliance Group U.S. during the time of the Global Iron project.

8. The study itself examined thirteen different attributes and a total of forty-eight attribute options. France was selected to represent the European Market, albeit an abbreviated market, for two reasons: cost and time. The same reasoning applied to the selection of Mexico as representative of a developing country.

9. In the mid-1980s Black & Decker acquired the General Electric Housewares Division. The brand name of the GE iron is now Black & Decker.

10. Russell Ackoff, *Creating the Corporate Future: Plan or Be Planned For* (New York: Wiley, 1981), p. 105.

Chapter 5. Organizing for Renewal

1. An excellent discussion of the impact of various formal and informal organizational approaches for the effectiveness of research and development activities may be found in Thomas Allen, *Managing the Flow of Technology* (Cambridge: MIT Press, 1977), pp. 206–28.

2. Hirotaka Takeuchi and Ikujiro Nonaka, "The New New Product Development Game," *Harvard Business Review,* January–February 1986, p. 137.

3. Jon Katzenbach and Douglas Smith, *The Wisdom of Teams* (Boston: Harvard Business School Press, 1993).

4. Charles Morris and Charles Ferguson, "How Architecture Wins Technology Wars," *Harvard Business Review,* March–April 1993, pp. 94–95.

5. Michael Cusumano and Richard Selby, "How Microsoft Competes," *Research-Technology Management,* 30, no. 1 (January–February 1996): 26–30.

6. James Brian Quinn, *The Intelligent Enterprise* (New York: Free Press, 1992).

7. Martin Gilber, *Churchill: A Life* (New York: Henry Holt & Company, 1991), p. 677.

8. Gordon W. Prange, *Pearl Harbor: The Verdict of History* (New York: Penguin Books, 1991), p. 290.

9. Allen, *Managing Flow of Technology*.

10. Corporations have pursued alternatives to relocating employees from different countries to one physical location. Some of the more intriguing opportunities involve computer-based solutions. IBM-Lotus Development (Cambridge, MA), for example, has developed a "team room" application on top of its Notes groupware product, where electronic documents in a variety of formats can be electronically distributed and the editing of them coordinated among team members. Other companies, such as Intervista Software (San Francisco), have developed prototypes of team rooms, using Internet-based virtual reality technologies, where individuals "go to" three-dimensional buildings and rooms to view information posted on virtual walls and conference tables. Video-conferencing among numerous individuals is also now possible on the Internet. However, even with such computer-based technologies, individual team members must still develop mutual trust and explore new ideas through close interaction. Computer networking can only augment—not replace—the face-to-face human element of team creativity.

11. Takeuchi and Nonaka, "New New Product Development Game," p. 140.

12. Vincent P. Barabba, *Meeting of the Minds: Creating the Market Based Enterprise* (Boston: Harvard Business School Press, 1995), pp. 161–62.

Chapter 6. Measuring the Performance of Product Families

1. E. Mansfield, J. Rapoport, J. Schnee, S. Wagner, and M. Hamburger, *Research and Innovation in the Modern Corporation* (New York: Norton, 1971).

2. James M. Utterback, Marc H. Meyer, T. Tuff, and L. Richardson, "When Speeding Concepts to Market Can Be a Mistake," *Interfaces*, 22, no. 4 (July–August, 1992): 24–37.

3. James Bryan Quinn, "Pilkington Brothers, Ltd.," Case Study B.P. 78-0148, Amos Tuck School of Business Administration, Dartmouth College, 1978.

4. For a complete discussion of Hewlett Packard's BET metric and how it was institutionalized, see Gregory H. Watson, *Strategic Benchmarking* (New York: Wiley, 1993), pp. 93–107.

5. Product Development and Management Association survey of two hundred companies, 1991.

6. For a specific categorization of various R&D metrics as well as a more

detailed discussion of the metrics presented in the next section, see Marc H. Meyer, Peter Tertzakian, and James M. Utterback, "Metrics for Managing Product Development Within a Product Family Context", forthcoming in *Management Science* and available as Working Paper 95-100, Center for Technology Management, 213D Hayden Hall, Northeastern University, Boston.

7. Industrial Research Institute, unpublished survey of 248 research directors May 17, 1993.

8. The reader may wish to refer back to Figures 2–1, 2–2, and 2–5 in Chapter 2 for a brief review of key concepts.

9. M. A. Maidique and B. J. Zirger, "The New Product Learning Cycle," *Research Policy,* 14 (1985): 299–314.

10. The development costs of the original CONTROLS 1.1 platform is added to that of CONTROL 1.2 as the denominator for the calculation, giving the full platform development cost.

11. In this particular company, one could not blame this decline on an eroding market. The rate of market growth was fairly constant at about 5 percent a year. The sales force, pricing, and practices associated with the MONITOR product family also remained fairly stable. However, when you use this measure in your own company, be sure to consider those and other related factors that might affect sales and development costs.

12. Note that in Figure 6–9, the management reduced the number of target segments to three—basic, standard, and premium—making sure that its top-of-the-line fixtures had comparable functionality to other "deluxe" suppliers but sold at a lower price point to recapture share. The seventy-two new styles each offered different functionality to customers and went out to trade at different price points. That is why in Figure 6–9 the CPR for each respective segment is shown as a range reflecting feature differences in various models within market segments and particular fixture lengths.

13. Henry Kissinger, *Diplomacy* (New York: Simon & Shuster, 1994), p. 27.

Chapter 7. Product Family and Platform Concepts for Software

1. For readers unfamiliar with by the term *client server computing* we offer the following explanation. With a client server architecture in software, one user working on a computer can request and receive data or programs residing on any other computer, regardless of size and location of that second computer. The requesting user (or computer) becomes the "client," while the providing computer becomes the "the server." The same two users can reverse roles, with the first

user becoming the server, dishing out data and programs to the second machine.

2. Related discussions of software product platforms may be found in Marc H. Meyer and Luis Lopez, "Technology Strategy in a Software Products Company," *Journal of Product Innovation Management,* 12 (Summer, 1995): 294–306, and Chapter 4 in Michael Cusumano and Richard Selby, *Microsoft Secrets* (New York: Free Press, 1995).

3. More complex systems will also generally have major subsystems for maintaining and preserving data in the event of some type of computer failure, and for handling users and access privileges.

4. There is a historical context to the engine, add-in module approach that we have suggested here. As noted by Peter Salus in *A Quarter Century of Unix* (Reading, MA: Addison-Wesley, 1994), the Unix operating system, as it has evolved over the past thirty years, reflects our approach. While the Unix operating system has not "taken over the world," the approach to software design and architecture found in Unix has indeed become ubiquitous, not only in other major operating systems but also in tools and applications. The basic approach has three simple tenets:

   1. Write programs that do one thing and do it well.
   2. Write programs to work together.
   3. Write programs that handle text streams, because that is a universal interface.

   While the third tenet has now been broadened to a richer context that embraces pictures, sound, and motion—all through industry standard universal interfaces that have emerged over the past decade—the basic idea remains compelling.

5. The awards include 1996 PC Magazine Editors' Choice Award, 1995 PC World Best Buy, Product Excellence Award of 1994 (Software Development Magazine), and numerous Ingram Best Seller List and Merisel Hot List awards. Visio Corporation reported revenues of $13.4 million in the first quarter of 1996, an increase of 63 percent over the last quarter of the prior year. Its international sales had also grown substantially, accounting for 33 percent of the total sales, selling Spanish, German, French, and Kanji versions of its software at the time of this writing. The company went public in the November 1995.

6. We wish to thank Russell Sueuer, Arthur DeTore, and David Hopper for providing the information used in this section.

7. Zona Research, Redwood, California, as reported in "Enter the Intranet," *The Economist,* January 1996, pp. 64–65.

8. JAVA, developed by Sun Microsystems, is an Internet programming language that allows architecturally neutral pieces of code, called "applets," to combine seamlessly through distributed networks.

9. Readers intrigued by this possibility are encourage to read Kevin Kelly, *Out of Control* (Reading, MA: Addison Wesley, 1994).

Chapter 8. Electronic Information Products

1. We are indebted to G. Thomas Aley of Ziff Davis Interactive Media and Development, to Paul Pinella of Individual, Inc., and to Andrew Campbell of CorpTech for their assistance in developing the data for this chapter.
2. "The World According to George," *The Red Herring,* February 1996, p. 44.
3. CommerceNet/Nielson, Internet Demographics Study, available at www.commerce.net.
4. For a more detailed discussion of the conceptual frameworks presented here, see Marc H. Meyer and Michael Zack, "The Design and Development of Information Products," *Sloan Management Review,* 37, no. 3 (Winter–Spring 1996): 43–59.
5. Andrew Campbell, president of Corptech, Inc., May 23, 1994, Northeastern University class presentation.

Chapter 9. Bridging to the Future

1. See Robert Cooper, "Stage-Gate Systems: A New Tool for Managing New Products," *Business Horizons,* May–June 1990, pp. 44–54.
2. C. K. Prahalad and Gary Hamel, "The Core Competence of the Corporation," *Harvard Business Review,* 68, no. 3 (May–June 1990): 79–91.
3. If objective measures are not available, can you obtain the subjective assessments of employees and customers on the quality of your market understanding, technological competencies, and distribution channels? For a discussion of subjective measures, see Marc H. Meyer and James Utterback, "The Product Family and the Dynamics of Core Capability," *Sloan Management Review,* 34, no. 3 (Spring 1993): 29–47.
4. Dwight Gertz, *Grow to Be Great* (New York: Free Press, 1995), p. 102.
5. "Top Corporate Performers of 1995," *Forbes,* January 1, 1996, p. 68.

Index

AGING SMARTER

The Ultimate Guide To Living Your Most Active & Healthy Life After 50

DR. MAT PARKER

CONTENTS

ABOUT THE AUTHOR

Dr. Mat Parker is a physical therapist and founder of San Diego's leading specialist physical therapy practice, Parker Physio (www.parkerphysio.com), for those over the age of 50 who want to live an active and mobile lifestyle well into their 60s, 70s, 80s, and beyond.

Mat attended San Diego State University, where he received a degree in Kinesiology with an emphasis on Athletic Training. During this time, he worked extensively with the Division I men's soccer and women's rowing teams.

He went on to earn his Doctorate of Physical Therapy from Western University of Health Sciences in Pomona, CA. After graduation, he spent a year in Kaiser Permanente's orthopedic residency program, specializing in musculoskeletal conditions.

Frustrated with the hospital and corporate clinic setting, he decided to start his own practice in order to give patients more individual care with highly personalized solutions. No aides, no assistants, just one-on-one care focused on getting people back to the things they love: walking on the beach, running a 5K, playing 18 holes of golf, or sleeping comfortably. He also works with the firefighters all over San Diego county as an injury prevention specialist.

In his free time he enjoys reading, traveling, spending time with friends, and being a coach for the *Challenger Little League* and a Big Brother for the *Big Brothers Big Sisters of America* organization.

ACKNOWLEDGEMENTS

There are countless people who have helped lead me on this journey. I know I'm going to forget plenty of people in this small blurb, but here it goes. I want to credit John Hansen for introducing and inspiring me to become a healthcare provider. Thank you to Dr. O for opening up my mind and making me think bigger.

I want to give a huge shoutout to my numerous clinical mentors, including Karla Plooster, Monique Peterson, Cassey Sia, and everyone at the Kaiser Permanente Orthopedic Residency program. Also Andrew Vertson and Rick Noda, for sharing my vision of what healthcare should be and helping me serve more people.

Thank you Paul Gough and Greg Todd for helping me realize the true impact and value I can give to the world. Thank you for all the support from the amazing communities I'm honored to be apart of, including SSPT and the 4% Club. Thank you Ryan Cannon and Anthony Rosetta for helping me with all the photos in this book.

Of course, I want to thank my family. Mike, Andy, Dad, and Katie, words can't begin to express how much your loving support means to me. I couldn't be more grateful for each and every one of you.

Finally, Mom, you have always been there when I need you most. When times are dark and foggy, you are always the light that brings me back. You always inspire me to be the best version of myself and have always shown me the importance of hard work; I can't thank you enough for all that you do, Ma!

I f you're reading thing, there is a good chance you are suffering from pain or injury that's been ongoing for months or maybe even years. I've suffered frequent back pain for most of my life. Throughout that time, I tried all of the standard remedies: NSAIDs, Acupuncture, yoga, and more. I would get some temporary relief, but my back pain would always slowly come back, usually with a vengeance.

It stopped me from hiking, walking, playing with my grandkids, and playing tennis, which was awful, because exercise is key to my physical and emotional health. Without it, I get depressed and tend to isolate myself.

I felt frustrated over my inability to exercise consistently. I also found that there is a lot of information, often conflicting, about how to treat back pain. Because of my willingness to try anything to make it better, I tried any and every solution short of surgery. I really didn't want to go that route, but the limited success I was having caused me to believe that back pain would be a part of my life for good and that surgery would eventually be my only alternative.

Until I had the pleasure of meeting Mat. I could immediately tell was different. He provided clarity, cleared up the confusion for me, and gave me hope that I could solve this perplexing problem. With his guidance and advice, along with some hands-on work and some specific exercises, I was able to rid myself of my back pain. I was able to hike in Hawaii, play with my grandkids, go to Disneyland with them, and get back to exercising.

This book is the exact same advice that helped me get over my back pain. Mat is someone that you can tell cares about his patient's well-being. He doesn't treat you like just another number. He gets results because he realizes that everybody is unique and so every treatment plan should be too. This book will help you head in the right direction—the direction of healing your long-standing pain.

-**Mark**, late 50's, former patient

INTRODUCTION

Your Golden Years. These are the years that are less focused on career accomplishments and more on leisure and family. It's a time for interacting with your loved ones and enjoying different activities, trying new hobbies, traveling to dream destinations.

Whether you're already in those golden years or are slowly approaching them, there are some disturbing trends, especially those over the age of 50. People are struggling with poor health and chronic pain that is limiting their ability to be active. It stops them from living a mobile lifestyle. It affects their independence and overall quality of life. Worst of all, many people believe it is normal. Many people just accept it or ignore help from experts because they believe it won't work for them or because they believe their problem is somehow different. Many people give up.

Poor health and chronic pain normally develop because of one reason: decision making. Deciding to hit the snooze button on your alarm instead of waking up to exercise. Deciding to take pills to mask pain and stiffness. Deciding to eat that extra piece of cake or drink a soda when you are trying to stick to better lifestyle choices. Deciding to take advice from a friend or family member instead of a health professional.

These small decisions over time can lead to heart disease, diabetes, unnecessary joint surgeries, a dependency on medications, and other health problems. Your chances of maintaining independence and mobility while living free of painkillers will always come back to these decisions. When facing them, it's important to have reliable information from a specialist. That's what this book is all about.

This book is for those who are looking to better understand their bodies. It's for those who value their health and plan on being active and independent into their 60s, 70s, and beyond. It's for those who are willing to put in the time and take action towards becoming the healthiest version of themselves. It's to help you age smarter while avoiding things like pain pills, injections, and surgeries.

There is such a vast amount of information on the internet and YouTube that it can be difficult to decipher what information is actually true and what isn't. This book was created to provide more clarity.

The information and recommendations given here are not conjecture. Everything is based on the exact methods that have helped hundreds of my patients get incredible results. However, this book was not created to diagnose yourself. It is for those that feel stuck and have "tried everything" without getting the solutions they're looking for. It is written to help guide you on the path to better health without using complicated medical and anatomical terminology.

I can't make any big, bold guarantees without knowing your exact health background, but I can tell you that after reading this book you will have much greater clarity. My goal is to give you quality information so that you can have confidence in making the best decisions about your health. The advice given in this book may not be considered "sexy." There are no revolutionary techniques to acquire better health, just simple guidelines that are often overlooked. In fact, you may believe many of these recommendations are too simple to do any good, but I promise that if you put them into action, the difference will be remarkable.

Let's get started!

CHAPTER 1

What If Everything You've Been Told About Aging Is Wrong?

The human body is one of the most intricate and misunderstood structures in existence. Although many medical advances have been made over the past decade, healthcare practitioners are still trying to understand how each system in the body operates in unison, especially when pain and stiffness begin to affect our lives. With the power of social media and the internet, more and more bad information is out there. I want to provide you with good information so you can make better decisions about your health.

Having low back, neck, shoulder, knee, or hip pain should not be a life sentence, and you shouldn't accept a lower quality of life because of it. There are a TON of false beliefs out there. Let's go through the most common ones I hear from family and friends as well as current and past patients.

"Being in pain is just part of getting old."

I once heard a patient say, "My doctor told me that if you're over 50 years old and you wake up <u>without</u> any pain, something is significantly wrong with you."

Yikes!

Where does this belief come from? A multitude of places. In American society, we portray aging as a negative stereotype. From birthday cards to movies, "old people" are made out to be weak and feeble creatures, always needing a walker or cane to get around. They are painted as forgetful, hard of hearing, constantly repeating the same story over and over again.

Meanwhile, throughout our lives we are told by parents and grandparents how we should cherish our youth because when you get older, "everything hurts." Many physicians then tell us that after age 50, being in physical pain is normal.

When the media, loved ones, and physicians all promote the misconception that being in pain is just part of getting old, it's easy to believe it's a fact of life. This negative belief can have dramatic consequences. But what if you refused to accept this fate? What if you decided to look at aging as a privilege? As a great opportunity for INCREASED mental and physical activity?

A study done in the Journal of Gerontology found the beliefs about aging itself can have enormous effect on your quality of life. Researchers followed 433 people aged 50 over an 18 year period and found those who had positive self perceptions about aging were significantly healthier and lived, on average, 7.5 years longer than those with a negative self perception about aging.[1]

The negative belief from patients and healthcare providers leads to those over the age of 50 being vastly undertreated for pain and stiffness.

Many of you reading this may already have some sort of ache, pain, or stiffness. Maybe you have trouble just getting out of bed because you currently feel like the Tin Man from the Wizard of Oz. Activities that used to be simple—putting on pants, donning a bra, or putting on a shirt—are

---

[1] Levy BR, Slade MD, Kasl SV. Longitudinal benefit of positive self-perceptions of aging on functional health. *J Gerontol B Psychol Sci Soc Sci*. 2002;57:409–417.

dreadful because everything hurts. Some days are better than others, but your pain is slowly worsening and becoming more constant. You finally decide to see your doctor.

You've always trusted your doctor. Why wouldn't you? From when you were a kid seeing your pediatrician to now going to your general practitioner, you have never been let down. At your physician's office, he or she listens to your story, gives you a prescription for anti-inflammatories, tells you to rest, and says to come back in 6 weeks if it hasn't improved. Unfortunately, you don't really know what "rest" means. Can you still exercise? Are you supposed to lay in bed all day? What if trying to do your favorite activity still makes your pain worse? It's all incredibly frustrating. The pain improves a bit with the medications, but as soon as the pills wear off, it all comes roaring back.

Six weeks pass, and you still feel the same, so now you begin to be concerned that the pain hasn't healed. You begin to wonder whether something more serious is going on. Am I going to need surgery? Am I always going to have to take these painkillers? Back at the doctor's office, you are told, "Well, you know, you aren't in your 20's anymore. This is the normal."

PAUSE.

I have heard this story or a close variation of it HUNDREDS of times. People believe that nothing can be done to help their situation except take pills, get an injection, or go under the knife. That it's just time to accept it. That diagnosis of arthritis, osteoarthritis, or degenerative disc disease is a lifetime curse.

Being in pain is NOT a normal part of getting older. With appropriate treatment, you can get back to golfing 18 holes, playing tennis, being active with your grandkids, walking on the beach, and traveling.

There are cases of people doing extraordinary things well into their 50s and beyond. A few years ago, an 80-year-old hiked to the top of Mt. Everest. Or maybe you've heard of Ernestine Shepherd? She is currently the oldest female bodybuilder at age 80, and she didn't start exercising until she was 56! As I'm writing this book, supreme court justice Ruth Bader Ginsburg is 85 years old, and her workout routine consists of push ups, planks, and the bench press.

I know what you're thinking, "But Mat, they are all genetically gifted. The average person can't do that." If you honestly believe that, please go ahead and close this book now. My most successful patients are the ones whose doctors have told them nothing could be done but who refused to accept that answer. They strongly value their health and have specific goals to stay active and independent for as long as possible. They don't want their kids to worry about them. More importantly, they don't just want to live–they want to THRIVE.

Not all healthcare providers are created equal.

My goal isn't to bash on other healthcare providers, but it's critical to understand that there are good and bad practitioners out there, and it can be difficult to recognize the difference.

It's similar to taking your car in to see the mechanic. If you're someone like me who can barely check their oil, you go to the mechanic without a clue of what's wrong with your car and nod when he tells you, "The reverse main seal is leaking," pretending you know what he's talking about. You don't really know if it's true, but you trust the mechanic because he has a bunch of 5 star reviews on Google and a couple plaques on the wall. Secretly, you're praying you aren't getting ripped off and going to end up on an episode of 60 Minutes.

You don't really have a reason not to trust your doctor. He or she is wearing a white coat and has a ton of degrees up on the wall. It's his job to know what's best for you, right?

But it's not always so simple. Most physicians are well intentioned—we all get into medicine because we love to help people—but the current health-care landscape makes it difficult to provide high-quality patient care. Physicians today are vastly overworked and forced to document behind a computer screen for hours each day. Many physicians can only provide 7 or 8 minutes of interaction time with their patients before they have to see the next one.

Your physician is asked to make an accurate diagnosis very rapidly after asking you a few questions and doing minimal to no physical examination of your pain or injury. Forget about having the time to ask all the questions you may have. Heck, Dr. House isn't even that good. He always needs a one-hour episode to solve all his patient's ailments. To give you a frame of reference, I spend at least 30 minutes to get a solid understanding and perform an examination in order to determine the root cause of your particular problem. You can see why it's easier to give the quick answer of arthritis or that it's just part of getting older.

Am I telling you that your physician is a hack and you should stop seeing him or her? Absolutely not! I have the privilege of working with some incredible primary care physicians and orthopedic specialists who help hundreds of people. I just want to bring to your attention that even if you have been let down in the past, there might be another solution for your problem.

Maybe your physician has referred you to try physical therapy and you didn't get the results you were looking for. Remember, not all physical therapists and physical therapy clinics are created equal either.

The story goes like this: you get a referral from your doctor for PT. At that point, you are given a list of physical therapy clinics, and you decide on one that's close to your house or has the best reviews on Google or Yelp.

When you call the clinic, the very first thing they ask you on the phone is for your name, date of birth, group policy number on your insurance card. THEN, what body part hurts? At your first appointment, you are given 20 pieces of paper to sign and fill out.

After your hand aches from all the paperwork, you finally get called back by a physical therapist. They seem nice enough. You talk to them for about 20 minutes while he or she types away on a computer with minimal eye contact. You do a few physical tests and are given an elementary explanation of what's going on. Before you know it, you're passed on to a college student who shows you a bunch of exercises.

The next time you come in, you do 45 minutes of exercises with 12 other patients in the gym doing the exact same thing, which is bothersome because you know you could do all these exercises at home. After 45 minutes, you finally get to see the physical therapist, and he or she gives you 8-10 minutes of time until you are put on an electric stimulation machine with an ice pack.

I tell you this because I was part of this system. It's why I left it to create a business that truly focused on patients and their personal goals, not billable insurance units. Having to see 20-25 patients per day, every day, five days per week was a daunting task. It was increasingly difficult to give people the care they deserve when you have to bounce from person to person every 10-15 minutes.

Similar to your primary care provider, this isn't necessarily the physical therapy clinic's fault. With insurance reimbursement dropping lower and lower, PT clinics must see more patients to cover their overhead costs. This hurts the most important person: YOU, the patient!

If you are just given a sheet of exercises and spend an average of only 10-15 minutes of one-on-one time with your physical therapist, you may not be getting the best treatment. Although there are different styles of physical therapy, I am a firm believer that exercises by themselves are never enough. There must be hands-on, soft tissue work in order to correct muscle imbalances and allow the body to heal properly.

The body must be viewed as a whole. The way you stand, sit (especially at work), lay in bed, lift things off the ground, and grab items off the shelf all must be taken into consideration to truly get to the root cause of a problem.

I have heard from people who have seen their chiropractor for years with the exact same back or neck problem. They continually go back just to get temporary pain relief. A chiropractor once told a friend of mine that if she doesn't keep going back for adjustments, her organs will shut down. What a claim! Have you ever turned on the news and heard, "Local woman, aged 54, dies today from organ failure due to not returning to see her chiropractor?" Yeah, me neither.

If your chiropractor tells you something like this or if your chiropractor isn't always striving to get you back to your favorite activity by changing the way you move, strengthening weak muscles, or stretching tight muscles, their motives may not be pure.

Sometimes people believe that their pain is hereditary because their mom or dad or family member had similar issues. This is also not true!

Chronic pain isn't something that is passed off into your DNA from your parents or grandparents. The assumption that when you get older you're supposed to be in pain is a false one. Like a classic car, you may need more maintenance, but pain isn't an automatic fact of life.

Another thing I hear all the time is, **"Mat, my MRI or x-ray shows I have arthritis (or degenerative disc disease or stenosis or a herniated disk),**

so what can you really do to fix it?" It has been ingrained in most of us that when you've had pain for a significant period of time and conservative treatment hasn't helped, an MRI is the next logical step because it will tell you exactly what's wrong. Yet, more and more research shows that MRI's and x-rays are terrible at discovering the source of your pain.

In 2014, a huge research study was performed with 3000 people without low back pain. These were completely pain-free adults aged 20 to 80 without any history of low back pain. All 3000 subjects were given some sort of radiology, either an MRI or CT scan. Researchers found 80% of people in their 50s showed disc degeneration of their lumbar spine. Even 37% of people in their 20s had some form of disc degeneration. Disk bulge prevalence increased from 30% of those at age 20 to 84% of those at 80. Remember, <u>not a single subject had ANY low back pain</u>.[2]

Maybe you've been diagnosed with a rotator cuff tear? A patient of mine had an MRI resulting in the diagnosis of a full thickness rotator cuff tear and significant pain in his right shoulder. He went under the knife, only for his surgeon found his entire rotator cuff was normal and intact, with no tear whatsoever.

Maybe you've been told you have knee arthritis and are "bone-on-bone"? Most people who are told this believe nothing can be done or they have to get a total knee replacement. Yet many patients I work with who are diagnosed with "bone on bone arthritis" can get back to walking as far as they like without pain or difficulty.

So when people tell me they had an MRI or some sort of radiology done showing arthritis, rotator cuff tears, meniscus issues, degenerative disc disease, etc. it's just a tiny piece of the puzzle. Studies continue to show even people without pain have these diagnoses. What's important is how you

---

[2] Brinjikji W, Luetmer PH, Comstock B, et al. Systematic Literature Review of Imaging Features of Spinal Degeneration in Asymptomatic Populations. *AJNR American journal of neuroradiology*. 2015;36(4):811-816. doi:10.3174/ajnr.A4173

move. How long have you had pain? Do you have significant weakness? Is your pain constant or does it come and go? All these questions must be answered to get to the root cause of your problem. The human body can accomplish incredible things when you start to factor in posture, body mechanics, and the quality of your movement.

Am I some sort of magician or guru? Far from it. I just believe people don't know that quality care exists and that surgery or pills isn't the only answer. Does this mean nobody should get a total knee or hip replacement? Absolutely not! But what if you could delay surgery for another 2, 3, 4 years? What would that mean for your quality of life?

Just remember that when you get a consult from an orthopedic surgeon, the surgeon only has a couple options. He or she can prescribe you medications, give you an injection, or cut you open to perform surgery. Many times people believe surgery is a relatively quick fix. It's just a couple hours on the operating table. How long can rehab actually take, right? Well depending on the type of surgery and what your goals are you're talking months to more than a year to get back to all your favorite activities.

More and more studies show that for operations such as rotator cuff repairs and knee meniscus surgeries, the results are the same or even better when getting physical therapy instead of going under the knife. There is an appropriate time to get surgery, but I always recommend quality conservative treatment first.

"What about cortisone injections?"

Cortisone injections can be very useful when there is inflammation present, especially for knees, shoulders, and low backs (they are referred to as epidurals when injected into the low back). Unfortunately, the effects of cortisone injections tend to be temporary when you don't have a specific incident that caused your pain or injury, such as falling off a ladder or lifting something too heavy.

You may not know how your pain started. Maybe it gradually got worse with time until you finally decided to do something. Normally, when injuries start this way it's because there is some sort of movement imbalance, meaning the way you are sitting, standing, lifting things off the ground, or taking off your shirt is not correct and causing pain. If these movement faults aren't fixed, the cortisone injection won't matter, and the pain will slowly creep back into your life.

My recommendation for cortisone injections is that if you are suffering from excruciating pain which limits your ability to sleep or walk, it's okay to get an injection. But go see a qualified healthcare specialist like a physical therapist to help make sure you keep the pain away for good so you can return to your favorite activities. Don't depend on cortisone injections every few months as your sole source for pain relief. A recent study showed receiving a cortisone injection every few months for a long period of time for knee pain has been linked to accelerating cartilage loss.[3]

All the information discussed thus far may lead you to ask the million dollar question: why has my pain or injury not healed?

Understanding this is vital to improving your health. I try to explain it to each of my patients. To illustrate this, let me tell you about Nicole. She was in her mid 50s and had struggled with chronic back pain for many years. It got to the point where Nicole couldn't walk or stand for more than 15 minutes because she had pain and a feeling of tightness going down both of her legs.

Nicole has two beautiful grandchildren, and her goal was to be able to be able to walk her grandkids to and from school everyday, which was approximately half a mile away. When you initially start having pain, you begin

---

[3] McAlindon TE, LaValley MP, Harvey WF, et al. Effect of Intra-articular Triamcinolone vs Saline on Knee Cartilage Volume and Pain in Patients With Knee Osteoarthritis: A Randomized Clinical Trial. *JAMA*.2017;317(19):1967–1975. doi:10.1001/jama.2017.5283

to move differently. No matter what part of you hurts, your body will do everything it can to avoid being in pain. For Nicole, when she walked into my clinic, I noticed she was limping mildly. She said she had been walking like that for many years without realizing it.

When you limp or change the way you naturally move for long periods of time, you begin to create muscle imbalances. Some of Nicole's low back muscles had begun to shorten and tighten up. While those muscles tightened up, her glutes, had become weakened. This issue had to be addressed, or her pain would never truly go away.

With Nicole, we were able to fix these muscle imbalances, mobilize her stiff joints, and allow her not just to walk her grandkids to school but also train for a 5k! Your case may be different, but you shouldn't be satisfied living in pain and discomfort. There are always more options, no matter what you've been told.

"I've had pain for YEARS and have tried everything. Nothing can be done!"

I hear something along these lines almost every day. Normally, it's from people who have done injections, pain pills, physical therapy, chiropractic, acupuncture etc. but are still being limited by pain or stiffness. This belief causes people to feel hopeless and stuck. It leads them to live a lesser quality of life than they deserve. Just because you've tried some things and were let down doesn't mean you are doomed.

I tell patients with this belief that even if your problem can't be 100% solved, what if it could improve by 10%? 20%? 30%? Wouldn't that be worth your time? What would it mean for your quality of life if you could spend 15 to 20 more minutes walking with a loved one? To be able to go upstairs with significantly less pain? To get a bra on and off without pure agony? To bend over to put on shoes without fear?

There is always something that can be done. It starts by reading books like this one. Just by reading this you are someone who is motivated to improve their quality of life. Someone who strongly values their health. Someone who is looking for answers. That's more than half the battle. You are going to keep trying everything you can to live the happiest and most active life. If you understand these false beliefs and the mistakes commonly made, you can avoid them and work on getting your energy and life back. Now let's keep going!

CHAPTER 2

The Most Common Mistakes People Make About Their Health

The false beliefs from the previous chapter lead to mistakes that can keep you in pain and stop you from living a life where you are excited to get out of bed every morning and filled with energy, drive, and passion. A patient once told me, "You live in pain for so long, you do everything you can to ignore it, and when if finally does disappear, the results are life changing." Having back, neck, shoulder, or knee pain is not a life sentence. Natural solutions are out there, but first, let's talk more about the things you shouldn't be doing.

Mistake #1: Rest is almost NEVER the answer

This is BY FAR the most common mistake I see. One day while you are driving your car and reach to grab something out of the back seat, you feel a bit of a shoulder ache. You don't think anything of it at the time, but the next day the shoulder ache is still there. Initially, it's not too concerning. Maybe you can take a couple ibuprofen, ice it, and everything is fine.

Weeks pass and the shoulder ache doesn't improve. The ibuprofen just seems to mask the symptoms. Sleeping has become wildly uncomfortable, and you feel a jolt of pain in the shoulder every time you take off your shirt or reach to pick up a gallon of milk. Now you begin to become more worried. Did I tear something in my shoulder? Am I going to need surgery? So you begin to use your shoulder less and less because you don't want to do any further damage.

At this point, several months have passed before talking to your physician. When you finally can't take it anymore, you set up an appointment, only to get a prescription for an anti-inflammatory and asked to return to the doctor's office in 6 weeks if the shoulder pain is still there. This is a story I hear all the time from patients.

It doesn't matter whether it's shoulder pain, back pain, or knee pain. When pain strikes, our brain goes into protection mode. Our parents always told us as little kids to "stay off it" or "put some ice on it" or "rest." Yet the key to solving your pain is actually the opposite. One of my favorite phrases is, "motion is lotion." For a ligament that is sprained or a muscle that is tight, incorporating some gentle movement will greatly accelerate the rehab and healing process.

If you are struck with low back pain, you may have the urge to lay in bed, but that's always a recipe for disaster. To eliminate back pain for good, walking (aka motion) is vital to recovery. It increases blood flow to the whole body and allows for improved healing.

Are there exceptions to this? Of course, and I'll be discussing some of them in upcoming chapters.

Mistake #2: Painkillers and the opioid epidemic

If you've watched the news, then you know the United States has a huge opioid problem right now. The majority of patients I see have been prescribed at least one opioid medication in their past. Some patients absolutely hate taking pain pills, which is a big reason why they come to see me. But other patients with severe cases of chronic pain and long surgical histories use opioids just to get out of bed in the morning.

Opioids are medications chemically similar to endorphins, a substance we make naturally in our body to help alleviate pain. Opioids are prescribed to treat severe to moderate pain and include drugs you've probably heard of: oxycodone, oxycontin, percocets, morphine, vicodin, and fentanyl. These drugs are prescribed by physicians to help patients with pain after surgery, pain from cancer, or chronic pain.

Opioids block pain messages sent from the body to the spinal cord and into the brain. They have also been shown to cause a large release of dopamine in the brain, which triggers feelings of euphoria and relaxation. You can begin to see why these pills have the potential to be so addictive and dangerous.

The most common side effects include depression, significantly slowed breathing, addiction, severe withdrawal symptoms, and of course overdose. These drugs do not help with inflammation. These pills aren't improving the way you move, walk, or lift things off the ground. They are strictly used to mask your pain. In fact, several musicians, including Tom Petty, Prince, and rapper Mac Miller, all passed away from overdoses involving opioids, specifically fentanyl.

The critical part I want to bring to your attention is that **pain is always a symptom**. Pain is never the root cause of your problem. For example, you may have pain shooting down the back of your leg, which is known as sciatica. The sharp, shooting pain isn't just there for fun. The sciatic nerve is being irritated somewhere along its path. The cause of sciatica is normally significant stiffness in the lower part of your back (the lumbar spine) or tightness in the piriformis muscle in your butt (piriformis syndrome), which aggravates your sciatic nerve leading to pain down the leg. Opioids aren't going to make the joints in your lumbar spine less stiff or your hip muscles move better. They are just going to cause a temporary traffic jam and stop the pain signals from getting from your sciatic nerve to your brain. Yet opioids are normally the first line of defense when seeing your physician.

Opioids are being prescribed more and more in the United States, and according to the Centers for Disease and Control Prevention (CDC), in 2017, there were almost 58 opioid prescriptions written for every 100 Americans. That's a lot of dangerous pills being prescribed!

Is there ever an appropriate time to take opioids? Of course. They can help cancer patients feel more comfortable and help us feel better after significant surgical procedures. However, if you've had chronic pain for more than 90 days and all you've been given are a combination of opioids, muscle relaxants, and anti-inflammatories, it could be time to find a healthcare provider who can understand where the root cause of your pain is coming from rather than trying to mask your symptoms with pills.

Mistake #3: Trusting the Internet

Thanks to Steve Jobs and Apple, we all have small computers in our pockets with access to an infinite amount of information. If you want to know who won the gold medal in the shot put at the 1992 Olympics, find a new recipe for baking asparagus, or hail a ride to the airport, it can all be done on our phones with a few taps of our thumbs.

The answer to any question we could possibly have is only a Google search away. So when things like back or knee pain creep up, it's normal to head to Google to find out what's going on. Websites such as WebMD and the Mayo Clinic allow you to plug in your symptoms and instantly get a diagnosis. Unfortunately, reaching an accurate diagnosis on the internet is never that easy. There are so many other factors involved when making an accurate diagnosis, especially with musculoskeletal pain. It's necessary to consider stress, diet, exercise, other diseases such as diabetes, and more.

Then there is YouTube, which is quickly becoming more popular than Google itself. Anything you need, from how to wallpaper your house to how to fix a leaky faucet, can be found on Youtube. Many people search "best exercises for back pain" and get THOUSANDS of video results.

Normally these videos are titled "The 5 BEST Low Back Pain Stretches To Erase Back Pain In 5 Minutes Or Less!!" If these videos actually worked, I would be out of a job and a lot less people would be walking around with aches and pains.

I also know that these websites frustrate many healthcare practitioners because people come in convinced they have a certain problem or diagnosis. Personally, when patients come to me with self-diagnoses from WebMD or the Mayo Clinic websites, I actually get excited. It tells me that the person values their health and is actively looking for a solution to their problem.

All that is needed is a bit of education on the true source of your pain or dysfunction from a specialist who is known to get the results you want.

Mistake #4: Getting General Advice or Exercises

A generalist such as a primary care physician has to know about a TON of things, from understanding medications to diagnosing different diseases. I have great respect for primary care physicians and the stress that is put upon them. Many are asked to see 3-4 patients an hour, chart all their notes, write prescriptions, communicate with staff, etc. all while trying to listen to their patients and make the most accurate diagnosis possible. That's a tall order!

It's easy to give you an answer of resting for 6 weeks while taking a pain or anti-inflammatory medication. Many times, physicians won't even recommend seeing a musculoskeletal specialist, mainly for two reasons.

One, some physicians are actually incentivized to reduce expenses of your insurance company by not recommending physical therapy. They are also incentivized by pharmaceutical companies to prescribe certain medications. Said another way, physicians are offered a bonus at the end of the year from insurance companies for not recommending other treatment options and from pharmaceutical companies for prescribing certain medications. Neither of these have your best interest at heart.

Am I saying your physician is cashing checks every Christmas? Absolutely not. I know a ton of them with incredible integrity, but many are affected by the incentives whether they realize or not, and some doctors cash in intentionally. Dateline has done several reports on it if you'd like to investigate for yourself.

The second reason is that most physicians are not thoroughly trained to know orthopedic injuries or understand certain physical pains well enough to determine who would actually benefit from physical therapy. Shocking, but very true nonetheless.

Therefore, getting specialist advice is critical to recovering from pain and returning back to your favorite physical activity. Be sure to look for someone who takes the time to really listen to what's going on and has had success with your type of injury. The key to discovering a true specialist is to ask questions. What is the root cause of my problem? How long will it take to fix? What's the exact rehab plan to get to my goal? If they cannot answer those three questions with confidence, look for another provider.

Too often, friends and family ask me for "some exercises to fix my back pain." Unfortunately, without spending the time to truly understand the root cause of your problem, general exercises won't help you like you hope. One of the most common mistakes I see is people doing exercises at the wrong time, for the wrong diagnosis, and with improper technique. There is definitely a time and a place for exercises, but to give you "cookie-cutter" style exercises in this book or online would be irresponsible and potentially dangerous for your long term health.

Mistake #5: "Mat, have you ever heard of....?"

If I had a dollar for every time a friend or patient asked me, "Hey Mat, have you ever heard of...(fill in the blank)?" I'd have enough to take an Uber from LA to New York. These devices or treatments usually include inversion tables, laser therapy, KT tape, cryotherapy, traction machine, knee or lumbar braces, a new topical cream, or a "breakthrough" treatment that was featured on Dr. Oz.

All of these are marketed as quick fixes that require minimal work from the potential buyer, you. Buy the product, slap on the cream or brace, and VOILA! Your knee pain will vanish! Sadly, there is no academic research that supports most of these devices, but they are wisely marketed using testimonials of people portrayed to be oddly similar to you. The commercial or online ad will show a video of someone that looks like you and mention the exact things you are feeling and have someone using the product with INCREDIBLE results. Then they will have paid physicians tell you they recommend the product to all their patients.

Please do not fall victim to this kind of marketing. Understand that these things don't ever fix the root cause of the problem. They are band-aids at best. They will provide some pain relief and maybe make you look cooler if you are wearing different colored KT tape. Do I recommend KT tape or certain braces? Yes, I do. However, it's always in conjunction with quality physical therapy treatment. Moving the joints that need to be moved, strengthening weak muscles, doing soft tissue work on tight muscles. fixing how you sit, stand, walk, or run. That's how you get better and stay healthy for the rest of your life.

Mistake #6: Forcing A Yoga and Pilates Routine

"I feel so stiff all the time. If I were only more flexible, I'd feel better. I need to do yoga or pilates."

This is another statement I hear frequently, and one that can cause more harm than good. I love doing both yoga and pilates myself, but caution must be taken before performing either of them when you've had pain for more than a few months.

Back, neck, shoulder or hip pain can be aggravated during yoga and pilates, especially if your teacher isn't properly trained to deal with complex pain and injuries. Every yoga and pilates studio is different; some teachers are also physical therapists and understand when it's appropriate to do a certain maneuver over another while rehabbing from an injury. Others do not, in which case you might have to come see someone like me after things have worsened.

I always recommend to see a specialist before going to a yoga or pilates studio. Many times, my patients are able to do both simultaneously as long as they are following certain guidelines based off their specific pain or injury. Other times, I have them wait until they have done a proper rehabilitation program before sending them off to yoga or pilates. Both are incredible workouts, but my advice is that it's better to be safe than sorry.

Mistake #7: Going to the Gym and Working Through It On Your Own

I tend to see this more often with men with women, but it can happen with anyone. You have been working out in a gym for years and have always been able to work through aches and pains. I'll be honest, many times this strategy can work. Unfortunately, if you are dealing with something like an Achilles' tendon or rotator cuff injury, there is a risk you can completely rupture a muscle—not good! Both of those injuries take close to a year or more to get back to full participation of activities such as playing volleyball or running a 5k.

The other statement I hear quite frequently from people is, "Yeah, I just avoid squatting or lifting anything heavy so that I don't aggravate my (insert body part) pain." I normally say, "If we could eliminate your pain and minimize the chance of it coming back, would you go back to lifting heavy?" There is usually a long pause. This thought doesn't often cross people's minds. The belief is that, when you reach a certain age, pain is supposed to start setting in and you have to live with limitations. That's not true!

Now, you might not be able to bench 300-plus pounds like you could in your 20s, but you should feel more than capable of doing the bench press comfortably well after your 50s and 60s. Don't forget 80-year-old Ernestine Shepherd, who started lifting at 56 years old and can still bench press 115 pounds! Discussing your problem with a specialist to figure out how to appropriately modify and scale exercises is the key component to avoid injuring yourself while working out.

Mistake #8: Indecisiveness and Doing Nothing

You may be suffering with some pain or stiffness right now and know you should do something about it. Unfortunately humans have this terrible tendency to do nothing when we are overwhelmed with information on how to solve a problem. Nobody likes making the wrong decision, myself included. When bombarded by recommendations from loved ones, WebMD, Youtube, chiropractors, acupuncturists, physical therapists, etc., a sense of anxiety can set in over trying to make the best decision for your health. If this sounds like you, you're not alone. Most people I work with tell me a similar story.

Finding a healthcare provider you trust can be difficult these days. And with all these "cutting edge" treatments being marketed, it's hard to know what's real and what's not. But continuing to do nothing only makes the recovery process more arduous. While you wait, your problem may begin to worsen, leading to a decreased quality of life.

If you've been let down in your past by other types of treatment, you may feel stuck or that nothing can be done. Remember, there is always something that can be done. There are plenty of different types of treatment methods out there. You just may not have found what works best for you yet.

Understanding why these mistakes occur and how to properly avoid them can help you prevent pain and injury or expedite the healing process if you are currently suffering.

Next we are going to move into more specific topics, including back pain, knee pain, shoulder pain, neck pain/headaches, wellness, nutrition, and fitness. If you are suffering from a specific type of pain or you're interested in a specific topic, you may be tempted to jump ahead to that chapter, but please consider reading everything in its entirety. A better understanding of your body as a whole will help you achieve long term health!

CHAPTER 3

Back Pain

To say that low back pain is an epidemic would be a vast understatement. Low back pain remains the most common cause of disability and lost work time among working-age adults in industrialized countries.[4] Another study showed that chronic low back pain (pain lasting more than 3 months) in the United States may be as high as 30%.[5] That's a TON of people suffering unnecessarily!

My goal is to help you better understand your back pain and why it may not have healed properly. Even if you don't have low back pain, it's still incredibly useful information to help protect you from it.

All Back Pain Isn't Created Equal

There are many different types of back pain. Just because someone in your family or your neighbor has back pain doesn't mean it's the same kind of back pain you have. That's why there is no one-size-fits-all approach when trying to fix low back pain, but there are patterns to help you recognize what kind of back pain you have so you can beat it once and for all.

---

[4] Bogduk N. Management of chronic low back pain. Med J Aust . 2004;180(2):79-83.
[5] Johannes CB, Le TK, Zhou X, Johnston JA, Dworkin RH. The prevalence of chronic pain in United States adults: results of an Internet-based survey. J Pain. 2010;11(11):1230-1239. doi: 10.1016/j.jpain.2010.07.002.

How long you've had low back pain can greatly affect your recovery. When you initially get low back pain from lifting up your 5-year-old granddaughter or a heavy laundry basket, it is considered acute low back pain. Most of the time, acute low back pain tends to improve in anywhere from a couple weeks to a couple months.

Unfortunately, after having acute low back pain once, you are significantly more likely to have occasional flare ups or the feeling that your back "goes out." It's important to know that flare ups are **normal**, but the key is to recognize any triggers to these episodes and then utilize the right tools to recover from them. Many times the pain not only affects the low back but can shoot down your leg, causing increased numbness and tingling. This is commonly known as sciatica.

When these flare ups aren't dealt with correctly, acute back pain quickly becomes chronic back pain, or back pain lasting more than 3 months. Acute low back pain is like having common cold. A common cold can be frequent in nature, annoying, but it goes away quickly.

Chronic low back pain is the equivalent to developing persistent low-grade pneumonia and can be described as continued pain and disability. Luckily, no matter how long you've had low back pain, you can make a full recovery. Your body is an amazing machine, and given the right inputs and proper movements, you can get back to the life you deserve.

Words Are Powerful

A mentor of mine taught me that the words we use are incredibly powerful in how we make ourselves and others feel. The right words can make us powerful beyond measure, but the wrong words can hurt and weaken us. In medicine, the words we use are critical, and too often I see healthcare practitioners who are lazy with their communication.

For example, if you went to your physician in your mid 50s and were told you "have the back of a 90 year old" or "this is the worst case of degenerative disc disease I've ever seen!", how would that make you feel? I know if I were told that, I'd be terrified and begin to label myself as old and broken.

Or maybe somebody told you that your hips are out of alignment or your S.I. joint is "out"? This terminology is not doing anything for your recovery, and if your S.I. joint or hips were actually out of alignment, you would be in excruciating pain and on your way to a hospital.

These words and labels are not helping you, **especially** with low back pain. I once had a patient in her late 50s who, after hurting her back picking up her 3-year-old granddaughter, was told by a physician that she had herniated a lumbar disc. She saw a chiropractor, who then told her she was not allowed to bend over or lift anything over 5 pounds for the rest of her life and would require weekly sessions for the foreseeable future. Fearful that she would need back surgery, she had to have her husband and kids help her with everything from putting on pants and tying her shoes to doing all the grocery shopping and cooking.

It began to negatively affect her relationship with her husband, and she couldn't be as active with her grandkids due to fear and pain. She was taking pain pills daily, wearing a bulky back brace, and was barely sleeping. She lived like this for two years before a friend sent her my way. During our first meeting, she seemed distant and initially believed there was nothing that could be done.

I let her know that back pain is not a lifetime curse but can be beaten with the right steps. We also discussed how herniated or "bulging" discs naturally reabsorb after several weeks and that bending over isn't going to re-injure anything in her spine. We then developed a plan just for her and took baby steps, first reintroducing how to bend over safely, how to turn on the core muscles properly, and then improving hip and leg strength.

After one month, she was able to walk a mile without difficulty, and after 8 weeks she could lift heavy laundry baskets without ANY pain.

If she came in and I told her, "This is the worst case of bulging discs I've ever seen; I don't even know how you are standing right now!" her recovery would be doomed before she even started. Instead, I explained that what she had was common and that she just had some normal wear and tear. This allowed her to relax and focus on the rehab process. So please be mindful of which healthcare practitioners you're seeing and, more importantly, how you define yourself.

You Are NOT Your MRI

Earlier, I discussed how MRI's and x-ray exams are not all they're cracked up to be. After a few weeks of having back pain, the first reaction people have is to want an MRI. It makes sense. We believe the MRI will identify exactly where the source of our pain is coming from so it can be eliminated. Unfortunately, that is normally not the case.

MRI's and x-rays are only snapshot images, meaning when you get an x-ray or MRI, you are laying down and perfectly still. As you know, back pain is never 100% constant. It fluctuates up and down depending on the activity you're doing and the position you are in (i.e. sitting or standing). A great physical therapist named Jason Silvernail gave an explanation to better understand this. MRI's show you how the tissues of the low back LOOK, not how they FEEL, and it's critical to understand this difference.

If I were to take a picture of you at the park, the picture would tell you what you looked like but not what you felt like at that exact moment. It couldn't show whether you were anxious or happy, annoyed or craving food. In the absence of a major injury, these scans don't do a great job of actually identifying your pain.

Back pain is almost always aggravated by a certain posture or movement. The way you lift things off the ground. The way you stand. The way you walk. The way you sit in a chair for long periods of time. You don't do any of these things in an MRI scan, and it is a big reason why they are not the end-all-be-all when determining the source of your low back pain.

When they're debating getting an MRI, I ask my patients, "There is a good chance that you'll have a diagnosis of degenerative disc disease (arthritis) and possibly a herniated disk or spinal stenosis, so if this is the case...then what?"

Usually, it comes with a confused look and a response along the lines of, "What do you mean? After I get a diagnosis then you and the physician can better treat it!" Unfortunately, it doesn't quite work like that. You don't really treat bulging discs or spinal stenosis.

What I help people with is walking further, increasing their activity, safely bending over to put on their socks and shoes. And getting them back to picking up their grandkid without having the fear or expectation of excruciating low back pain. My most successful patients are always the ones who don't focus on an exact diagnosis. They understand that they have chronic low back pain and have a positive mindset that their situation WILL improve. Because with the right help, it usually does.

Surgery is always the LAST Option

According to the Agency for Healthcare Research and Quality (AHRQ), about 500,000 Americans go under the knife each year for low back pain problems, spending approximately 11 billion dollars for these operations. Yet the John Hopkins Medicine team recently released a report that **fewer than 5 percent of people with back pain are good candidates for surgery**.

That's a pretty startling statistic! If you believe you are in that small 5 percent of people appropriate for back surgery, then you may have any of the following signs or symptoms. These guidelines come from world famous back pain researcher Stuart McGill.

- At any point in time you begin to lose bowel or bladder control that is considered a medical emergency and need to go to the emergency room ASAP

- SIGNIFICANT neurological issues–if you begin notice one or both of your legs buckling when you're walking or significant muscle atrophy (muscle loss) of one of your leg muscles

- SIGNIFICANT trauma, broken bones/vertebrae from a car wreck or a brutal fall

- Severe and UNRELENTING pain for an EXTENDED period of time, meaning at least six months

If none of the above applies to you, you more than likely fall in the 95% of people who are not good candidates for low back surgery. Here are some of the signs and symptoms of people with low back pain that SHOULD NOT get low back surgery.

- If you have ever described your back pain as having many "good and bad days," you are NOT a good surgical candidate.

- If you haven't completely exhausted ALL your conservative options. Even though you may have had physical therapy, chiropractic care, acupuncture, or massage once and it didn't work, that doesn't mean there aren't other therapies or trained professionals more appropriate for you.

Beware of "Institutes" that offer to view your scans and advise you on surgical options without fully assessing you, meaning they don't actually assess how you move/walk/stand/etc. in person. You also want to be on the lookout for any new "cutting edge" treatments or "technological advances," as more often than not they don't pan out.

Every couple years the surgery field will have a new type of procedure or new type of equipment to use; laminectomy, foraminotomy, discectomy, lumbar disc replacement, or a new type of fusion. These are all to be avoided at all costs, especially fusions. Your lower back joints, the lumbar vertebrae, need to be able to move, slide, and glide a bit. When they can't do that, you begin to stress the joints above them (your upper lumbar spine) and below them (the SI joint, tailbone, and hips) in a way they are not designed to handle. This isn't good and can begin to cause pain in different areas of the body.

Those who get low back surgery, many times, have the same pain they had prior to surgery, and sometimes their pain actually gets worse. If you've already had low back surgery in your past and are still being held back by pain and discomfort, don't worry. We'll get you going in the right direction in the next section.

Many patients I see have had SEVERAL low back surgeries and were severely limited in regards to their overall mobility. It's a story I hear all the time! With a customized plan and a little time, we can get them back to living a more active lifestyle with their loved ones.

Getting Back to the Basics

We've talked about the background info of low back pain, but let's move into some actionable advice you can start doing right away. Every back pain patient I have starts with these same strategies regardless of their diagnosis or how long they've had back pain.

There are 168 hours in a week. You could be a professional athlete getting treatment everyday for 3 hours a day and it would only equal 21 hours of treatment a week. That still leaves 147 hours where you still must consider how you are moving and what position your low back is in. Therefore, these 3 steps are incredibly critical to defeat low back pain.

Step 1: Breathe better! "Mat, I have been breathing my whole life. I'm pretty sure I've got this breathing thing figured out." Well, let's find out. Lie down on a flat surface with one hand on your belly and the other on your rib cage. (See picture below)

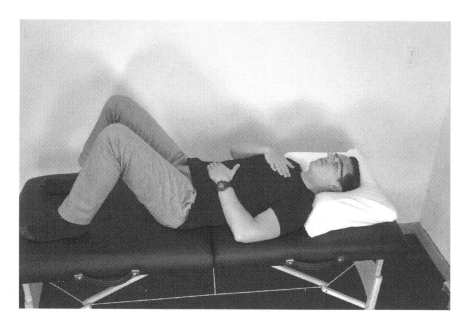

Now, take a deep breath and notice which hand goes higher. Is it your top hand that's on your rib cage or your bottom hand on your stomach? If it's your top hand, you would be classified as a "rib breather." If your bottom hand goes considerably higher, you are classified a "diaphragmatic breather." If you can't tell or feel like it's about even, that's okay, because with back pain (as well as shoulder and neck pain for that matter) we want to be breathing with the diaphragm.

This means you want your bottom hand to be moving higher than your top hand. The reason that this is important is when we fill up our bellies with air, we create increased air pressure in our midsection, adding increased support to your lower back. Not only does this kind of breathing help with your lower back, but it also helps with decreasing stress, as this kind of breathing is closely associated with meditation.

Step 2: Since we now know that breathing with the diaphragm is vital to the low back, change your hand position. Place both hands on your sides as in the picture below.

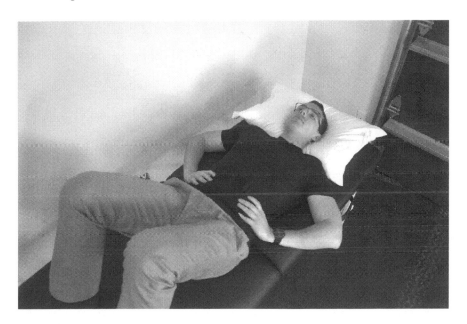

When you inhale, expand your stomach into your hands in an outward direction. Consciously think about filling up your abdomen like a balloon and letting the air press into your low back, stomach, sides, and even your pelvic floor.

This is how you want to breathe from now on!

Step 3: Brace for impact! Now that we've gotten breathing going in the right direction, it's time to learn how to brace your core muscles correctly.

First, it is helpful to understand what exactly is your core. Many people be-lieve it's just the six pack muscles you see on the cover of Women's or Men's Health magazines, but it's actually all the muscles of your midsection, low back, glutes, and hip flexors. These muscles, used in unison with one another, can help provide your low back with increased support and decrease low back pain.

It's easy to believe that having a strong core means you'll never get back pain, but that's not the case. What's significantly more important is your ability to activate these muscles at the right time. If you learn how to do this, you won't need to wear a back brace because these muscles all serve as your internal back brace.

How do we activate these muscles properly? Whenever I ask patients to "brace their core," they suck in their stomach or pull their belly button into their spine. I'm here to tell you that there is a more effective way to properly engage our core.

Lay on your back, keep your knees bent, and place your index and middle fingers about 2 inches to either side of your belly button (see photo below).

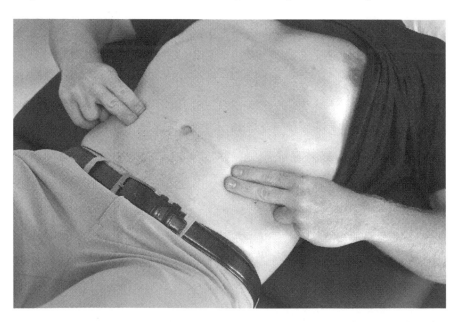

Now, press your abdominal muscles into your fingers as though another person were going to punch you in the midsection and you are going to break their fists with your strong trunk muscles. This is a proper abdominal brace! Side note: please DO NOT hold your breath!

The key is to combine the diaphragmatic breathing from step 2 and combine it with proper abdominal brace. You will feel like you can't take as big an inhale and you'll want to let go of your brace as you exhale. That's normal! You are now using your diaphragm and core muscles in a way you haven't in the past, so your body is adjusting. This is a difficult skill to learn initially, but it gets easier with practice.

It's one thing to be able to do this while laying on your back, but it's critical to start applying the breathing and bracing to everyday life. If you are lifting up a box of groceries from Costco, your back will thank you for activating those abdominal muscles properly while breathing correctly. When you get good at bracing, you should begin to use it like a volume dial, adjusting how much force you are putting into your brace.

When you want to pick up a grandkid who is quickly approaching the 100 lb threshold, you may want your abdominal brace turned up to an 8 or 9 out of 10. But if you're just pulling a couple of small items out of the back of the refrigerator, your brace only needs to be a 2 or 3 out of 10. Start practicing, and play with your volume dial! Your back will thank you for it!

Are You Practicing Spinal Hygiene?

Here is another term I am shamelessly stealing from back pain researcher Stuart McGill. Spinal hygiene is similar to dental hygiene but for your spine. It's something that must be performed daily, and the quicker you can incorporate these strategies into your daily life, the better off your back will be. This is a critical component to back health, and this advice alone has helped many of my patients improve their back pain immediately. They may seem trivial and unimportant, but don't be fooled. Doing all of these things properly can drastically improve or eliminate back pain.

Sitting

As soon as you read the word "sitting," you may have immediately worried about how you sit with bad posture. I'm actually here to tell you that sitting with perfect posture is overrated. Your body does not like to stay in any one static (or frozen) position for long periods of time, so even if you sat with perfect textbook posture for 8 hours at work and never moved from that position, you would still feel like the Tin Man from the Wizard of Oz when trying to go home at the end of the day.

The key is to move around more often. Try standing up every 20-30 min to allow your muscles and joints to loosen up. If you're at a standing desk, work in a sitting position for a bit, or vice versa. Your spine loves position changes! Now, if you can combine position changes with sitting with a little better alignment, then you'll be cooking with gas.

Everyone knows sitting in a slouched position like you see in the photo below isn't the best for your low back (or shoulders and neck for that matter).

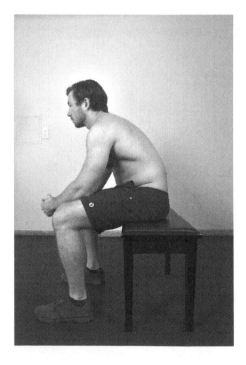

I would argue the bigger mistake I see is those that are sitting with an over-corrected posture. Yes, you can sit with an overcorrected posture, and I see it quite frequently with my patients who have low back pain. Overcorrected posture looks like the photo below, with the low back overly arched, causing the muscles on the left and right side of our spine, called paraspinals, to be hyperactive. When these muscles are hyperactive, it compresses the joints in your low back, which can aggravate low back pain.

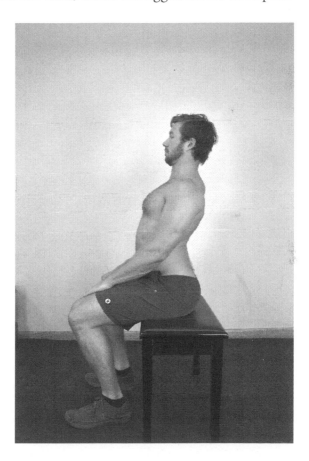

The goal is to be somewhere in the middle of these two postures, in a position called neutral spine. To find neutral spine, slouch or round your back as far as you can, then arch your back like I described earlier, and finally find a comfortable spot in the middle of these two positions. This is neutral spine. To help sit in the most ideal posture, you should sit in chairs with good lumbar support or utilize a pillow or small, folded dish towel. You don't need a large pillow for good low back support. It can look like this.

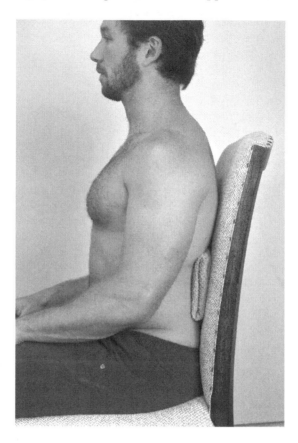

You can see there is a small curve of the low back, but it's not too rounded or overarched. It's right in between. Perfect! Moving around every 20-30 minutes or so is much more helpful than sitting in one static position, but if you have to sit for long periods of time, ensure you are in neutral spine with good lumbar support. When sitting at your desk chair, ensure that your feet are resting flat on the floor with your knees and hips at 90 degree angles. Your ears should be in line with your shoulders and your arms in line with your body with your elbows at 90-degree angles.

Standing

Standing is another critical position that we take for granted, and something that we do all the time. If you have back pain when standing in a long line for a cup of coffee, for example, it definitely doesn't feel great. Standing in a pain-free, optimal position is helpful to healing.

Normally, those that have back pain have overactive low back muscles, similar to the overarched or overcorrected lower back I discussed when sitting. To assess this yourself, stand up right now. With one hand, feel your low back just to the left and right of your spinal column. If these muscles are hard as a rock and feel like cords, you must learn how to relax them to decrease pressure on your low back.

Keeping your hand on those low back muscles, SLIGHTLY lean backwards until those muscles shut off and feel soft and relaxed. Now slowly lean forward until the low back muscles become hard again. The goal is to find the most UPRIGHT standing posture without your low back muscles turning on.

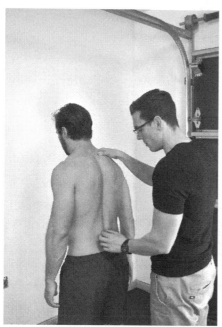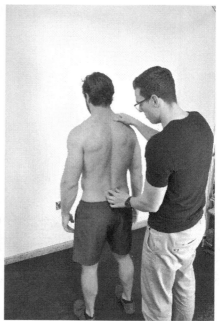

In the photo on the left, you can see my left hand assessing the low back muscles or paraspinals. When he is leaning forward, his paraspinals are working too hard and are tight like cords. In the photo on the right, you can see he is standing more upright and there is less paraspinal activity, meaning more comfort for your low back. (Note: if you're having trouble, try standing with one foot in front of the other to see if it works better for you). This will be your new safe standing position. Again, being as upright as possible with the low back muscles turned off is ideal.

Your neck positioning also affects the low back muscles. If your head or neck naturally protrudes forward (sticks out), it will also force all your back muscles to turn on. So while standing in your new, relaxed position with one hand on the lower back muscles, try sticking your head and chin until your back muscles engage. Now draw or pull your chin in until they turn off like the photo below.

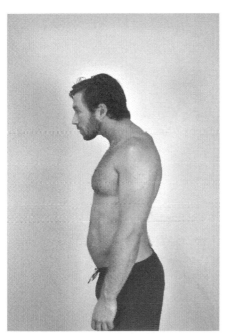 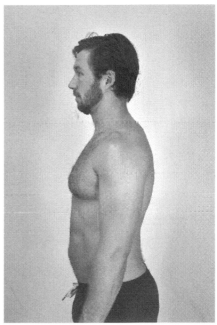

Remember, keeping the low back muscles turned "off" is always ideal so keeping your chin and head pulled back and keeping your head in line with your shoulders and hips is ideal for your low back. Additionally, If you allow your shoulder to round, your lower back muscles will turn on. If you pull the shoulders back, then the low back muscles will relax.

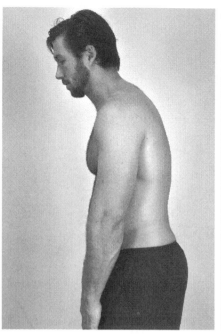

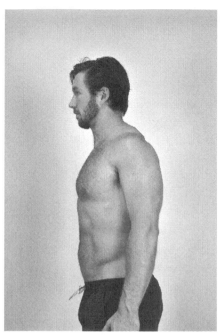

The low back muscles will also activate if you cross your arms over your chest. They will then relax if you put both hands behind your back.

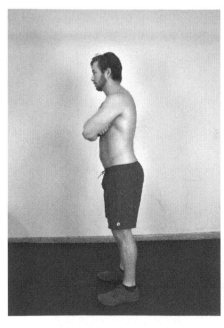

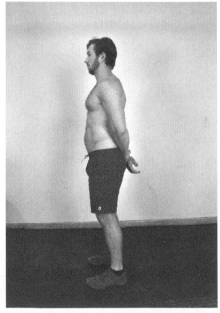

Hopefully, this experiment shows you how small adjustments can force your back muscles to engage or relax. Keep experimenting until you are in a comfortable, upright position that allows your low back muscles to stay relaxed. This can be difficult to do yourself, so if you have trouble, please consider seeing a trained specialist such as a physical therapist.

Lifting and Bending

Bending over to put on shoes or lift things off the ground can both be painful and difficult when not done correctly. The key is to perform a good hip hinge whenever you bend over. What's a hip hinge? Great question!

Normally, when people bend over to pick things up off the ground (especially with back pain), it looks something like the photo below.

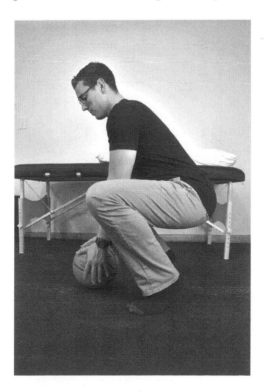

In this photo, you can see that my trunk is vertical and my knees are collapsing over my toes. This puts excess stress on the back and knees.

The way to perform a hip hinge properly is to begin with your feet a little wider than shoulder width apart. Then push your hips back as if you were going to sit in a tiny chair behind you. When your hips are far enough back, the knees will naturally begin to bend.

If you are having difficulty doing this, place your hands on your thighs. Then slide your hands down until they are resting on top of your knees. You are now performing a perfect hip hinge.

Important note: the hips move first and then your knees next! It should look like this photo below.

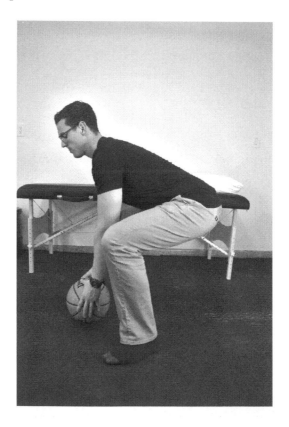

My hips are back as though I'm sitting in a chair, and my trunk is leaning forward and not vertical as in the previous photo. The hip hinge is critical for protecting your low back. When people use the phrase, "lift with your legs," this is to what they are referring to. In this position, your hips and glutes are doing the work instead of your low back.

Another note: if you are lifting anything off the ground, it should be directly underneath you. The farther away the object from your center of mass, the more stress you put on your low back. So please be cautious when grabbing heavy grocery bags out of the back of your car.

Don't forget that when you lift anything with significant weight, always use your abdominal brace and proper breathing. For heavier items, your inner abdominal brace should be turned on more forcefully. For smaller items, having a lighter abdominal brace is perfectly fine. Just be sure to use the brace!

Sleeping

We spend a third of our lives sleeping, yet it is often overlooked when it comes to a healthy lifestyle. Getting 7-8 hours of sleep allows your body to heal itself when it's injured. Unfortunately, having back pain can affect your ability to sleep. Quite the conundrum, I know. Luckily, there are several things you can do to help get more comfortable.

First, we can break down sleeping positions into three separate categories: back sleepers, side sleepers, and stomach sleepers. If you switch into more than one position, it only matters what position you start in. For example, I consistently wake up on my side, but I always start sleeping on my back, so I'm a back sleeper.

For back sleepers, place pillows under your knees and thighs to elevate your legs. By elevating your legs, your low back is placed in a less com-promising position, allowing maximum comfort. Experiment with the amount of pillows you use. Some people will feel more comfortable with just one pillow where others feel more comfortable with two or three. If your mattress has the ability to lift the foot of your bed, experiment with it as well. Just try it out.

At this point, someone usually asks me "Mat, what if I end up kicking the pillows?" This is normal, and it's ok. Even if your pillows only last an hour or two, that is an extra hour or two of improved sleep quality.

After the pillows, the next best thing to do is to get a small dish towel and place under the small of your back when you're sleeping. Having this small towel under your back may seem silly, but many times it allows your low back muscles to relax so you can actually get some shut-eye. Experiment with this prior to bedtime. Grab pillows and a towel and figure out what is the most comfortable for you. It should look something like this:

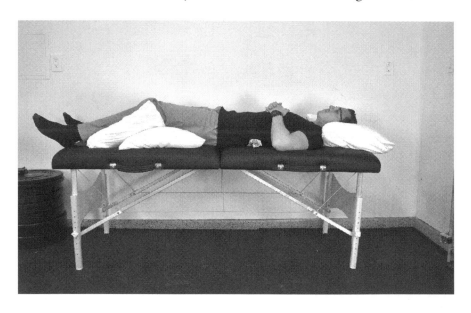

For the side sleepers, placing a pillow between your legs will keep your pelvis in an optimal position. Many people place pillows in a horizontal position, but it's best in a vertical position, meaning the pillow should go from your upper groin area all the way down to your ankles. SImilar to back sleepers, putting a rolled up dish towel underneath your side, below your ribs and just above your pelvis, will give your back more support.

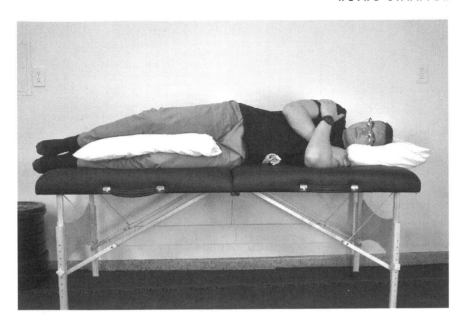

For stomach sleepers, place the center of your pillow underneath your belly button. This will allow your back to be in good alignment and let you sleep in significantly more comfort.

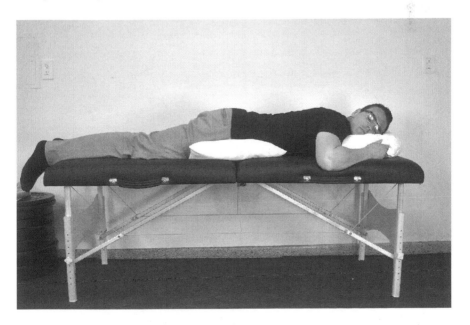

"I Have Back Pain Because My Hamstrings Are Tight!"

I hear this from patients and have read it on the internet, so let's nip this back pain myth in the bud right away. There is NO research that shows a correlation between hamstring tightness and low back pain.[6] If you're spending a large amount of time on a foam roll or lacrosse ball to work those hamstrings, please stop.

If you are feeling a constant tightness wrapping around your hips, it's easy to assume it's due to tight hip flexors or tight hamstrings. The perception of tightness is a protective mechanism from your nervous system that indicates another group of muscles is not working properly. It's generally a sign that you have weak glutes (and poor abdominal bracing/endurance, as we discussed earlier).

Most patients with back pain have weak hips, specifically weak glutes or butt muscles. The glutes play a vital role in stabilizing your pelvis and supporting your lower back when you walk, hike, go upstairs, lift things off the ground, etc. The risk for back pain increases when your glutes are weak and aren't activating correctly. This can be attributed to the significant amount of sitting we do on a daily basis and a lack of appropriate strength training. We sit at desks. We sit on couches. We sit in our car. We sit at the toilet. All of this sitting weakens our glutes and increases the amount of work our low back has to do. Not great for long term spine health. So in addition to getting better at doing your abdominal brace, don't forget to strengthen your butt!

If you want more in-depth low back pain tips, go to our webpage at https://parkerphysio.com/back-pain/ to download your free report titled, **"8 Simple Ways To End Back Pain & Stiffness Without Painkillers Or Injections."**

---

[6] Relationship Between Mechanical Factors and Incidence of Low Back Pain. Mohammad Reza Nourbakhsh and Amir Massoud Arab. Journal of Orthopaedic & Sports Physical Therapy 2002 32:9, 447-460

If you want more tips for dealing with sciatica, go to our webpage at https://parkerphysio.com/sciatica-hip-pain/ to download your free report titled, **"7 Natural Ways To Ease Sciatica & Hip Pain Even If You've Had Pain For Years."**

Summary

- Having an episode of low back pain is normal, but chronic low back pain (lasting more than 3 months) is not. Chronic low back pain doesn't go away by itself and will take more than just rest or painkillers to solve.

- Words are powerful. Be careful working with healthcare practitioners that tell you your back is "out of alignment" or that you "have the back of a 90-year-old."

- Don't put too much weight into your MRI exam. Discs reabsorb. Arthritic joints can be mobilized. Weak muscles can be strengthened.

- Learning to breathe with your diaphragm and activate your core muscles will help support your low back.

- Practice good spinal hygiene. Sit, stand, sleep, and lift with good form and technique. Your back will thank you.

- Don't forget about your hips and glutes, which play a vital role in supporting your entire spine.

CHAPTER 4

Knee Pain

One of my favorite phrases about the human body is, "little hinges swing big doors." I can't think of a more accurate way to describe the knee joint. The knees allow you to sit, stand, walk, jump, and exercise. Your knees are designed to absorb and cushion whatever impacts you throw at it. Unfortunately, your knees can take a pounding over the years from running on hard surfaces, playing golf, or intense hiking.

This can lead to wear and tear on the cartilage in your knees, causing it to wear thin and possibly creating clicking or popping noises. Enough damage to the knee can lead to significant pain and stiffness. In fact, after low back pain, knee pain is the most common diagnosis we work with at Parker Physio.

In this chapter, I'll go over an in depth look at knee pain to give you a more thorough understanding of why knee pain happens and the strategies to eliminate it.

Between a Rock and a Hard Place

Your knee doesn't have a lot of options. The knee is connected to both your hip and your ankle/foot. If your hip is weak, your knee will have to take on more force to help stabilize your leg when you do activities such as walking or climbing stairs. If the ankle/foot are in poor positioning, as with flat feet or a bunion, it can also play a role in the alignment of the knee and the amount of force the knee must absorb. So when I see clients with knee pain, the hip and foot must be assessed as well.

If you look at the illustration below, you can see what I mean about the knee being influenced by your hip and foot. This drawing represents a still shot of a person with knee pain walking, the moment the right foot is planted as the left leg is swinging. Look up near the pelvis. See how the pelvis is not horizontal but is tilted at an angle? The pelvis dropping due to a weak right hip, more specifically due to a weak right glute (the gluteus maximus). When the pelvis drops like this, the femur (the thigh bone) will begin to turn inwards, causing excess stress on the inner portion of the knee.

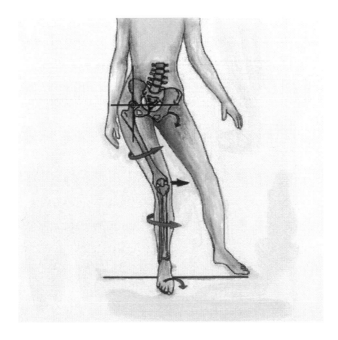

Someone with a history of knee pain and significant hip weakness will normally present with "knock-knees," anatomically known as "knee valgus." To test this, stand in front of a mirror with your feet shoulder-width apart. If your knees look like they want to kiss each other, you would be considered knock-kneed or having knee valgus. Having knee valgus for years can add a significant amount of stress on the inner portion of your knee, leading to increased knee pain.

Foot problems can also cause knee valgus. Take a look at the foot in the picture above. When the arch of your foot excessively collapses, it can cause the tibia (the big lower leg bone) to turn inwards, causing knee valgus. Arches excessively collapse if the small muscles of your feet are weak or if you don't wear proper shoes with good arch support.

If this happens every time you step down on that leg and you walk like this for thousands of steps per day, day after day, it can add up rapidly. Also notice how everything, especially in the lower half of your body, is connected. Having a problem at one joint, such as the knee, can cause problems at other nearby joints, and vice versa.

Knee valgus and knee pain can be improved. When working with a specialist healthcare provider, they shouldn't just be treating your knee but also looking at the hip and foot to improve overall alignment and strength.

What Kind Of Shoes Are You Wearing?

Here in beautiful San Diego, CA, it almost never rains, so the weather is perfect 95% of the time. As you can imagine, being outdoors and going to the beach with friends or family are pretty popular activities.

Unfortunately, a common mistake I see with those suffering from knee pain is a poor selection in footwear. Although sandals may be fashionable, they are not friendly to your knees in the long run. The majority of sandals do not have proper arch support and can cause the knee to have excessive, unnatural movement, which then can lead to knee pain.

I always recommend wearing sandals as little as possible, but if you are adamant on wearing them, please be sure to invest in a good pair with proper support. Also, avoid the thong sandals that are worn between your first and second toe. Thong sandals tend to create imbalances between the small muscles in your foot and your glutes (aka your big butt muscles). When your glutes aren't working the way they should, it can lead to an array of problems, including in the knees, back, ankles, feet, and hips.

To all the ladies reading this, please sit down and gently brace yourself before reading this next sentence...

Wearing high heels is not good for your knees. When walking with high heels, you put increased weight on your knee joints, and they aren't designed to take on that much force. Not only that, but when your heels are up that high, it can begin to shorten your Achilles tendon, which can lead to calf tightness and to Achilles tendonitis issues down the line.

I also understand that sometimes you have to wear high heels, whether at a formal event or work. If you are wearing heels at a formal event, please bring a pair of sneakers or flats so you can change as soon as the event has ended. If you have to wear heels at work, (politely) inform your boss that wearing heels is making your knee pain worse and that you must wear sneakers. Most companies are trying to avoid spending money on employee injuries and should acquiesce to your request. (Side note: you will more than likely need a physician's note to bypass your office dress code policy.)

My go-to recommendation for footwear is a store like Road Runner Sports®. They will give you a custom walking or running shoe recommendation based on your type of feet. Great shoe brands include Saucony®, Hoka One One®, Asics©, and Brooks®.

The other recommendation I make is to try foot orthotics. They can help put your foot in better positioning, which will then allow your knee to move better. Orthotics are great because you can slip them right inside any pair of shoes you have. Many of my patients love buying multiple pairs for their work, walking, and exercise shoes. Don't worry about getting custom foot orthotics unless you have a significant history of foot problems or have foot deformities. The general orthotics at a sporting goods store or online are fine. My recommendations are Vasyli® or SuperFeet®.

If you would like more tips specifically on foot or ankle pain, you can check out my free report, **"The 6 Essential Tips To Reduce Foot And Ankle Pain In 14 Days"** at https://parkerphysio.com/foot-and-ankle-pain/. It has all my best tips for ending foot and ankle pain naturally.

Arthritis Isn't Your Enemy; Pain & Stiffness Are

"Mat, I have bone-on-bone arthritis! I saw the x-ray. Isn't physical therapy and exercise going to make it worse? I just know I'm going to need a knee replacement!" I've heard this countless times, especially from those over age 50 with knee pain. A total knee replacement sometimes is the answer, but not always. Let me tell you a story.

I once had a patient who we'll call Janet. She was 55 years old at the time and came to me after having more than 10 years of right knee pain. In her late 30s, Janet had a meniscus surgery on that same knee after twisting it during a hike. Janet began to tell me how excruciatingly painful it was to go upstairs or walk more than 10 minutes. Getting out of bed in the morning was torture due to the stiffness, and she could only stand in line at the grocery store by putting all her weight on her grocery cart.

Janet came to me out of desperation. Her daughter had just gotten a new job and had asked Janet to watch over her two beautiful grandkids while she was at work. She was terrified that she would end up being in a wheel-chair and wouldn't be as active and independent as she wanted.

So she was determined to find a solution to her knee problem. Unfortunately, she had been let down in her past. Cortisone injections. PRP. Synvisc shots. KT Tape. A copper sleeve. Knee brace. None of them worked. She even tried physical therapy at another facility for a few weeks but felt ignored.

She saw a certified physical therapist for 10 minutes before being given exercises to do at home.

Janet, still determined, ended up finding me on Google and liked what I had to say on the phone, so she came in for a free consult that we call our Taster Session. During the Taster Session, she told me all about her "bone-on-bone" arthritis and how she was going to need a knee replacement.

Janet was determined to avoid surgery at all costs, but she was terrified her family and friends were passing her by, that instead of taking care of her grandkids, she would need someone to take care of her.

Watching her walk around, you didn't need any medical training to see the severity of her limp and how she appeared to be sinking while walking. Janet's right knee was stuck in a slightly bent position, causing her to be unsteady.

Her balance was poor, quadriceps were weak, and glutes not activating properly. Her painful right knee could not straighten or bend half as much as her left knee. But she did have one thing going for her. She was open to the idea of trying something different and committed to getting a natural solution so she could avoid or put off a total knee replacement.

We developed a customized plan of care, and I let her know that arthritis isn't really the enemy. Again, arthritis happens in every joint of your body over time. It's the normal wear and tear of aging. However, sometimes arthritis can lead to stiffness, which leads to pain and inflammation. So it is stiffness that is the true enemy.

When you have stiffness, your joints can't move as freely as they are designed to. Picture an old, creaky door in your house that won't open or close all the way. The door continues to get stuck, but you have to get in and out of it, so you keep forcing it open and closed, causing increased stress on the door hinge. The same thing is happening to your knee when arthritis has turned into stiffness. You have to keep walking and doing your daily activities, but the knee doesn't always want to cooperate.

The knee joint stiffness then begins to cause pain and inflammation. In order to get the knee joint moving again, we have to apply some lubricant (think WD-40) to get the knee moving again. How do we do that? With proper hands-on work to improve knee mobility and then with specific corrective movements to keep the knee moving the way it's designed to. It involves getting the big hip muscles strong and resilient while improving the stability of the foot and ankle.

After explaining all this to Janet, she was excited to get to work. Was it easy? Nope. Was it an overnight fix? Nope. But Janet invested in her health and did everything she was asked. With the help of the hands-on work and specialist guidance, Janet is now able to walk as far as she wants without a limp. More importantly, she is active with her grandkids, all without knee pain. I still stay in touch with Janet, who is quickly approaching 60 and has maintained her health without getting a total knee replacement, taking pain pills, or getting more injections.

Can I guarantee that success for you? Unfortunately not. Occasionally, I do turn away patients with knee problems. Normally, it's because of one or more of the following reasons:

- They've waited too long to get specialist help

- Their pain is constant and doesn't change whether they are sitting, standing, or lying in bed

- The knee (or knees) is constantly swollen, severely limiting range of motion

- The knee joints are significantly bowed in or out

Please don't let yourself get to this point, Reach out for help sooner rather than later!

If you want to see whether your knee situation can improve, schedule a phone call at www.parkerphysio.com/free-telephone-consultation to talk more about your knee suffering and how we can help.

Be Wary Of Injections, Knee Sleeves, and Supplements

You've probably seen the commercial with Brett Favre wearing his copper knee sleeve. He is loading hay into the back of his truck, talking about his aches and pains since retiring from football, and ends with him playing catch with his dog. It's pretty cheesy, but the commercials are everywhere, as are commercials for different "joint health" supplements and "NEWLY APPROVED, CUTTING EDGE" injections. These are all A+ marketing tactics, but you should be wary of using any of them.

Let's start with the knee sleeve. This is normally one of the first things people try when suffering with knee pain. Hop on Amazon, look for the knee sleeve with the most 5-star reviews, add it to your cart, and get your sleeve in 2 days (because Amazon Prime is the best). You slide it on and start feeling great! Like you can conquer the world. But the pain relief from the sleeve is always temporary, and it doesn't give you the long term solution you are looking for. The same can be said of the more bulky knee braces. Neither are fixing the root cause of the problem. You are only putting a band-aid on a leaky faucet.

The same can be said of supplements. There are probably more commercials for supplements than there are for knee sleeves or braces. The magic pills from a small foreign country that doctors just discovered can eliminate knee pain and arthritis! Or the more classic supplements, glucosamine and chondroitin. There is nothing wrong with taking these pills, and if they make you feel better, continue to take them. But these supplements are exactly that...supplements. They are used to help supplement your health. It is not a true fix to knee pain.

Last but not least are knee injections. There are several different kinds out there. Cortisone, Synvisc, and PRP are the most common, but by the time you're reading this book I'm sure there will be a new injection out on the market. Each type of injection is used slightly differently.

Cortisone is predominantly used for inflammation, and most physicians will allow you to get 3-4 injections per year. Synvisc injections are done in a set of three injections over the span of a few weeks or there is Synvisc-One®, which is a single injection. The Synvisc injections are designed to help improve lubrication the knee joint.

With Platelet Rich Plasma, better known as PRP injections, a small portion of your blood is removed, put into a machine called a centrifuge to separate the various components, and then the platelets, the cells responsible for healing in your body, are injected back into your knee.

It doesn't matter whether or not you haven't had any injections or all three different types of injections. Just like the knee brace, knee sleeve, and supplements, the injections alone are normally not enough to get you back to walking on the beach, running in your neighborhood, or playing with your grandkids.

All those things can help you feel better, but none of them will truly fix the underlying problem. The knee is a complex joint, and there are many factors that must be considered.

So What Do You Do About It?

There are many recommendations to help with knee pain. I can't promise what has worked for most of my patients and clients over the years will work for you. However, reading and following these tips will be better than spending another day just resting, accepting it, and thinking it's just your age.

First, be mindful of what surfaces you are walking on. It's best to avoid walking on uneven surfaces such as at the beach or in the hills. Flat, even surfaces will always be the most friendly for your knees. If you are having pain when walking up stairs, here's a trick to significantly decrease knee pain.

When we walk upstairs, 99% of the time we stand straight, pressing up through the balls of our feet with our heel in the air, just like this photo below.

Going up stairs in this manner is similar to walking around in high heels. You put a large amount of body weight and force on your knee joints that can worsen knee pain. To decrease the force on the knee, you want to do a couple of things. First, instead of putting your heel up in the air, put your foot flat on the step and when you push up make sure the force is coming through your heel. Then you want to lean your trunk slightly forward. Doing both of these things will instantly engage your glute muscles and take significant force off your knee joints. It should look like the photo below.

In the photo above, my foot is flat on the step, and my trunk is leaning forward. When I drive up, I'm pressing through my heel and squeezing my left butt cheek. This allows my hips to work more and let's my knees take a break, meaning less pain. Your glutes are much better equipped to help you go upstairs than your knees and quadriceps muscles. Give it a try and feel the difference!

My next recommendation is that if you're overweight, **shed a few pounds**. Research has shown when you lose weight it decreases force on the knee joints and can lead to decreased pain.[7] The two biggest factors in losing weight? Nutrition and exercise. In chapter 7, we'll go over in-depth nutrition principles that I commonly see people overlook and which stop them from achieving their weight loss goals (and why I hate the word "diet").

On the topic of exercise, working out can be difficult when you have significant knee pain. High impact activities that include a ton of running and jumping can aggravate your knees if not performed correctly. However, there are several safe cardio exercises that can be done.

One of the best exercises for cardiovascular health and decreasing force on your knees is swimming. Swimming or even walking in a body of water, whether the pool or the ocean, is great for your knee joints. The best part about being in water is that you partially float. That takes bodyweight off of your knees, allowing you to exercise safely. Other things you can try are an exercise bike or elliptical. Both of these are gentle on the knees and great for cardiovascular health.

All of those things I mentioned can be found in commercial gyms, and if you are a baby boomer over the age of 65, you more than likely qualify for a program known as Silver Sneakers. A Silver Sneakers memberships offers a massive network of gyms with no cost to you, so you can use the pool, bike, or elliptical.

Now that we've discussed a little bit of cardiovascular exercise, what about strength? Yes, having strong knees is important for living the active life you want. Unfortunately, many people believe just doing some simple exercises is the answer to fix any problem or physical pain. Yes, exercises are **one** of the secrets to heal knee pain naturally, but there is a right way and wrong way to go about it.

---

[7] Felson DT, Zhang Y, Anthony JM, Naimark A, Anderson JJ. Weight Loss Reduces the Risk for Symptomatic Knee Osteoarthritis in Women: The Framingham Study. Ann Intern Med. 1992;116:535–539. doi: 10.7326/0003-4819-116-7-535

If you're doing exercises that increases your knee pain or causes the knee to become swollen, this is the wrong way to go about it. Swelling and inflammation of your knee is not your friend, and I see too many people try to push through it, believing in the old mantra, "no pain, no gain." This is not only foolish, but it's stopping you from getting any closer to reaching your goals.

My advice is to strengthen your quads (your big thigh muscles) and your glutes (the butt). The quads help support your knee, and when they are strong, they can decrease wear and tear on your joints. Just as important are your glute muscles, which are the "role model" for the knee. If the glutes are strong, they positively influence your knee to be in good alignment, but if the glutes are weak, they negatively influence your knee to begin to bow in or out. The knees bowing in or out isn't good for long-term knee health.

Regardless of your method, exercises alone will not solve your knee pain. It's one part of the healing process. There are many different types of knee pain, from meniscus and ligament injuries to patellofemoral issues and osteoarthritis. Each of these requires a different treatment protocol and specific exercises, but everyone with knee pain can benefit from strengthening their glutes and quads.

"A Song Of Fire And Ice"

One of the most common questions I get asked when it comes to knee injuries is, "Should I use heat, or should I use ice?" The answer I always give is, "It depends." If you just went for a long walk and are struggling with pain AND swelling, ice will be your best bet. Swelling and inflammation are not your friends, and they limit your knee's ability to move freely, which isn't great for being able to walk or do your favorite types of exercises. Use ice 15-20 minutes at a time a few times per day.

If your knee is stiff and there isn't any significant swelling, heat can help it feel looser. Using a heating pad or hot pack first thing in the morning when the knee is the most stiff can help you start your day, but as with the knee sleeve, this is a temporary sensation. When it comes to knee stiffness, riding the exercise bike for 10-15 minutes is a much better option because it increases blood flow and provides more lubrication to the knee joint.

Meniscus and Total Knee Replacement Surgery

Meniscus repairs and the total knee arthroplasty (also known as a total knee replacement) are two of the most common knee surgeries performed today. When people are told by their physicians that they have a meniscus tear or that it's time for a total knee replacement, they often believe they don't have any other options. I want to bring your attention to a few things you may not know about these surgeries. But first, we need some helpful background information.

The meniscus consists of two cartilage rings that sit on top of your tibia (the big lower leg bone) and provide a cushion for your knees. Meniscus issues tend to occur in the younger population (under 50), usually while playing sports or running and attempting to change directions too quickly while the knee is in a bent position. Those with meniscus issues tend to complain of the classic signs of "catching" or "locking" while they are walking and have difficulty pivoting to change directions.

When the meniscus is torn, you have to have surgery to get it fixed, right? Maybe not. In 2013, the New England Journal of Medicine performed a study comparing meniscus repair surgery vs. physical therapy in adults over 45 with knee meniscus tears and mild-to-moderate osteoarthritis. Half of the patients in the study had a surgical meniscus repair while the other half of the patients had a standardized physical therapy regimen. After 6 months and 12 months, the researchers found no significant difference in pain or overall function.[8]

The New England Journal of Medicine published another article in 2013 in which they compared meniscus surgery versus a "sham" surgery by placing people into two groups.[9] In the sham surgery group, patients were taken in the operating room and the surgeon simulated meniscus surgery using suction and a mechanized shaver (without the blade) but didn't actually repair anything. The other group had a traditional meniscus repair surgery. What did they find?

There were no significant differences in knee pain or function between the two groups.

This means that you always have more options and that surgery isn't always the answer. If your physician tells you that you need surgery, ask to try physical therapy first. It's a cheaper, less invasive option, and if it doesn't work, you'll still have the ability to have surgery after. I have plenty of patients who were able to save themselves from getting meniscus surgery after receiving specialized physical therapy. In chapter 9, I'll let you know what quality physical therapy care looks like so you be sure to pick the right facility for you and your needs.

If you've had a meniscus or ACL surgery in your past, there is a higher chance to later develop the "Big 3": pain, stiffness, and swelling. When the Big 3 begin to take their toll, your ability to walk and do other every-day activities becomes increasingly difficult. By far the biggest mistake I see people make with chronic knee pain is to procrastinate on making a decision to do something about it.

---

[8] Katz, J.N., Brophy, R.H., Chaisson, C.E. et al, **Surgery versus physical therapy for a meniscal tear and osteoarthritis.** *N Engl J Med.* 2013;368:1675–1684

[9] Sihvonen, Raine, et al. "Arthroscopic partial meniscectomy versus sham surgery for a degenerative meniscal tear." *New England Journal of Medicine* 369.26 (2013): 2515-2524.

They secretly hope that tomorrow will be a "good day," although it rarely is. I cannot stress enough that there is always something that can be done, and even if your knee pain improved by 10, 20, or even 30 percent, what would that do to your quality of life?

Too often people come to me after it's too late. Please don't let that be you!

If you want to find out how we can help you, go to <u>www.parkerphysio. com/free-taster-session/</u> for information on a free session, where you can get the confidence and clarity to understand what's going on with your knee(s) and make the best decision about your health.

Summary

- The knee is influenced by your hip and foot, so both body parts must be considered when caring for your knees

- Having arthritis is normal, but if you suffer from the Big 3 (pain, stiffness, and swelling), that is abnormal, and getting specialist help sooner than later becomes critical to long-term knee health

- Be wary of knee sleeves, braces, injections, and supplements. They can all be helpful but normally won't provide a long-term solution

- If you have knee pain and want to exercise, try swimming, riding a stationary bike, or using an elliptical

- Ice and heat can help reduce knee pain. Use heat if you're stiff and have minimal to no swelling; use ice if your knee is swollen and painful

- It's always a good idea to strengthen your quads and your glutes to help support your knee joints

- Many times, trying physical therapy can get you the same or better results than knee surgery

- When in doubt, get a specialist to check out your knee to help you make the best decision about your health

CHAPTER 5

Shoulder Pain

The shoulder is one of my favorite joints of the body. Unlike the knee, the shoulder has significantly more freedom of motion. It can go up, down, behind your back, sideways, rotate inwards, or rotate outwards. These motions allow us to eat, lift stuff, play sports, and do our daily activities. Unfortunately, because the shoulder joint allows for more motion, it has a higher risk for injury and pain.

Shoulder pain happens for many different reasons. Things like frozen shoulder, impingement, rotator cuff tears, labrum injuries, and tendonitis, just to name a few, can cause you to grab your shoulder in agony. In this chapter, **I want to give you a better understanding of the shoulder and ways to ease your shoulder pain**.

Sometimes shoulder pain starts after a big incident occurs. For example, spiking a volleyball over a net, lifting something heavy with a jerking motion, or falling on your outstretched arm. More often, though, shoulder pain begins to creep up on you with no warning and no explanation. When it first occurs, you don't think anything of it, but it slowly gets worse and worse until it becomes so unbearable you can't sleep at night.

How did this shoulder pain creep up without telling you it was going to affect your active, on-the-go lifestyle? It's usually an accumulation of damage done over many years of repetitive motions and poor body positioning (aka bad posture). It may be sitting at a computer all day, scrolling through Facebook on your phone, reading in bed, or cleaning the house. These small, trivial motions and positions slowly begin to take a toll on your body.

When shoulder pain strikes, we naturally begin to use our other arm to do the majority of our daily activities. And why not? That's why we have two arms, right? Not exactly. As you use the painful shoulder less and less, it begins to become stiffer. When you try to move your arm to get rid of the stiffness, you feel a sharp, stabbing pain. This cycle can continue until you develop something known as adhesive capsulitis, more commonly known as frozen shoulder.

I'll be blunt; frozen shoulder sucks. It takes a large amount of hands-on work and appropriate stretching to fix. Please don't let your painful shoulder get to that point. I'm not trying to do any fear mongering. My goal is to bring awareness to letting unnecessary shoulder pain linger around for longer than it should. Nor is the purpose of this book is to assign you a diagnosis. Diagnosing shoulder pain is much more complex, and you should always see a specialist when getting help.

Posture Problem?

Let's take a closer look at your posture. Stand to the side of a mirror. Are your shoulders rounded forward? Is the upper part of your back starting to develop a small hump? Are your head and neck protruding forward? If you said yes to any of these questions, your posture may be greatly affecting your shoulder's ability to move properly. Let me show you why.

Keep standing in front of the mirror, round your upper back as if you are curling up into a little ball. At this point, you should look something like the Hunchback of Notre Dame. Now reach your arm up in the air as far as you can while you're hunched over. Not very far, is it?

Now, stand at attention with your back straight as an arrow. Reach your arm up in the air again as high as you can. Notice the difference? When your standing in an upright posture, your shoulder can move higher and more freely. This is why, when trying to improve shoulder health, it's critical your upper back, also known as your thoracic spine, must also be thoroughly examined and fixed to get the long-term relief you want.

Your neck is another body part that must be closely examined. The shoulder and neck greatly affect one another. Many times, people come to me thinking they have a neck problem when they actually have a shoulder problem. Or vice versa, people come to me with a shoulder problem when it's actually a neck problem. If you are having any numbness, tingling, or burning sensation shooting down your arm and affecting your fingers, you more than likely have a neck problem, not a shoulder problem. Don't worry, I will discuss more about your neck in the next chapter.

If you've read everything so far, you may begin to notice a pattern that everything in your body is connected. My patients get the best results when treatment isn't centered around the symptom, in this case shoulder pain, but treating the whole body. This allows people to get back to living an active and mobile lifestyle. When the stiff joints of your neck and upper back are unlocked, your shoulder is able to move freely and comfortably.

Everything You Need To Know About Your Rotator Cuff

The rotator cuff is one of the more misunderstood structures of the body. It's a group of four small muscles that surround your shoulder and keep it centered in the joint, allowing it to perform all of its amazing different motions. When these tendons are pulled on or stressed repeatedly, they can become irritated, leading to tendonitis or possibly a rotator cuff tear.

"If my MRI says I have a rotator cuff tear, the only way to fix it is surgery, right?" Not necessarily. What if I told you that having a rotator cuff tear could be a normal part of aging? In multiple studies, researchers found that after the age of 50 there is a **1 in 5 chance you already have some sort of rotator cuff tear but don't have ANY symptoms.**[10] [11] And as you continue to get older, these odds drastically increase. What does that mean for you? It means there is a possibility that you already had a rotator cuff tear prior to having any shoulder pain.

How is that possible? Because your body is an incredible machine. The reason the shoulder can have a rotator cuff tear without pain or weakness is quite fascinating. When something in the human body doesn't work properly, the body will adapt and ask another part to help out. For the shoulder, this is usually a muscle called the deltoid, which has the strength and ability to substitute for a compromised rotator cuff. Your shoulder has the ability to do this automatically, without pain or loss of strength.

Other times, as I mentioned earlier, MRI's aren't as accurate as you may think. I once had a client in his early 50s who had been a construction worker his whole life and gradually began having right shoulder pain. His MRI results came back with the diagnosis of a full thickness rotator cuff tear, and his surgeon scheduled him for an arthroscopic rotator cuff repair. When the surgeon went in to perform the repair, he found no tear whatsoever in the shoulder. The surgeon just cleaned up a bit of scar tissue and then sent him over to me for treatment. After several weeks of hands-on treatment, we were able to eliminate his pain, regain his motion, and improve the strength in his shoulder, which allowed him to go back to work and provide for his family.

Does this mean your MRI always lying to you or that you can always avoid surgery by getting physical therapy? No, not always. The shoulder is complex, and there are times when rotator cuff surgery is necessary. There

---

[10] Yamamoto, Atsushi, et al. "Prevalence and risk factors of a rotator cuff tear in the general population." *Journal of Shoulder and Elbow Surgery* 19.1 (2010): 116-120.
[11] Tempelhof, Siegbert, Stefan Rupp, and Romain Seil. "Age-related prevalence of rotator cuff tears in asymptomatic shoulders." *Journal of shoulder and elbow surgery* 8.4 (1999): 296-299.

are many factors that must be considered when assessing the shoulder. What kind of tear do you have? A partial tear? Full thickness? Do you have significant shoulder weakness? Are you over the age of 50? How long have you had the tear? Are you a diabetic (diabetes affects healing time)?

The answers to these questions must all be considered in combination with seeing a trained specialist. But what if you could avoid costly surgery and get back to being as active as you want? If you've been diagnosed with a rotator cuff injury, ask your physician about getting specialist physical therapy. I'll discuss what specialist physical therapy looks like more in chapter 9. In the meantime, keep reading for more tips on what to do and what NOT to do when you have shoulder pain.

Sleep Like A Baby

One of the most common complaints I get with the shoulder is the inability to sleep comfortably without pain. When you can't sleep at night, it drains your energy. Your mood decreases, you become irritable, and the relationship with your loved ones is affected. I once had the sweetest woman with shoulder pain tell me, "I need to be able to sleep again! I feel exhausted and am acting like a real b*tch towards my husband!" Luckily, after a few short weeks of working together, she was able to return to sleeping comfortably throughout the night, no longer fearing the deep, agonizing ache. (And they are still happily married!)

Poor positioning is the number one reason shoulder pain happens at night. When the muscles, tendons, and nerves of the shoulder are irritated, trying to stay in one position all night is a tall task. You may sleep with your arm tucked underneath your pillow or just let it lay by your side without support. Doing this puts the muscles and nerves of the shoulder in a slightly stretched position. After a few hours of being in this state, pain can rear its ugly head. The position of your shoulder matters.

To get in the optimal sleeping position, place a small, flat pillow underneath your armpit while keeping your elbow at a 90-degree angle. If you start your night on your back, I also recommend placing a rolled up dish towel or an additional small pillow underneath your upper arm. These two things help create more comfort for your shoulder, allowing you to improve the quality of your sleep. Your sleep setup should look something like the photo below.

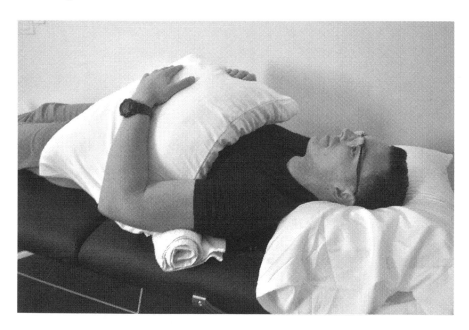

Another mistake I see frequently is lifting everyday objects when your arm is in an outstretched position, what I call "No Man's Land." I commonly have patients come see me after reaching into the back seat of the car to grab something or lifting a heavy grocery bag from deep inside the trunk, causing a jolt of pain to the shoulder.

The reason this is harmful for your shoulder is because it puts extra force on your rotator cuff muscles, which aren't designed to lift that much weight when your arm is outstretched from your body. Whenever you reach out to grab something, the shoulder is in a position where it has minimal stability and strength, a perfect recipe for an injury. The following photo is lifting in "No Man's Land."

do heavy lifting with your legs, not your back or arms. Your arms should serve to secure objects close to your body so that your legs can do the hard work. Next time you need to get something in the backseat, please get out of the car and walk to the closest car door to grab it. As for groceries or any other heavy objects, get as close as possible and hug the object with your arms while letting the legs do the lifting. Or hold it by your side.

 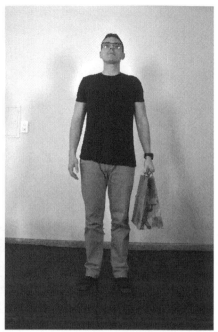

Speaking of heavy lifting, many of my female patients carry incredibly heavy purses. I'll sometimes tease them that they're carrying mini suitcases, because they have everything from Kleenex to chapstick to allergy medicine in there. When I ask if they carry their purse on one shoulder more than the other, the answer is generally yes. Carrying a purse or other heavy objects on your shoulder for long periods of time stretches the muscles, tendons, and nerves of the neck and shoulder. Doing this over many years can eventually take a toll on the shoulder as well as the neck and begin to cause uncomfortable shoulder pain.

If you are going to use a purse, please make it as light as possible. Yes, I understand that can be a tall task for some of you, but your body will thank you for it. My other suggestion is to constantly switch carrying your purse from one shoulder to another. This will even out the force the weight of the purse puts on your body.

What About Cortisone Shots?

We briefly discussed cortisone in previous chapters, but when it comes to the shoulder, cortisone can be an effective tool to help improve shoulder pain. A cortisone injection consists of some sort of anesthetic, such as lidocaine, and a corticosteroid, which is a powerful anti-inflammatory agent. The purpose of a cortisone shot is to help reduce inflammation inside the joint, hopefully decreasing the pain.

I have had some patients who had a traumatic incident, got a cortisone injection, and POOF! The pain went away and stayed away. Unfortunately, for most of you reading this who've had a gradual onset of shoulder pain with no big inciting incident, the injections are never quite as successful. Getting a cortisone injection usually will give you temporary relief, sometimes lasting months, sometimes weeks, or sometimes just days before that pain begins to creep back.

Why? If you spend years and years of sitting at a desk or watching TV, certain muscles of the shoulder will begin to tighten up, affecting your ability to move your arm freely. These tight muscles can then lead to your shoulder not moving properly. If you get a cortisone shot but don't fix the tight muscles and the quality of the shoulder motion, your pain more than likely will return, causing even greater frustration.

Cortisone injections also do have some possible side effects, including nerve damage, joint infection, weakening of nearby bone (osteoporosis), temporary increase of blood sugar (important for diabetics), and muscle tendon weakening or rupture. Therefore, physicians will normally limit the amount of injections to 3 or 4 per year.

What's my recommendation? It always depends on your personal situation. If you are adamant about not getting any injections and don't want to risk any of the side effects, definitely look into getting hands-on treatment from a specialist. If you like the idea of getting a cortisone injection, talk to your physician first to see if it's appropriate for you. If it is, my patients get the best results when getting physical therapy treatment in conjunction with the injection. The shot helps with the inflammation so we can work on loosening those tight muscles and getting your shoulder to move safely.

Side note: even if your shoulder pain decreases to a 0/10 after the injection, it's still a good idea to get looked at by a specialist to ensure the shoulder is moving correctly and all the appropriate shoulder muscles have good strength. If those things aren't corrected, you are at risk for the shoulder pain to return.

"What If I Have Arthritis?"

As I mentioned throughout this book, having arthritis is normal but being in pain is NOT. Being diagnosed with osteoarthritis doesn't mean a life of stiffness, pain, and misery. I'll give you an example.

Another client, whom we'll call him Dave, came to me after severely injuring his shoulder doing heavy weightlifting back in the 1980s. Now in his early 70s, he suffered for almost 30 years with shoulder pain and stiffness. He couldn't lift weights like he wanted and decided to come see me when he could no longer put on his shirt or lift up his morning cup of coffee. His MRI and x-rays showed he had "severe arthritis" and "significant rotator cuff damage." His physician said all that could be done was to get total shoulder replacement surgery. Dave was adamant about not getting surgery and had the goal of going back to lifting free weights.

We developed a customized plan just for him, and Dave was able to get his motion back and return to the gym with minimal to no pain. How did we get there? A combination of treatments involving plenty of hands-on work, loosening stiff joints and muscles, followed by precise exercises to get the shoulder moving properly and safely.

Most of the time, especially with shoulder problems, people are able to live with the pain that they are suffering with–they just don't want to. To ensure we are the right people to help you, we always recommend starting with a phone call. We love spending at least 15-20 minutes on the phone to truly understand your problem and allow you to express your concerns and ask questions. To schedule a time to talk to us on the phone, please go to https://parkerphysio.com/free-telephone-consultation.

Is There Anything Else I Can Do?

Absolutely! Ice and heat are both your friends and can be utilized to help control pain and stiffness. If your shoulder is feeling achy or painful, use ice for 15-20 minutes. If your shoulder feels stiff and you've had shoulder pain for longer than 3 days, use a heating pad or hot pack for 10-15 minutes at a time.

Another factor to consider is your resting posture. Sitting or slouching for long periods of time can cause the muscles of the neck and shoulder to tighten up. My first suggestion for posture-related issues is to avoid being in any one specific posture for too long. For every 30 minutes you spend sitting, spend a couple minutes standing up and moving around. Roll your shoulders forward and backward. Pinch your shoulder blades back and hold for a few seconds. Lift both your arms in the air and stretch (as long as it's relatively pain-free). These small things can go a long way into helping you feel better.

If you do have to sit for long periods of time (for example, working at a desk job), you want to be in good positioning. When sitting at a desk, your feet should rest on the floor, not dangling in the air. Your hips and knees should create nice 90-degree angles. You want your chair to give a bit of low back/lumbar support. Keep the upper parts of your arms down to your sides with your elbows at a 90 degree angle. Therefore your keyboard should be 8-12 inches from your body. Then keep your shoulders slightly pulled back and your ears in line with your shoulders. It should look something like this photo below.

If your office offers an ergonomic service, definitely take advantage of it so you can maintain good sitting health.

You may be wondering whether I can give any stretches or exercises, and I could give you 50 of them. But without knowing your individual condition and understanding your medical history, I would be doing you a disservice by giving you exercises that could possibly make you worse and cause you more pain. If you would like more advice and tips on shoulder pain, go to https://parkerphysio.com/shoulder-pain.

Summary

- The shoulder can do a wide variety of incredible movements, but that can also increase the risk for shoulder pain/injuries.

- Your neck and upper back (thoracic spine) play a significant role in shoulder health. Make sure your sitting and resting postures don't include rounded shoulders or a head protruding like a turtle.

- When sleeping, use a pillow and dish towels to help prop up your shoulder in a safe resting position so you aren't waking up every hour with pain.

- Be careful when lifting heavy objects with your arm outstretched from your body ("No Man's Land"), and always keep everything you lift as close to your body as possible. Side note: when driving don't reach into your backseat to grab stuff.

- A cortisone injection can help decrease inflammation and pain, but it's normally temporary (and has side effects). Always think about getting specialist help in conjunction with the injection, even if you don't have any pain.

- Don't accept arthritis as a curse; there is always something that can be done to improve your situation.

- If you work at a desk all day, make sure you are sitting with optimal alignment. If your office offers an ergonomic assessment, do it!

CHAPTER 6

Neck Pain & Headaches

Your neck has a ton of responsibility. Similar to the knee, your neck is between a rock and a hard place. It has to hold up your head, which weighs between 8-12 pounds on average, while also helping support your shoulders. First, it's important to understand your neck and shoulders are closely related. What seems like shoulder pain may actually be a neck problem. Or a neck problem could actually be a shoulder problem. This chapter will help provide you with a little more clarity on all things neck pain and headaches.

As we age, the frequency of neck pain increases, with the greatest prevalence occurring in our 50s, and it's estimated 22-70% of the population will have neck pain some time in their lives.[12] [13]

By far the most common complaint I get with necks is the overwhelming feeling of tightness in the upper traps and surrounding neck muscles. Many people believe that it's where they "carry their stress," which can be partially true but is usually not the root cause of the problem. The feeling of tightness is the effect. The cause is often a combination of factors. It's

---

[12] Miller MB. The cervical spine: physical therapy patient management utilizing current evidence. Wilmarth MA, ed. ISC 21.2.6, Current Concepts of Orthopaedic Physical Therapy. 3rd ed. La Crosse, WI: Orthopaedic Section, APTA; 2011.
[13] Cleland JA, Childs JD, McRae M, Palmer JA, Stowell T. Immediate effects of thoracic manipulation in patients with neck pain: a randomized clinical trial. Man Ther. 2005;10(2):127-135.

an old neck injury that didn't quite heal right, sleeping with two pillows instead of one, spending years at a desk staring at a computer, or looking down at the phone to text or read the newspaper every day.

You may believe these things are trivial, but the combination of them all over many years can cause a compound effect leading to neck pain, especially for those over the age of 50. Again, the average human head weighs somewhere between 8-12 pounds, which is the equivalent of a bowling ball. Picture a bowling ball balancing on a bamboo stick, which is your spinal column. Life is good when the bowling ball is balancing on a relatively straight, vertical bamboo stick. However, if you begin to let the bowling ball drift forward when you look down to text or use a laptop, then the bamboo stick, your spine, begins to bend. The further your head drifts forward, the more bending and force is placed on your spine.

While it's fine to do this occasionally, spending 8 hours in this position at work for 40 hours a week over many years can cause pain and tightness in your neck and all the muscles around it. It can also lead to horrible headaches.

I had a patient, Barbara, who came to me in her early 60s. She worked as a secretary at a dentist's office. In her free time she loved sewing, especially making quilts, and spending time with her four grandkids. Unfortunately, she suffered from severe right-sided neck pain. It started at the base of her skull and radiated down to the inside of her right shoulder blade.

Barbara told me how painful and unsafe she felt driving because she couldn't turn her head to the right side. Her pain affected her quality of sleep, and she was starting to get headaches at work. Barbara and her husband planned to work for a few more years before retiring and moving to Arizona, but her pain was beginning to jeopardize that future. She tried going to a massage therapist to work out all the tight and painful muscles but only got temporary relief. Barbara hated taking pain pills, but felt she had no other options, until a mutual friend recommended she come see me.

Barbara's situation is an increasingly common problem. I explained that the cause of her neck pain stemmed from years of sewing and sitting in front of a computer at work. We created a plan to optimize her desk and sewing setup to make sure the neck was in a safe position. Then we began working on moving the stiff joints of the upper back and neck as well as strengthening the shoulder muscles that help support the neck. Barbara was an incredible patient who was determined to get better. After a few short weeks and some mild ergonomic changes, Barbara was able to reclaim her health. To this day, she still sews without pain or discomfort and is getting closer to her plan to retire in Arizona.

Deskwork and Posture

In general, posture doesn't matter as much as you may think. Don't let the media fool you; there is no such thing as "perfect posture." The key with posture, forever and always, is to not be in one static position for an extended period of time. If you've been sitting at your computer desk for an extended period of time, stand up and move around. If you're at a standing desk and haven't moved anything but your fingertips for an hour, go for a walk. Why do many people feel so stiff in the morning? Because you've been in bed, hopefully sleeping like a log, and your joints haven't moved for 6+ hours.

If you absolutely must be in a sitting position for an extended period of time, for instance, when sitting in your car during rush hour traffic, then your sitting posture becomes much more important. Whether you are at a traditional desk or sitting in your car, the rules of good sitting remain the same. We already discussed the first step: keep your ears in line with your shoulders. You should also have some sort of small low back support. Many chairs and car seats already provide this, but if yours does not, place a folded towel between your chair and the small of your back.

Next, your torso should be upright or slightly leaning backwards. Your knees should be at a nice 90-degree angle with your feet resting comfortably on the floor. If you are driving, you shouldn't be reaching for the gas pedal and shouldn't be a mile away from your steering wheel with your arms outstretched. When in doubt, being a little bit closer to the steering wheel is better for overall alignment of your spine and neck.

If you are at your desk, keep your monitor just slightly below eye level. Also, ensure that your monitor is directly in front of you. This is vital for your neck. I have a friend, Jaime, a contractor, who came to me one day with severe neck pain. He told me he was struggling turning his head side-to-side and was nervous to drive because his neck hurt so much when trying to switch lanes or parallel park. Jamie, by trade, does a ton of manual labor and thought he must have injured it while lifting something heavy or working underneath a sink he was building.

After investigating further and asking him more questions, he told me that although he spent a ton of time building things, the majority of his time is sitting at a desk looking at a computer. When I asked about the location of his monitor, he told me he had 2 monitors but the one he spent the most time looking at was located approximately 60 degrees off to his right side.

Picture sitting at your desk with your body facing forward but your head turned to the right. Then imagine sitting in this position for hours, every single day, for months, even years. It's no wonder Jaime's neck was very unhappy and led to intense neck pain. I actually didn't do any hands-on work or give him any exercises. I just told him to move his monitor so it was directly in front of him. In one week, 100% of his pain went away.

Can I guarantee the same results for you? No, but I can promise that if you don't optimize your environment, no amount of physical therapy, massage, chiropractic, or acupuncture will be effective. You'll end up being a hamster on a wheel, cycling between short periods of pain relief followed by increased pain.

The goal is to always try to keep your ears in line with your shoulders no matter what position you're in. Improving neck positioning is that easy. For example, if you are reading or texting, stop holding your phone down by your belly button. Lift it up towards eye level. Will you look funny texting this way? Probably! But your neck will love you for it. Same thing if you like to read prior to going to bed. Personally, I love reading before falling asleep. Unfortunately, laying flat and holding my book on my stomach while looking down isn't great for my neck. Therefore, I force myself to sit upright and hold my book at eye level.

Get Some Quality Shut Eye

When sleeping at night, I always recommend using one pillow. If you want some more neck support while you sleep, grab a small dish towel and wrap it around your neck. Having this towel around your neck provides support and tells your neck muscles to relax. When these neck muscles are relaxed, the vertebrae in your neck are less compressed, which can decrease neck pain and give you better quality sleep. It should look something like the photo below.

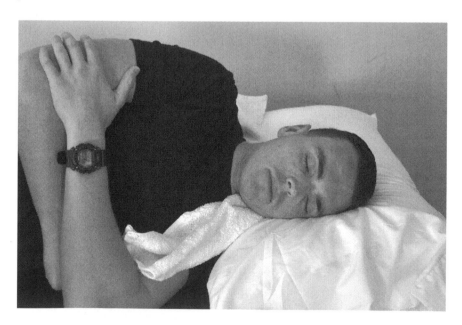

Many people ask me all the time what the best neck pillow is? There is no one-size-fits-all pillow. There are TONS of them out there, ranging from bamboo pillows to custom-fit ones. The best recommendation I can make is to try a couple different kinds. When in doubt, purchase a flatter pillow that also provides some neck support. If the pillow doesn't provide enough support, remember to try using a dish towel.

If you wake up throughout the night because of numbness or tingling in the forearm, hand, or fingers, this can be a sign the nerves around your neck are being irritated. Normally what I find is that people who have these symptoms sleep in the position below.

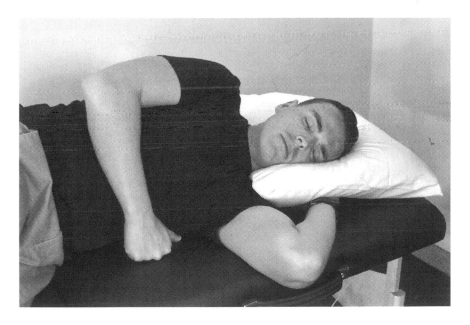

Sleeping in this position for a few hours compresses nerves in the neck which connect all the way down to your fingertips. Like an electrical wire, it can cause an uncomfortable numbness and tingling sensation, causing you to wake up. Not fun! Instead, try hugging a pillow. By hugging a pillow, you place your shoulders and neck in a friendlier position for your nerves, allowing them to breathe. Is there a good chance you throw the pillow away after an hour or so? Yup. But being in a better position, even for a few hours, will allow you to sleep better and increase your energy levels. In case you need a photo of what hugging a pillow looks like, check out the photo below.

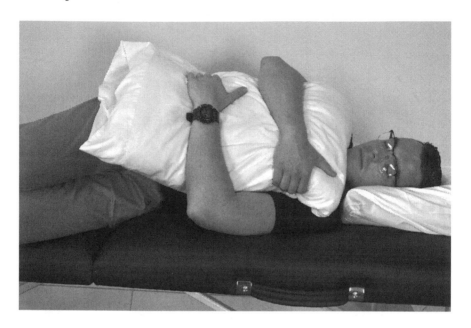

Car Accidents, Severe Neck Pain, & Whiplash

Car accidents do happen, often leading to pretty severe neck pain and tightness. Normally, the pain and tightness doesn't kick in until the day after the accident. Right after an accident, your body goes into "fight or flight" mode, and your adrenaline levels shoot up. When the adrenaline levels decrease as you go to bed that night, the muscles around the spine and neck will begin to tighten and can lead to headaches and a feeling of deep pain. These symptoms together are more commonly known as whiplash.

By the way, it's always a good idea, after being in a significant car accident and your head does a "snapping" movement backwards, to get an x-ray to rule out any kind of neck fracture. Nobody likes to wait in the ER, but having the x-ray will give you peace of mind that nothing more serious has occurred.

In regards to whiplash, the best recommendations I can give you involve what NOT to do after symptoms have set in. The first thing I want to tell you is if you don't have a neck fracture, PLEASE avoid wearing a neck brace. Although your neck will feel better in the short term, as you wear a neck brace, the muscles of the neck can begin to turn off and weaken. This can end up causing even more pain and dysfunction down the line. If you do have to wear a neck brace per physician order, try not to be in one for an extended period of time.

There was a randomized study done where a group of subjects with a whiplash injury were separated into two groups. One group of those with whiplash were told to return to their normal activities, meaning no sick leave from work and no cervical collar. The other group of those with whiplash were told to go on sick leave from work for 14 days and be immobilized with a cervical collar. At 6 months, the "act as usual" group had much better results in regards to pain, stiffness, memory, and concentration.[14] So avoid wearing that neck brace and get back to living your life!

Next up, be wary of getting any kind of massage in the first two weeks after your car accident. When a car accident occurs, your body automatically does everything it can to protect your central nervous system (aka your brain and spinal cord). Your body does this by tightening up all the muscles surrounding your skull, neck, and often your low back as the accident is occurring. Your body is pretty cool, right?

Unfortunately, these muscles tend to stay tight and stiff for weeks after the accident occurs, and when this happens, pain can come with it. So it's normal to believe that if the muscles are tight and stiff, a massage will loosen up these muscles and make you feel better. And it does...temporarily. The

---

[14] Rosenfeld M, Gunnarsson R, Borenstein P. Early intervention in whiplash associated disorders: a comparison of two treatment protocols. Spine 2000;25:1782.

day you get a massage you'll feel like you are walking on a cloud, and you'll begin to feel like your normal self again. Then the next day arrives, and you feel like you've been hit by a ton of bricks.

This happens because in the early phases of whiplash recovery, those muscles surrounding your spine like to stay in protection mode. Many times, a massage can temporarily loosen these muscles, but the body will slowly revert back to being tighter than ever. Therefore, I normally recommend waiting 2-3 months, depending on the severity of the car accident, prior to getting a massage.

In the meantime, the best thing you can do to help speed up recovery is to have a positive mindset and keep moving! Many people think they have to rest and lay in bed all day. This is never a recipe for success. Reengaging in your normal activities as soon as possible is the best solution. Take a loved one on a brisk walk for at least 10 minutes. If you are at work, be sure to take movement breaks every 20-30 minutes. If you've been standing for a while, sit for a few minutes. If you've been sitting for awhile, stand and move around. Just don't allow your body to stiffen up.

On the other end of the spectrum, if you enjoy high-intensity exercise and weightlifting, hold off until the deep ache, tightness, and headaches significantly decrease in intensity, normally around 2-3 months. You want to allow your body to heal safely, and the demands of high-intensity exercise can trigger more pain.

If you want to further speed up your recovery, go see a specialist who works with car accident victims. Someone like a physical therapist will not only help you get back to sleeping more comfortably and exercising safely but will give you the confidence and peace of mind in making the best decision for your health.

Headaches vs. Migraines

Understanding the difference between a headache and a migraine can help you make a better decision on treating the root cause of your issue. Headaches (more specifically, tension headaches) can be treated with interventions such as physical therapy. True migraines are normally more severe and tougher to diagnose, but the frequency and severity of migraines can improve with specialist help.

Symptoms of tension headaches include the following:

- Pain or stiffness at the base of the skull
- Restricted neck movement and ability to turn your head side to side
- Symptoms caused by being in one position for too long (e.g. sitting at a desk with your forward head and rounded shoulders)
- Tender or aching muscles in the shoulders
- Pain shooting down to the shoulder blade
- Difficulty finding a comfortable sleeping position

Symptoms of a migraine headache or a "migraine aura" normally consist of the following:

- Nausea
- Pain behind the eyes
- Pain in the temples
- Vomiting
- Seeing flashing lights or spots
- Extreme sensitivity to light
- Temporary loss of vision

People often tell me they have migraines and are taking migraine medications when they actually have a tension headache. The cause for tension headaches normally goes back to your resting posture. If you spend hours everyday with your head protruded forward and your upper back and shoulders in a rounded position, the joints of your neck and spine get stiff and can lead to tension headaches.

If you are suffering from true migraines, it's important to avoid your migraine triggers. These are different for each person but normally include things such as emotional anxiety, contraceptives, alcohol consumption, or menopause. Stress reduction techniques such as meditation and a warm compress can help control symptoms as well. In addition, physical therapy can also help decrease the intensity and frequency of migraines.

If you would like a more in depth look with even more tips and advice on neck pain and headaches, download them at www.parkephysio.com/neck-pain

Summary

- Years of looking down while reading and letting your head protrude forward like a turtle when using the computer can eventually lead to neck pain, headaches, and tightness of the upper traps.

- Perfect posture doesn't exist; the goal is to have frequent breaks where you can stand up and move around. If you are required to sit for long periods of time at work or in your car, be sure to:

  - Keep your ears in line with your shoulders
  - Trunk at 90 degrees or your chair slightly leaning backwards with good lumbar support
  - Make sure your feet can easily rest on the ground
  - Keep your computer screen directly in front of you, just below eye level

- When sleeping, use a dish towel to provide support for your neck and keep your spine in good alignment. Please use ONE pillow under your head.

- After a car accident, try to resume your regular life activities and be careful of getting a massage or returning to high-intensity exercise too soon. Better yet, go see a physical therapist to help you get more guidance and recover more quickly.

- Understand the difference between headaches and migraines. Know both can improve significantly with the right relaxation techniques and help from a professional.

CHAPTER 7

Nutrition & Fitness

We can't talk about health unless we discuss nutrition and fitness. Both are vital to living an active and healthy life. Please notice that I used the term "nutrition" and not "diet." I hate the word diet because it implies that it's temporary. Diets tend to fail, but don't worry if you're someone who has struggled with staying consistent with good nutrition. This information will help you head in the right direction. The goal isn't to jump from diet to diet but to consistently make good quality food choices by understanding how to develop good habits and discipline.

"You are what you eat" is probably a phrase you've heard thousands of times. It is 100% true. You can't put low-quality fuel in a Ferrari and expect it to run at full capacity. I only understand these nutrition principles because I struggled with weight throughout my youth and all the way through college. I tried all kinds of diets, including Paleo, Atkins, Keto, intermittent fasting, vegetarian, etc. Each of them worked, but my results were always temporary. The weight kept coming back. Each time I failed, I felt worse about myself, which led to more eating and more weight gain. I got to a point of such self disgust that lead to the next new fad diet. It was a vicious cycle, and my self esteem suffered because of it. This story may sound familiar to many of you.

I'm not here to bad mouth any specific diet, because many of you reading this may have gotten positive results with one that I attempted. I am also not here to tell you which diet or style of eating is best. There are much better resources you can read to choose what's right for you. Most of you already know HOW to eat better, but the act of actually doing it day in and day out is forever and always the challenge. That's what we are going to dive into.

I was finally able to lose the weight and keep it off by understanding my unhealthy triggers and how to develop better habits. You can absolutely sustain a healthier lifestyle, but first you must set yourself up for success.

To get started, remove all distractions and grab a pen and paper (or my personal favorite, a whiteboard). Think back to times your previous attempts at healthier eating failed. Was it after you were assigned a stressful project at work? Maybe it happened after you went out to eat with family at a restaurant such as Claim Jumper. Maybe after a long day you got home and didn't have any healthy food prepared, so you just grabbed In-N-Out. Whatever it is, don't spend time judging yourself for past failures. Just write.

Now look at your paper or whiteboard. Notice any patterns? For myself, I recognized a few. First, I would eat a ton of chocolate chip cookies (aka my kryptonite) the night before an important exam. Having an exam always gave me anxiety, and chocolate chip cookies would give me a temporary sense of comfort, quickly followed by an upset stomach and a feeling of guilt. Anxiety and stress were a trigger for me to eat unhealthy and even worse, after the exam was over I "celebrated" by eating something else I shouldn't, maybe a cheeseburger and french fries, stopping any progress I was making towards eating healthy and losing weight. I never really understood why I did this prior to exams until doing this writing exercise, so please make sure you do it right now!

Another trigger of mine was if I came home at the end of the day and didn't already have healthy food premade in the fridge, I would go out and eat garbage. It would be the end of the day, and I would feel exhausted with zero desire to do any cooking. Personally, I have never really enjoyed the act of cooking, so I always preferred to go out and grab something fast. The emotional fatigue (and lack of preparation) led me to eat stuff I know I wasn't supposed to. The feeling of guilt would quickly return because I didn't follow my new diet to perfection. So of course I would quit eating healthy altogether, and the pounds would come back with a vengeance.

Recognizing your own patterns will allow you to better prepare so that when you do go out and decide to eat some ice cream or a big steak with potatoes, you have a plan to get back on track.

Let's say you have decided to make a lifestyle change to eating healthy consistently and workout. You eat salads, healthy fats, good proteins, everything you're supposed to eat in addition to finishing all your workouts. You also love ice cream, so you decide you'll have one "cheat" meal on Saturday night and keep a half gallon in the freezer to reward yourself for eating healthy. Your week starts strong, but then Friday rolls around.

You've had a long, productive week, and you finally get home to kick your feet up on the couch. In the back of your head lurks the thought of ice cream. You begin to tell yourself, "I've worked out and eaten healthy all week, so it won't hurt to have a little ice cream tonight then have my cheat meal tomorrow." You grab the half gallon and what was supposed to be a couple bites quickly turns into an empty carton and you feeling like Chunk from the movie Goonies.

My question is, why even have the half gallon of ice cream in your house in the first place? If you know you are going to have one cheat meal (or dessert) on Saturday, then go out and buy ONE serving of ice cream at your favorite ice cream shop. Eliminate the necessity of exercising self control by not having the option to eat the ice cream at all.

Using myself as an example, the first thing I did was I made sure to not have any unhealthy food inside my house. More specifically, no cookies.

Each of us only has so much self control prior to giving in to indulgences. I was fine throughout the day, but as the test days got closer, I would eat an entire box of Oreos in one sitting. How did I eliminate this problem? I stopped buying cookies. If it's not in my house, I don't have to use any self control not to eat it. The cookies no longer stared me in the face, so I didn't have to constantly choose not to eat them.

It's incredibly difficult to stop a habit cold turkey. It's much easier to replace a bad habit with a good one. When anxiety from an upcoming test began and the craving for cookies started, I decided I would go for a brisk walk instead. I argue that walking is one of the best forms of exercise in existence. You get your body moving, the heart rate slightly raised, and get your brain working more optimally...a win, win, win. Maybe you always eat something unhealthy when there is a deadline at work or after you get in an argument with a loved one. Instead of using unhealthy food, try something different and go for a walk. You'll feel great afterwards, and it improved my test scores in school.

The other thing that you can do to minimize urges and sustain healthy eating is to do meal prep one or two times per week. We all have to make hundreds of decisions per day, from picking out what we are going to wear to what kind of gas we are going to put in our cars. Making these decisions uses up brain power, and the end of the day is normally when we are at our weakest. One of my favorite phrases used by my friend Rick Noda of T3 Body and by the British Army is known as the 7 P's, "Prior Proper Planning Prevents Piss Poor Performance."

Taking time one day per week to write down what you're going to make and what groceries are needed goes a long way to reaching weight loss and healthy eating goals. Then you can spend a couple hours (preferably on Sunday) to make your meals and have them ready to go. Having food ready after a long day of running errands or working is incredibly helpful. Personally, I spend a couple hours on Sunday and Wednesday baking a bunch of chicken and veggies and placing them in individual containers for consumption. Many people I know also love using a crockpot, because you can create really creative (and yummy) dishes that cook while you are at work!

Food, Inflammation, and Pain

Once we've figured out the emotions surrounding our eating habits and have created a plan to stick to sustained healthy eating, we can begin to get a bit more granular with the types of foods to incorporate into our daily lives. One of the biggest movements in nutrition today is decreasing inflammation in the body. Why is that important? It is said that cardiovascular disease, cancer, and diabetes account for almost 70% of all deaths in the United States, and all these diseases share inflammation as a common link.[15] Diets that increase inflammation are normally high in refined starches, sugar, saturated and trans-fats while being low in omega-3 fatty acids, natural antioxidants, and fibers from fruits, vegetables, and whole grains.[16]

If you are suffering from back, neck, shoulder, or knee pain, then you will want to do everything you can to reduce inflammation in the body and promote healing. You already know what foods you shouldn't be eating; candy, cookies, frozen meals, etc. All increase inflammation, and you should always start by cutting these things out first.

The foods that are high in omega-3 fatty acids, fiber, and whole grains are also known as Superfoods. They are rich in natural anti-inflammatories, and consuming them daily can help your body with recovery. Don't try to add everything I list here. Just add one or two at a time and build from there. Be aware that many of these you can't eat with certain styles of eating such as Keto, Paleo, or vegetarianism, but incorporate what you can.

---

[15] Aggarwal BB, Shishodia S, Sandur SK, Pandey MK, Sethi G. Inflammation and cancer: How hot is the link? Biochem Pharmacol. 2006;72:1605–21.

[16] Giugliano D, Ceriello A, Esposito K. The effects of diet on inflammation - Emphasis on the metabolic syndrome. J Am Coll Cardiol. 2006;48:677–85.

Herbs & Spices

- Garlic
- Ginger
- Turmeric
- Cinnamon
- Cayenne Pepper
- Sage
- Rosemary

Green, Leafy Vegetables

- Kale
- Spinach
- Collared Greens
- Arugula

Berries

- Blueberries
- Raspberries
- Strawberries
- Cranberries

Legumes

- Lentils
- Kidney Beans
- Black Beans
- Peas

Nuts & Seeds

- Almonds
- Pecans
- Pistachios
- Walnuts
- Cashews
- Brazil Nuts
- Macadamia Nuts
- Sunflower Seeds
- Pumpkin Seeds
- Chia Seeds
- Flax Seeds
- Hemp Seeds

Proteins

- Salmon
- Eggs

Miscellaneous

- Avocado
- Artichokes
- Sweet Potatoes
- Seaweed
- Dark Chocolate (in small amounts!)

Teas

- Green Tea
- Lemongrass Tea
- Cinnamon Tea

I often have patients ask me what other supplements to take to help improve recover from pain and injury. The popular ones for joint health include fish oil, chondroitin, and type-II collagen. The honest truth is I would be less concerned with the supplements and more focused on the actual food you're eating.

If you want to learn more about certain supplements, check out Examine.com. They have the largest database of nutrition and supplement research available. They are not affiliated with any supplement or food company and are independently funded, so all their recommendations are as unbiased and science-based as possible. No gimmicky marketing or commercials with over the top testimonials. Just facts. As their website says, "We're not here to tell you what to do. Instead, we simply tell you what the evidence says. And in cases where the research is mixed, we make that clear too." I can't recommend their website enough when it comes to anything related to supplements.

Don't Be "Watered Down"

Drink more water! In my opinion, this is by far the quickest and easiest way to improve your health. Our bodies are almost entirely made up of water, and the benefits of water are countless. According to Harvard Health, some of the benefits of water include: carrying nutrients and oxygen to your cells, flushing bacteria from your bladder, helping with digestion, preventing constipation, stabilizing heart rate, improving blood pressure, cushioning your joints, protecting organs, and regulating body temperature.

Unfortunately, many of us aren't getting enough water to drink, especially older adults. Why not? Research suggests one reason is that older adults don't sense thirst as much as they did when they were younger.[17] This can be a serious problem if you are using a medication that may cause fluid

---

[17] Kenney, W. Larry, and Percy Chiu. "Influence of age on thirst and fluid intake." *Medicine and science in sports and exercise* 33.9 (2001): 1524-1532.

loss, such as a diuretic. When I make the recommendation to drink more water to patients, they normally ask, "How much?" The old school way was to drink eight 8-oz glasses of water, but research coming out says some people may need more or less than the standard 64 ounces of water. Medications, exercise, sex, and environment can all influence the exact you amount you need.

Don't base how much water you should drink by thirst, because as I mentioned, your sense of thirst decreases as you age. To drink enough water, monitor the color of your urine. The color determines how hydrated you are, the lighter the better. If your urine is a darker yellow, you are more than likely dehydrated and need to increase your water intake.

The other recommendation I make is to drink a couple glasses of water when you first wake up, and then carry a LARGE water bottle with you throughout the day. I constantly see people with small 12-24 ounce water bottles, which is great, but too often people don't refill the bottles throughout the day. If you start your day by carrying a larger water bottle that holds 48 to 64 ounces of water, you increase your chances of drinking more.

Fitness

The second component of this chapter is fitness. I choose the word fitness instead of exercise because exercise can be misinterpreted and is a bit too general. The term fitness is defined by the Center for Disease Control and Prevention (CDC) as "the ability to carry out daily tasks with vigor and alertness, without undue fatigue, and with ample energy to enjoy leisure-time pursuits and respond to emergencies." This includes cardiovascular fitness, muscular endurance, muscular strength, flexibility, balance, speed, etc.

Since you are reading this book, you are someone who values their health and understands the benefits of fitness and consistent exercise. Too often

I see people, especially over the age of 50, who are making one of the following 3 mistakes:

1. Not exercising enough (or at all)
2. Not exercising with enough intensity
3. Only doing one type of exercise

Not Exercising Enough (Or At All)

This is probably the most common and (theoretically) the easiest to fix. Everyone wants to exercise and start on the path to being fit, but they either don't know where to start or are currently struggling with some sort of lingering pain which limits their activity.

If you don't know where to start and don't like going to a traditional gym, I recommend you start with walking. Even if you suffer from back pain and can only walk for 10-15 minutes prior to pain setting in, you should still go for walks. Just incorporate periodic sit breaks before the pain starts. Getting a Fitbit is a wonderful way to track how many steps you take per day, and challenging a loved one is an even better way to ensure you take enough steps.

The key is to not overcomplicate it. Just get out and walk. I normally advise creating a routine and doing it at the same time every day. Whether it's first thing in the morning or right after work with a significant other, you have to make it non-negotiable. No matter what, it has to get done! Create a steadfast rule for yourself that you are going to walk (or do some sort of exercise) every single day, rain or shine. If you don't trust yourself, tell somebody your goal and make them hold you accountable. This is your health and your life; you can do this!

After you start building momentum, you'll want to walk further. Then start incorporating different types of exercise. Maybe ride a bike, start running, or go to a bootcamp class. Use the momentum to your advantage and get moving!

If you suffer with ongoing pain, stiffness, or injuries, try physical therapy. There is no faster way to get back to living an active life doing the things you love than with the help and guidance of a certified physical therapist.

If you would like more information on recovering from the most common sports and running injuries, be sure to check out "**The Ultimate Guide To The Most Common Running & Sports Injuries: Rehab Like The Pros And Get Back To Your Favorite Sport!**" at https://parkerphysio. com/sports-running-injury/

Not Exercising With Enough Intensity

You may have been in a gym and have seen an older gentleman (or two) sitting on an exercise bike holding up a newspaper who is kind of, sort of pedaling. He sits there for approximately 30 minutes, followed by talking to his buddy for 30 minutes, and then heads home. He probably does this 5-6 days per week and brags about how often he works out to everybody he possibly can. Please don't be that guy (or gal)!

It's great that he makes an effort to go to the gym, but glorified sitting is not the key to becoming fit and healthy. Let's talk about ways to safely improve your exercise intensity. But please make sure to check with your physician if you have any current or previous cardiovascular issues before following any of these recommendations.

First, you need to get that heart rate up. What's the ideal heart rate when exercising? To find your maximum heart rate, a good guideline is to do 220 minus your age. So if you're 50 years old, your max heart rate would be 170 beats per minute (bpm). The rule is you want to be between 65-85% of your maximum heart rate. So 65-85% of 170 bpm you want to be somewhere between 110 and 145 beats per minute. Yes, you should be sweating, and yes, you should be breathing hard.

The best way to measure your heart rate is to purchase a heart rate monitor. The goal is to spend 30-40 minutes in your ideal heart rate zone after a proper warmup. If you do this 4-5 days per week, your life will improve across the board. The physical and cognitive benefits are numerous, and it can change your outlook on life. Do the physical activity you love the most, whether it's tennis, running, or swimming.

Make sure to perform a nice warm-up and cooldown before and after exercising. Not doing these things often leads to pain and injuries, which will slow you down from reaching your health and fitness goals. If you want to learn more about how to safely perform a proper warm-up or cooldown, as well as other health tips, go to https://parkerphysio.com/blog and subscribe to our weekly updates.

Only Doing One Kind Of Exercise

The last mistake I see frequently are from the avid runners, swimmers, cyclists, tennis players, etc. They are die hard about a specific sport, and they do that activity four, five, or six days a week. If this sounds like you, then first let me tell you, "Congratulations, and keep being AWESOME!" You are getting that heart rate up and maintaining good physical fitness. I love working with people that actively value and take care of their health. What I want to bring to your attention is that doing one specific type of exercises with repetitive motion can take a negative toll on your body and joint health.

For example, when you run for miles and miles, you put excess stress on the knee joints. When you play tennis and overhand serve repeatedly, you put a ton of stress on the shoulder joint. If you like rowing, it's a large amount of stress on the joints of the low back. This begins to take a toll as you pass the age of 50, and it commonly leads to pain and injuries. To improve joint health, it's important as you age to incorporate something called movement variability.

Movement variability, simply put, is doing different forms of exercise. If you love running 5-6 days per week, try instead to run 2-3 days per week and swim 2-3 days per week. Swimming is great because there isn't any hard impact on your joints. If you love weightlifting, make sure you incorporate some yoga and flexibility work. You get the idea. Just make sure you are mixing it up. Remember, fitness incorporates muscular strength, muscular endurance, cardiovascular endurance, flexibility, and balance. The more of those things you incorporate into your fitness regimen the better!

Summary

- You already know HOW to eat healthy, but the action of eating healthy is what's hard. Instead of worrying what diet to choose, focus on what emotional triggers lead you to eating unhealthy food

- We all only have so much self control, so remove unhealthy foods from your house and prepare healthy meals in advance so you can minimize temptation

- When trying to stop a bad habit, try to substitute it with a better, healthier habit

- Inflammation in the body leads to a series of terrible diseases, so be sure you are minimizing sugar and processed food and incorporate more Superfoods

- If you want to try a certain supplement, talk to your physician and check Examine.com to see if there is academic research that supports what the supplement claims to do

- When it comes to fitness, be sure to exercise consistently with appropriate intensity and to include some variability in your routine

CHAPTER 8

Wellness, Health, & Everything Else

S o far we have discussed different parts of the human body, why certain aches and pains occur, and ways to combat them. We also talked about nutrition and fitness. This chapter will be more of a smorgasbord of vital health topics that help with healing and can drastically improve the quality of your life. In fact, each section of this chapter could be its own book, but I'm going to give you the highlights.

First, a disclaimer. There is a large amount of information in this chapter. Please don't be overwhelmed or feel the need to do everything I mention. If you do just ONE thing from this chapter, you'll be doing better than the majority of people out there!

Mental Wellness & Stress

I'll start with a story. Before starting my business and understanding the importance of mental health and stress, my days would look like the following. The alarm on my phone would go off. I'd hit snooze a couple times and tell myself, "PLEASE just a few more minutes!" After the third snooze button, I'd roll over, grab my phone, and then check my Facebook and Instagram to see what the world was up to.

After mindlessly scrolling through social media, I would scan my email inbox, which contained a combination of junk and requests from work.

"Ugggh!" (Side note: I hate having the red notification bubble next to my apps on my phone. So yes, I read all my emails, and I might be a bit OCD). Finally, I would hop a quick shower and be off to the office, barely making it on time. Not a great way to start the day. After work, it was home for dinner and back to scrolling my phone while watching the news or Netflix. This would then lead to me going to bed way too late, starting the whole cycle over again.

Sound familiar?

Although technology keeps advancing and is allegedly supposed to make our lives easier, I would argue the exact opposite. We have never been more plugged in. From the time we wake up to the time we go to bed, we are constantly bombarded by emails, text messages, and notifications. Our bosses and clients want immediate replies. Kids and grandkids need to get picked up and dropped off for school, sports, and extracurricular activities. Trying to squeeze in a workout and eating healthy becomes a hassle because of the time commitment needed. This can cause a feeling of stress, the feeling that you are always busy, the feeling that you don't have true control over your day.

How do you take back your day and improve the overall quality of your life? Before we take a closer look at my story, it's important to understand cause versus effect. Running out of gas and being stranded on the freeway is an effect. The cause was not filling up the gas tank when the gas light came on.

My old feelings of stress and being overwhelmed were an effect. What was the cause? Many people would say it's how I started my day by hitting the snooze button repeatedly. But I would argue that was still an effect. The actual cause goes back to the night before, mindlessly scrolling my phone while watching the news or Netflix, pushing my bedtime later and later. This was the first thing I had to eliminate in order to take back control.

I'll talk more about optimizing sleep in the next section, but getting 7-8 hours of shut-eye a night is vital for good health.

Was getting rid of the news and Netflix while scrolling through my phone easy? Hell no! But the effect of getting quality sleep will make you feel like Superman or Wonder Woman the next day. It gives you the energy to hit the ground running.

When waking up, the best recommendation I can make is to create a morning routine. The power of a morning routine will help improve your mood and give you a sense of control over your life, something which doesn't happen when you sleep for 4 hours and have to hammer the snooze button. What makes a good morning routine? I'll tell you mine to give you some ideas of things you can do.

Upon waking up, I immediately make my bed put on some coffee, because I'm a coffee addict. While the coffee is brewing, I'll do a little bit of stretching for 3-5 minutes. When it's done, I grab my coffee and meditate for 10 minutes. I also review my daily planner, seeing what tasks I need to get done that day, and I write down the 3-5 things that I'm grateful for. It may be a person from my past, a material possession, my health, etc. Then I work out for 45-60 minutes, normally a combination of weightlifting and running. I come back, shower, and start my day.

It helps to understand the reasoning behind all of these activities. Making my bed gives me the feeling that I accomplished a task. Although a small task, it's all about developing momentum for the day. The coffee, in combination with a bit of stretching, gives me a bit more energy, which also adds to the momentum.

Afterward, meditating for 10 minutes is arguably the most important part of my morning routine. Meditation once had a stigma that it required a "spiritual awakening" or "finding your center." And meditation can be that if you so choose, but the most powerful benefit for meditation is a better understanding of your own thought processes. Most of us spend so much time worrying about things that happened in the past or anxious about what might happen in the future. Meditation can give you the mindfulness to better recognize these thought processes and focus on the present.

Meditation has recently exploded in popularity. Everyone from CEOs to famous actors have made this a daily habit. Not to mention there is tons of research showing people who meditate have lower blood pressure, decreased cortisol (stress) levels, and are overall more happy.[18]

If you've never meditated before but want to start practicing, there are plenty of resources available. I strongly recommend starting with guided meditation. Guided meditation is when someone coaches you through the process of meditation, what you should focus on, what you shouldn't focus on, etc. Some apps I highly recommend are Headspace (free), Calm (free), and my personal favorite, Waking Up (paid). Each of these have guided meditations that will help you through the process.

It may be difficult when you first start. Many days you'll feel like you were zoned out and not paying attention at all. But if you keep at it and spend just 5 minutes practicing a day, you will begin to feel an incredible change in your life!

Continuing on in the morning routine, writing down 3-5 people or things you're grateful for is an awesome exercise. The process of thinking about people and things you're grateful for will immediately improve your mood. You'll begin to stop worrying about the trivial things in life and focus on the people that truly matter, those who have always loved and supported everything you do. Whether that be a significant other, parents, kids, grandkids, or an influential mentor, it doesn't matter.

---

[18] Grossman, Paul, et al. "Mindfulness-based stress reduction and health benefits: A meta-analysis." *Journal of psychosomatic research* 57.1 (2004): 35-43.

Expressing gratitude for them on a piece of paper with the reasons why you are grateful for them can vastly improve your overall happiness. Trust me, you can't be grateful and anxious at the same time. You can't be grateful and stressed at the same time. I can't recommend doing this enough!

Moving along, the daily task list helps keep my day organized. I am a firm believer that using an old school planner and a pen is best. Something about physically writing things out, at least for me, helps organize my thoughts and actions better compared to using a phone or tablet. Using the planner, you can more easily figure out whether you are truly working towards your goals or working on minutia.

Ask yourself everyday whether the tasks you are working on today are going to get you closer to your one-year, five-year, ten-year goals? If you don't have goals written down, start there! What do you want to achieve personally in one year? Do you want to learn a new instrument? Maybe learn a new language? What do you want to achieve in your career? Maybe you want to retire soon? What do you need to do financially to achieve that? Then you can work backwards to break it up into monthly, weekly, and daily goals.

What about socially? Maybe you want to spend one day a week doing a fun activity with the kids or grandkids. Or you want to commit one night a week to having a date night with your significant other.

Writing down all your goals may sound stressful at first, but doing it will allow you to design the life you want to live. Many times, we get sucked into "putting out fires," answering emails, talking to clients on the phone, running errands, etc. and don't take the time to focus on the bigger picture of where we want to go.

Finally, I work out for 45-60 minutes. I like to run and lift weights. Maybe you like to swim, walk, or do bootcamp classes. Whatever it is, just get the heart rate pumping and remember the principles I talked about in the last chapter.

Do you have to do all these things? Of course not. I don't get to all of them every single day, but if I can do at least two or three from that list, I consider that day a win. I also wouldn't recommend trying to do all these at once. Pick one and try it for a month. Building a habit takes somewhere between 21-66 days, according to research.[19] So don't overstretch yourself. Just try to be 1% better than yesterday.

Also, I would strongly recommend trying to avoid your phone at all costs in the morning. Getting sucked into social media and emails as soon as you wake up is not a great way to start the day. I like to use the out of sight out of mind method. If I can't see my phone, I can't be tempted to use it. So I keep it in the kitchen until my morning routine is over.

The Lost Art Of Sleep

A third of our life is spent sleeping, yet most of us never take the time to optimize the quality of our sleep. To meet life's demands, we continue to sacrifice sleep in order to get more stuff done, and that can take a negative toll on our health. Getting a good night's rest has countless benefits. Mentally, sleep improves energy, mood, alertness, and memory. Physically, sleep helps every tissue and system in your body, including stress hormones, growth hormones, your immune system, appetite, breathing, and cardiovascular health (to name a few). Therefore, getting quality shut-eye is imperative to recovering from injuries and chronic pain. It's something I consistently stress to my patients early on in the rehab process. The ones who practice these things tend to get the best results.

---

[19] Lally, Phillippa, et al. "How are habits formed: Modelling habit formation in the real world." *European journal of social psychology* 40.6 (2010): 998-1009.

On the other side of the coin, by some estimates sleep deprivation affects approximately 70 million Americans of all ages. A lack of sleep has been shown to increase the risk for depression, diabetes, cancer, and obesity. A study done in *Occupational and Environmental Medicine* showed sleep deprived subjects have slower responsiveness similar to those that are intoxicated.[20] Another study done in *The Journal of Pediatric Orthopaedics* linked adolescents who are chronically sleep-deprived have a higher risk for suffering a musculoskeletal injury.[21]

EVERYTHING health-related comes back to sleep and the quality of sleep. In fact, athletes such as Serena WIlliams, Lebron James, Roger Federer, Maria Sharapova, and Usain Bolt will sleep 10-12 hours a day!

How can you begin to optimize your sleep? Great question. Let's dive in!

The first thing may be common sense, but it's important. Drinking caffeine close to bedtime can be detrimental to your sleep quality. If you love caffeine like myself (I'm a big coffee guy), make sure you aren't drinking any coffee or caffcine after 2 pm. This will give your body time to shut down appropriately when it gets closer to bedtime.

Speaking of drinking, I would also shy away from drinking too much wine or alcohol. Yes, the antioxidants in wine are good for you, but as soon as you cross the one to two glass threshold, you begin to risk not getting to the REM sleep cycle (the most important cycle of sleep).

Continuing on our list of things to avoid, minimizing nighttime "blue light" exposure is another critical component to awesome sleep. What is

---

[20] Williamson, Ann M., and Anne-Marie Feyer. "Moderate sleep deprivation produces impairments in cognitive and motor performance equivalent to legally prescribed levels of alcohol intoxication." *Occupational and environmental medicine* 57.10 (2000): 649-655.

[21] Milewski, Matthew D., et al. "Chronic lack of sleep is associated with increased sports injuries in adolescent athletes." *Journal of Pediatric Orthopaedics* 34.2 (2014): 129-133.

blue light? Look at a rainbow and you'll notice it consists of red, orange, yellow, green, indigo, violet, and blue colors. Sunlight is the combination of all these colors to create a white light. Each of these colors have different wavelengths and different amounts of energy. Blue light has shorter wavelengths and higher energy.

Sunlight (and blue light) are great for you during the day. It enhances mood, reaction time, and attention. However, basking in blue light at night can be damaging to our internal biological clock, otherwise known as our circadian rhythm. It tricks our brain and our body into thinking that the sun is still up, not allowing us to shutdown for a good night's rest. Blue light is emitted from our cell phones, laptops, TVs, and LED light bulbs.

Fortunately, there are many ways to decrease your nighttime blue light exposure. The easiest is to start by setting a "reverse" alarm clock for about 30-60 minutes before bed. This alarm will alert you to start turning off electronics, including televisions, laptops, and cell phone screens, to get ready for bed. I also recommend turning all your electronics to "night shift" mode. For you iPhone users, go to "Settings," tap "Display & Brightness," then "Night Shift" to automatically shift the colors of your phone to the warmer end of the spectrum. I would schedule it from "Sunset to Sunrise." Laptops have the same capability. If you are a Mac user, you can go to the app store and download a free program called "f.lux" to turn on the same settings.

If you want to get extra fancy, purchase a pair of blue light-blocking glasses to wear during the evening. The glasses filter out blue light from your laptops, lights, cell phones, and other technology so you can increase your melatonin production. I don't have any specific company recommendations, but I do have a pair of blue light-blocking glasses from Felix Gray that I love.

Speaking of melatonin, it's a hormone that is naturally produced by your body. When it's dark out, your body secretes increased melatonin. You can also take this as a supplement that normally comes in pill form to aid in sleep. However, before running to the drug store to buy melatonin, be sure to talk to your physician and pharmacist about the proper ways to take it. Another supplement that is great for sleep is magnesium. There are many different forms of magnesium to help with different body functions, but the magnesium shown to help with sleep is called magnesium citrate.

Again, please do not take any supplements without talking to your physician first. If you want more natural sleep supplements, try drinking a cup of chamomile or lavender tea, which you can buy at any grocery store.

How else can you optimize sleep? Go to bed at the same time every night and wake up at the same time every day (yes, weekends too). This allows your body's internal biological clock or circadian rhythm to stabilize and allows you to feel more wakeful during the day and more sleepy at night. Sleeping in on the weekends may feel nice, but it can actually make you more tired and lethargic when you have to wake up earlier during the week.

When shutting it down for the day, having a regular routine is always best. Begin by shutting off all technology. In fact, I charge my cell phone in the kitchen to ensure I am not tempted to stare at the screen while trying to get a good night's rest. My friends and patients always ask how I can do that? What if there is an emergency? I have been doing it for almost 5 years and have never had any issues, although I keep my ringtone set on loud, just in case.

After your reverse alarm clock goes off and technology is put away, I love to read for 15 or 20 minutes. Preferably something personal development-related to help prepare my mind for positive dreams. After reading, I do a brain dump. I get out a sheet of paper and begin to recap my day. What went well? What can I improve? What is currently causing me stress and what can I do to eliminate it? Good or bad, just get it all out on the paper. This helps clear the mind, which can accelerate your ability to fall asleep. Afterward, I brush my teeth and officially go to bed.

Your routine doesn't have to go exactly like this. This is just what works for me. You can change the order. You can do some foam rolling. Or give your significant other your undivided attention and recap each other's day. Whatever it is, just make it a consistent routine at the same time every night.

Now let's talk about your bedroom. We have already discussed the negative effects of blue light, and when it comes to sleeping, the darker your room the better. Your room should be a cave with no light seeping in. Blackout curtains are great. I would also consider blocking any little red or white lights coming from your television or laptop. If you are someone who likes falling asleep to your television, PLEASE put on a sleep timer.

You also want your bedroom to be relatively cool in temperature. Somewhere between 66 and 68 degrees is ideal. Depending on where you live in the country, you'll want to adjust accordingly. The cooler temperatures while sleeping helps improve your circadian rhythms.

A few other miscellaneous notes. Many people are raving about weighted blankets. The theory behind these blankets goes back to when we were infants. As an infant, when we cry or are upset, we are held tight by our parents or swaddled in a blanket. The pressure applied from our parents' arms or a swaddle blanket decreases our sensory output, allowing us to calm down and, more importantly, stop crying.

The weighted blanket companies have proposed that they help decrease stress and anxiety. There really isn't any academic research to defend these claims (yet), but I have patients who absolutely love their weighted blankets and tell me they literally "sleep like a baby."

I have not personally used one of these before, but I plan on experimenting with them in the near future. If you are going to buy one, it's recommended to get one that is approximately 10% of your body weight.

The other note I have is about white noise. White noise is a noise that contains every frequency a human can hear. White noise is utilized to help drown out any background noise that may come about while you're trying to sleep, such as a noisy neighbor or a cat meowing. A fan can produce a nice white noise, and there are several different phone apps that can as well. Is this a necessity? No. But it is another tool you can use to improve sleep quality, especially if you're a poor sleeper.

Finally, in regards to sleep is the power of naps. Not everyone reading this may be able to make naps happen due to family or work obligations, but short naps can definitely give you a significant boost of energy and brain power if utilized correctly. Naps should only last 20-30 minutes. No more, no less. The best time is usually between 1 and 4 pm. If these naps last any longer than 30 minutes, you risk the dreaded "grogginess" feeling. Studies have also shown that these power naps are more powerful than an afternoon cup of coffee when it comes to motor skills, memory, and learning ability.[22] So if you have the ability to take the occasional power nap...do it!

Totally Random (but Helpful) Tidbits

Everybody Poops

Have you ever had difficulty going to the restroom? Maybe you have difficulty with hemorrhoids or constipation? If that sounds like you, I would strongly consider getting something called a Squatty Potty®. In our Western culture, using a traditional toilet and sitting at a 90-degree angle isn't optimal for going #2. When sitting, we are partially blocking our colon, which makes elimination difficult. Our bodies are designed to poop in a squatting position. While in a squat, the colon opens up and your rectum can relax. No straining or significant pushing needed.

---

[22] Brooks, Amber, and Leon Lack. "A brief afternoon nap following nocturnal sleep restriction: which nap duration is most recuperative?." *Sleep* 29.6 (2006): 831-840.

That is where the Squatty Potty® comes in. It's a company that makes foot stools to place under your feet while going #2. The stool lifts your legs up and puts you more into a squatting position. If you don't want to buy the Squatty Potty®, you can just put a few books underneath your feet instead. Either way, your pooping experience will SIGNIFICANTLY improve when your legs are elevated, and you get closer to a true squat position.

Pick The Safest Home Possible

Are you close to retirement and looking to move? Maybe you want to move to a new state to avoid the California taxes and cost of living, or maybe you're helping your parent or grandparent pick a new home. Here are a few things to look for when picking your new residence. After you turn 65, the last thing you want to do is suffer from a fall. In 2016, it was reported that 30,000 people over the age of 65 died as a result of a fall. So let's minimize the risk of this ever happening to you!

First, pick a one-story home or a bottom floor apartment. As you continue to age, stairs become more difficult to navigate, and there is always a risk of slipping or falling. Eliminate the risk by staying in a single-story residence. If you do have stairs, make sure there is a sturdy railing to hold onto as your go up or down.

Next, walk-in showers are always more favorable than those with a shower/bathtub combo. Stepping in and out of a bathtub in order to shower increases your risk for falling, and it unfortunately happens all the time. The walk-in shower eliminates this risk. Grab bars and somewhere to sit inside of your shower are also huge bonuses.

The last thing I recommend is to remove ALL throw rugs! Throw rugs move, so they have the potential to slide out from underneath you. This immediately puts you at a significant fall risk. Please get rid of them!

If you are concerned about yourself or a loved one falling due to weakness or poor balance, consider seeing a specialist physical therapist. They will be able to determine any deficits you may have by assessing your strength, checking for any nerve issues, and developing a customized plan to decrease the risk of falls.

Summary

- Develop a morning routine to get your day started on the right foot and help manage your stress. This might include:

  - Practicing gratitude
  - Meditation
  - 45-60 minutes of exercise
  - Using a daily planner to discover what tasks need to get done to achieve your goals
  - Avoiding your cell phone to focus on the things that truly matter

- Optimize sleep by decreasing your screen time prior to bedtime. Keep your room dark and cool while minimizing all light (especially blue light) so you can get a good night's rest. When needed, a 20-30 minute power nap in the afternoon is a great tool to re-energize you.

- If you want to poop more efficiently, think about purchasing a Squatty Potty®.

- When you are deciding on a residence, consider choosing a single-story home with a walk-in shower and no throw rugs to decrease your risk of falling.

- When in doubt, see a specialist physical therapist.

CHAPTER 9

Finding The Right Healthcare Provider (And FAQ's)

H as our healthcare system ever let you or a loved one down in your past? Do you hate calling to make a doctor's appointment or getting a prescription refilled because of long wait times and talking to an automated robot who can't understand you?

Maybe you were trying to tell a physician or another healthcare provider something but you know they weren't really listening. Or you were expecting to talk to a physician or physical therapist but actually got a physician assistant or physical therapist assistant instead.

Have you been annoyed that your healthcare provider is always running late, appears rushed, and only spends 6-7 minutes with you before he or she is out the door? Does it bother you how deductibles keep skyrocketing while the quality of care is plummeting?

I worked in this system, and I hated it! I couldn't give all the focus and care I wanted to before I had to move onto the next patient.

Maybe you've tried physical therapy in the past, but for those of you that haven't, I'll explain how the traditional process works. Let's say you are suffering with back pain, so you go see your physician. Your physician recommends you try physical therapy. (Side note: only 7% of those with back pain are actually referred to physical therapy[23]).

You are given a list of physical therapy clinics, and you call the one that has the best reviews on Google. Or you try a place a friend recommends. When you first call the clinic and tell them your doctor said to try physical therapy, they'll ask you for your name, date of birth, what body part hurts, and group insurance policy number. You are never asked how your back pain started, how it happened, or what you've already tried thus far. Time isn't spent trying to truly understand the depth of your problem.

After getting the first visit scheduled, you go into the clinic, where you are given stacks of paperwork to fill out. When that is all done and your hand is severely cramping, you get called back for your initial evaluation. You spend a little time with a physical therapist and the rest of the time with an aide doing exercises you could be doing at home.

On the next follow-up visit, you find out that you have to spend the first 50 minutes doing exercises followed by 10 minutes with the actual physical therapist. If you breakdown the 10 minutes, the first 2-3 minutes are catching up to see how things are going followed by 7-8 minutes of actual hands-on work.

It doesn't matter what physical therapist you see, 7-8 minutes is not enough time to effectively treat chronic back/knee/shoulder/neck pain. Most people don't see any results after a few sessions and give up. I don't blame them one bit. Why would you waste your precious time on something that's not working?

This is not what physical therapy should be. So after watching this process for many years, I decided to create a physical therapy clinic, Parker Physio,

---

[23] Fritz, Julie M., et al. "Primary care referral of patients with low back pain to physical therapy: impact on future health care utilization and costs." *Spine* 37.25 (2012): 2114-2121.

that is dedicated to serving the most important person: you! My clinic's process is a bit different.

We start with an in-depth phone call. When you call my clinic, there will be no mention of date of births or group policy numbers. No robot answering machine that you have to press a bunch of numbers or try to yell "Yes" or "No" a thousand times. You'll be connected straight to one of my incredible staff members.

We want to spend AT LEAST 15 or 20 minutes on the phone getting to know you in order to gain a deep understanding of you and your problem. What you've tried. What's worked. What hasn't worked. What your pain or problem is stopping you from doing. What your number one goal is. Etc.

To schedule a phone call, go to www.parkephysio.com/free-telephone-consultation

After talking on the phone, if we determine that we can help and are a good fit for you, we'll schedule you to come in for your first session, which is 100% free. We call it a "Taster Session." No obligations. No paperwork. No referral or prescription needed. You come get a feel for my clinic and gain a better understanding of your problem and how we may be able to help. We want you to have total confidence and clarity in making the best decision for your health.

At the free Taster Session we will dive into answering more in-depth questions. What exactly is wrong? This could include stiff joints, weak muscles, poor quality of movement, etc. What are your options to fix it? What are your goals? How long it will take to reach your goal? What is the actual cost to solve your problem? What you can do at home to speed up recovery?

By the way, "get rid of my pain" isn't the best goal. You can take pain pills for pain relief. A better goal is fixing knee pain so you can walk on the beach with your loved one for as long as you want without having to worry about your pain coming back. A goal is getting your back strong enough to lift up your grandchild without the impending fear that your back is going to go out. A goal is to get your shoulder to the point you can drive a golf ball 250 yards down the middle of the fairway. A goal is being able to work an 8-hour day without neck pain or headaches throwing off your focus and energy.

I tell patients, "Pain relief isn't the best thing we can do for you; it's just a happy byproduct. Guiding you to living an active, mobile, independent lifestyle with the confidence your pain won't come back anytime soon is by far the best thing we can do for you."

To find out more about our Free Taster Session, go to www.parkerphysio. com/free-taster-session

At my clinic, you will not find a hot pack, cold pack, or electrical stim unit. You can buy all that stuff on Amazon and do those things at home. At Parker Physio, we know that our patients get the best results when we use our hands, a table, a couple resistance bands, and a few weights when appropriate. That's it.

While the traditional PT clinics will only do 7-8 minutes of hands-on work, we spend at least 30 minutes per session. Why? Because when you've been in pain and stiffness for an extended period of time, that's what it takes to break down scar tissue, unlock stiff and creaky joints, and release muscle tightness. This is especially important early on in the rehab process.

What about exercises? That all depends on you. We will ask you at the beginning what it is you're looking for. If you know that you aren't great about being consistent doing exercises at home, we create a plan for that. If you are someone who loves doing things at home to speed up recovery, we create a custom plan for that too.

When it comes to exercises and homework, we will only ask for 8-12 minutes of your day. No more, no less. We respect your time and will only give you exercises that give you the most bang for your buck.

You will also not find any aides or assistants at Parker Physio. Just you and a certified physical therapist for the entire session, in a one-on-one environment, working together in a fun, upbeat atmosphere. Throughout the process, you will have access to our physical therapists 24 hours a day, 7 days a week through our text message service, where we respond within 24 to 48 hours of asking any questions or concerns you may have.

We believe it's this process that gets our patients back to feeling young again. To a life where they aren't dependent on pain pills or afraid of the of needing an unnecessary (and costly) surgery. To walking, hiking, running, swimming, or playing sports with loved ones and friends. To having the internal confidence that these aches and pains don't have to be a daily occurence anymore.

Some of our most proactive patients who truly value their health will invest in our year-long plan of care to come back for checkups throughout the year. This allows them to keep their body in tip-top shape all year round. If any of this interests you, and you would like to inquire about cost and availability, go to https://parkerphysio.com/inquire-cost-availability/

Frequently Asked Questions

Here are some other frequently asked questions about physical therapy. It is compiled from years of questions left on my patient message board, from inquisitive email replies, from people who walk into our clinic in person, those who call in on the phone, and even "live chat" their queries to us. They all come from men and women who value their health enough to make a simple inquiry about what they can do at the first signs of ill-health and to ask exactly how physical therapy can help them achieve their goal of returning to great health.

Q1. What is physical therapy?

A: Physical therapy is a proven strategy for easing the worries and concerns of people suffering from aches, pain, and stiffness, helping that person move freely again, bend further, stretch easier, and live an active and healthy lifestyle into their 50s, 60s, 70s, and beyond.

More, it lets that person live free from the worry that the same problem will come back to haunt them anytime soon.

Q2. How can physical therapy help me?

A: There are two ways physical therapy can help, and a good physical therapist will lift your concerns and ease your worries by telling you what's going wrong, often within 10-15 minutes.

Next, the speed at which the physical problem is eased is completely dependent upon your age, how long you've had it, how severe it is, your commitment, and the manual skills of the physical therapist.

Q3. Do I get personal support if I need it?

A: Yes. If you arrange to do physical therapy with us, you'll be given almost unrestricted access to your own physical therapist, who will be on hand to take your call and reply to your emails and texts for as long as you need.

Q4. Does physical therapy help someone like me?

A: Here's a list of the types of people physical therapy helps:

1. People still working (and who want to remain that way), especially salespeople, managers, civil servants, engineers, office workers, teachers, manual workers, nurses, healthcare workers, lawyers, even doctors. Why? Because they need to move easily and be able

to sit comfortably for long periods in order to perform well in their jobs.

2. People aged 50+ who are determined to remain independent. Why? Because many people see the impact that poor physical health has had on their parents.

3. Active and involved grandparents. Why? Grandparents who play games with their grandkids, help with school work, walk with them to and from school, take them places, or babysit often tell us that's why they felt the need to try physical therapy.

4. People who take their health seriously. Why? Many people who visit us are proactive about their health. That means they read up on foods, vitamins, health topics, try to eat right, take vitamins and other supplements such as cod or fish oil, and do their best to stay out of the doctor's office.

Q5. What happens if I'm not happy with my physical therapy at the end of my session?

A: I will personally refund your payment back onto the card you've used or you can leave without paying, NO questions asked.

Q6. What if I book physical therapy today, but before I get to you there's a positive change in my condition so that I don't need to come and see you anymore?

A: That's great! That's what we're shooting for. Just call and we will cancel your name in the schedule and ask that you keep in touch with your physical therapist to let us know how you're doing.

Q7. Am I going to have to take off my clothes during physical therapy?

A: You never have to remove large portions of clothing. To make your physical therapy experience as comfortable as possible please, keep in mind the location of your injured body part.

For example, if you have a lower back injury, shorts and a loose shirt would be ideal. Or if you're suffering from a shoulder or neck injury, a t-shirt would be great for guys or a tank top for ladies. Your physical therapist will always aim to remove as little clothing as possible, and we will never ask that you remove an item of clothing that may completely expose a large area of your body.

Q8. If I don't want to make another appointment after my first visit, do you take it personally?

A: Not at all. That's totally fine! My first priority is to tell you what's going wrong and what you need to do next by creating a custom plan. Whether or not to continue with your treatment plan is totally up to you.

Q9. How likely is it that physical therapist will be able to help me?

A: If your problem or concern is one of pain or stiffness in the muscles or joints of the following areas, it's 99% likely that physical therapy can help you, and there are various ways we might do that.

- Back
- Neck
- Shoulder
- Elbow
- Knee
- Foot/Ankle

Q10. Can I talk to a physical therapist before I book, just to confirm physical therapy is right for me?

A: Absolutely! You schedule a call on our webpage at www.parkerphysio. com/free-telephone-consultation or email me personally at mat@parkeprhysio.com

Q11. Will you do anything at the first session to help my pain?

A: Yes. It's always my intention to start making progress on the pain and or stiffness you've got, as well as help ease any other concerns and frustrations.

Q12. Isn't physical therapy just for younger people who are injured and who play loads of sports?

A: Absolutely NOT. I'll be the first to say that physical therapy helps people who do play sports, but physical therapy is actually much more valuable and better suited to people who are aged 50+ and who want to keep an active lifestyle for as long as possible.

Q13. Will I get any exercises or anything like that to take home with me?

A: Only if the time is right and we think performing them is not going to make your pain worse, and I'll give you as many hints and tips as possible to use when you go back home that night. We actually prefer to use videos to help guide you, and we will never ask for more than 8-12 minutes of your day.

Q14. What will happen if I don't choose to go and see a physical therapist?

A: Your current predicament may continue, and you'll run the risk of doing unforeseen and untold damage to the joints if they're not taken care of properly or if surrounding muscles aren't made stronger. A failure to adhere to the right recovery program post-injury could increase the risk of early onset of pain and stiffness in joints.

Q15. How long will it take for a physical therapist to get me active and healthy again?

A: Everybody's a little bit different, but for most problems that involve joints and muscles that we see in our physical therapy clinics, we've worked out a way to get it down to as little as 2-3 weeks before a person is comfortable and safely active again.

Q16. My injury only happened the other day, and I'm in a lot of pain. When should I see a physical therapist for help?

A: ASAP. There will always be ways we can help. Sometimes it's as simple as, "Do this, but don't do that" advice. The first will be to tell you what NOT to do. So many people make poor, misinformed mistakes when it comes to dealing with acute pain. Every decision that you get wrong in the first few days will, very likely, add to the length of time it will take to get better.

Q17. Somebody mentioned a chiropractor to me, but what's the difference between physical therapy and a chiropractor?

A: To be brief, a physical therapist looks for a cure. Our aim is to help you create an effective treatment plan so you will not need to constantly keep coming back to us. So a physical therapist will design a plan to work on stopping the injury happening again.

We do very similar techniques to osteopaths and chiropractors, such as mobilization of your spine, but we also add things such as massage and stretching and believe that the combination of that with exercises and posture correction will reduce your pain fast and also help you manage your pain in the coming years to avoid the need for repetitive visits to see us.

Osteopaths and chiropractors are both fantastically effective at reducing back pain, and many of the good ones will even refer their patients to a physical therapist for the things like massage and exercises that they don't provide.

Q18. I can't work this thing out. One minute I'm not bothered by it, then the next it can quite literally take my breath away. Just when I think it's getting better, it hits me again! If I come in and see you at a time when it's not hurting, will I be wasting my time?

A: Not at all. Immediate pain relief isn't really what we do! Physical therapy is about finding the source of your problem, whether that is poor posture, bad movement mechanics, etc. And if your injury is now a few weeks old, two things are likely to be happening. The first is that the joints and muscles are locked stiff or jammed in one place, so every time you get to a certain point they don't want to move, producing a sharp pain. The second is that now you're likely to have tight and weak muscles. The combination of that plus locked joints equals long-term problems.

Q19. Is physical therapy guaranteed to help me like I hope?

A: There are no guarantees (like most things in life), and no decent physical therapist will ever claim such a thing is possible. It simply isn't. But that's why we offer a firm, money back guarantee in case you're one of the unlucky ones we can't help. If it doesn't help like you hope, we always offer you your money back in FULL.

Q20. Does this sort of thing happen to other people like me?

A: Yes, we see many people with the same sorts of injuries all day long, particularly in the 50+ age group who suffer from aches, pains, and stiffness

Q21. How quickly will I be seen?

A: Often within a day or two. If you need an emergency appointment, please let us know on the phone or in your email so that we can arrange for a physical therapist to work with you within 24 hours or less.

Q22. Do you still use your hands? I just went to another place recently and they told me they didn't do that type of thing anymore. I left very

frustrated and disappointed, as I know the hands-on style treatment really worked for me before when I was in pain.

A: Yes! The care that we provide is predominantly hands-on. We believe that the old-fashioned way of deep massages, stretching and mobilizing stiff joints, in combination with improved movement mechanics, is the fastest way to return you to enjoying better health.

Q23. I'm not in any pain per se, but I'm experiencing lots of stiffness and tightness and am worried that something's not quite right. Am I right to be considering physical therapy?

A: You are PERFECT for physical therapy (and us). Some people think that physical therapy is about ending pain, but that's only one thing we do, and it isn't even the BEST. The aim is to stop you from ever getting to the point where you are in lots of pain by making you more supple, flexible, and stronger, able to withstand the amount of activity you want to do, no matter your age.

Q24. I'm a runner and not in any pain when resting or doing my daily activities, but it always flares up after a few minutes of running. Is that common, and do I need physical therapy?

A: Yes and yes. Most sports injuries settle down so that you can walk around and do simple everyday things without pain. But as soon as you step it up a level or two, if the problem is still there, it lets you know in the way of tightness, pain, swelling, or stiffness.

Q25. What's the difference between a good physical therapist and a bad one?

A: Three things:
   - The amount of care taken (easy to spot)
   - The hands-on techniques and skills being used
   - Ability to accurately diagnose an injury

Q26. Can physical therapy help me if I have arthritis?

A: Yes! But please understand that it can't CURE it. It can very easily help manage the symptoms. Many people come to physical therapy aged 50+ and suffering from wear and tear (arthritis) inside their knee joints, low back joints, etc. After a few short weeks, they are able to do more than they could have imagined.

Q27. I have had clicking, clunking, and cracking noises happening in my joints for a few years now, and it's beginning to cause pain. I'm 58. Is physical therapy for me?

A: Yes. You're an almost perfect candidate for PT. This is a typical story. Most joint problems begin with warning signs such as the clicks and cracks you've been hearing. A few years later, pain can begin to settle in, so get help before that happens.

Q28. I'm in the early days of joint pain and stiffness. I've made it to 50 without any problems, but I'm now worried I'm next in line for joint troubles like the rest of my friends of a similar age. I'm really active and love to play pickleball, hike, walk, and swim. Can physical therapy help someone like me?

A: Yes. It's a simple case of ensuring you have full movement of your joints and proper strengthening to limit the impact of arthritis. Physical therapy will give you hope and the confidence to get back to the activities you want.

Q29. Will physical therapy help me with my flexibility? I'm stiff as a board the first few hours after I've been out on my bike, and I know this is causing my achy lower back.

A: Yes. We'll walk you through a simple set of exercise routines you can do every day to help eliminate this. Oh, and we'll fix your achy back too!

Q30. Is there anyone that physical therapy ISN'T right for?

A: Yes. Anyone who is expecting a miracle and hoping to be fixed in one visit. This is rarely possible, particularly for injuries happening to men and women aged 50+.

Q31. Is physical therapy expensive?

A: It all depends on how much you value your health. Some people will shy away from getting specialist help because of the cost. But what is it costing you by not getting help? If your problem has caused you to be grumpy and irritable, what's it costing in the quality of your relationships with your family and loved ones? What's it costing you in the quality of your work? What's a lifetime of pain medications costing you? What's surgery going to cost?

It never makes sense to me that people will spend money to maintain their car or their house but won't invest in their own bodies. I hope by reading this you choose to make the best decision for your health.

Q32. Is physical therapy painful?

A: Not really. It is true that physical therapy is a very physical experience, and treatments can be a little uncomfortable at times, but we always aim to be as gentle as possible and cause the least discomfort we possibly can to get your problem solved as quickly as we can.

Before we do any physical therapy techniques, we will tell you exactly what is about to happen and whether or not it is likely to hurt and for how long.

Q33. Will I be in any pain after the treatment (i.e. the next day)?

A: More often than not any pain stops as soon as we do, so you only have to tell us to stop and we will. Pain is a side effect to physical therapy that is often unavoidable, and most patients eventually concede that the pain is a nice sort of pain, one they know is doing them some good and is often no worse than the pain that they are already in.

The discomfort usually reduces as treatment progresses, and we always advise you on things such as ice and heat to help reduce the soreness that might be caused by the treatment. If it's painful the next day, ice usually soothes it!

Q34. Will I get some tips that I can be doing at home to help myself get better more quickly?

A: Absolutely. The aim is to help you in every way we can. In the clinic, we will do everything for you, but you're only with us for 30-60 minutes depending on the type of session you choose, so we aim to arm you with tools, tricks, and tips that you can use to make a difference you will feel very quickly and on your own.

Q35. How important are exercises to my recovery?

A: Not as much as you've been led to believe. They're more important to stop the problem from coming back. They do play a role in your recovery, but most people do the wrong ones, at the wrong time, in the wrong order, for the wrong reasons. A good physical therapist will stop that from occurring.

Q36. Why did my doctor tell me NOT to try physical therapy and rest instead?

A: There are two common reasons for this to happen:

1. Physicians (in certain insurances) try to reduce the expenses of the insurance company, so rarely do any of them go out of their way to recommend physical therapy or any other form of treatment.

2. Most general physician practitioners are not trained to know the depth of orthopedic injuries and the symptoms of physical pains well enough to understand when one can benefit from physical therapy. Shocking, but very true.

Q37. How long does the session last?

A: Depends on which option you want to take. We have a 30-minute option as well as a very popular 60-minute session. The reality is that it will take as long as you need to get the help you came looking for.

Q38. Do I need a referral from my physician?

A: Nope. Just call us and book. If you're willing to invest in your health, you're very welcome to come see us without a referral.

Q39. Can I bring a friend or loved one in to the treatment room with me?

A: Yes. No problem! You do not need to inform us of this decision in advance. If you are accompanied by a friend or family member, we will often ask whether you would like them to join you in the physical therapy room during treatment. Alternatively, they can wait in reception if you would prefer.

Q40. How often will I need treatment?

A: That is always dependent upon the nature of your injury and how quickly you want to improve. Our aim is for you to return to full activity as quickly and safely as possible. Your physical therapist will be in a better position to answer this following your first session.

Big tip: getting in early nearly always means less time to recover and less physical therapy sessions needed.

Q41. How long will it take for the physical therapist to relieve my pain?

A: As long as it takes you to call up and book! If you had tooth pain, I bet that you'd call the very first day you noticed the pain, because you know that's the best possible way to get rid of that tooth pain quickly.

To answer the question, it will take as long as it takes you to make an inquiry and come in to see us. Know this: it will happen much quicker than if you leave it to time or chance by taking painkillers or going to see the doctor!

CHAPTER 10

Lights, Camera, Action!

We've been on quite a journey thus far. We debunked some of the most common health myths. We reviewed the most frequent mistakes made when pain strikes. We covered different parts of the body, including the causes for low back, shoulder, knee, back, and neck pain, not to mention ways to minimize and eliminate these pains. We discussed the basic principles of nutrition and fitness. We reviewed wellness topics ranging from sleeping to pooping. In the last chapter, we talked about what physical therapy is and how it may be able to help you get back to better health.

I appreciate you sticking around and hope you have found this book helpful. At the end of this chapter, I'll be including a ton of healthy gifts and goodies you can have for FREE! But before I get there, let's talk about THE most important thing you can do for your long-term health, and that is to **take action**!

Reading this book and learning new information is great, but it means absolutely nothing if you don't decide to do anything about it. Too often I talk to people who want to try physical therapy, make better lifestyle choices, and have better exercise habits yet do nothing. They know they should do something, but they continue to let their health get worse and worse. One of my all-time favorite quotes is from the Dalai Lama. He was once asked what surprised him most about humanity:

"Man. Because he sacrifices his health in order to make money. Then he sacrifices his money to recuperate his health. And then he is so anxious about the future that he does not enjoy the present; the result being that he does not live in the present or the future. He lives as if he is never going to die, and then dies never really having lived."

An incredibly powerful quote. Do you have to do every single thing mentioned in this book? Absolutely not! Start with one thing and decide to do it everyday. It doesn't have to be physical. Meditating and working on mental wellness is just as important. Starting a new habit is hard, and the best way to maintain a new habit is to have someone hold you accountable. Somebody who will call you out when you try to make excuses. If you don't have anybody, email me and I will personally hold you accountable. It's mat@parkerphysio.com. Remember, habits take 21-66 days for them to become automatic. I know you can do it!

I'm throwing the gauntlet down and challenging you. Again, start with just one thing from this book. It could be trying physical therapy, walking everyday, eating better, or starting a gratitude journal. I know I'm repeating myself, but only because action is so vital. It will create a compound effect in your life when you begin to make healthier choices.

Imagine, if you continue to do nothing, what your life will look like 6 months from now? How about a year? 5 years?

Now imagine, if you started just ONE healthier habit per month, what your life would look like in 6 months? A year? 5 years? In this scenario, your life could be COMPLETELY different.

This Doesn't Have To Be The End...

If you've enjoyed this book, you should know each week I write to hundreds of people from around the country on how to improve their health and overall well-being. The best part? The health advice is delivered right to your email inbox.

After reading a book like mine or watching a motivational video, it's easy to be inspired and live healthy for a couple days. Unfortunately, motivation and inspiration are always temporary feelings, and it can cause us to slide back into unhealthy routines.To maintain momentum, you need a continuous stream of positive and helpful health advice.

So the best thing to do next is to visit my website and leave your name and email address, then I'll know to send you more health tips like the ones you've enjoyed reading in this book. You can do that at www.parkerphysio. com/blog

FREE Healthy Bonus Gifts

If you would like more in-depth information and self help tips on common topics, please go to the website addresses below. When you get there, you'll see a special tips report I have written for you containing even more information on ways to get the help you need.

- **Back Pain And Stiffness:** https://parkerphysio.com/back-pain/

- **Sciatica/Hip Pain/Piriformis Syndrome:** www.parkerphysio. com/sciatica-hip-pain/

- **Knee Pain:** www.parkerphysio.com/knee-pain/

- **Shoulder Pain:** www.parkerphysio.com/shoulder-pain/

- **Neck Pain Or Headaches:** www.parkerphysio.com/neck-pain/

- **Foot/Ankle Pain:** www.parkerphysio.com/foot-and-ankle-pain/

- **Sports/Running Injury Recovery Guide:** www.parkerphysio.
  com/sports-running-injury

Talk To A Physical Therapist From The Comfort Of Your Own Home

If you would like to talk to a specialist about any health-related problem you are currently having, I can also offer you a free, 20-minute telephone consultation with a certified physical therapist from my own clinic.

You can schedule that by visiting www.parkerphysio.com/free-telephone-consultation/ and filling out a brief form.

Health Disclaimer

I make every effort to ensure that I accurately represent the injury advice and prognosis displayed throughout this book. However, examples of injuries and their prognosis are based on typical representations of those injuries that I commonly see in my physical therapy clinic.

The information given is not intended as representative of every individual's potential injury. As with any injury, each person's symptoms can vary widely, and each person's recovery from injury can also vary depending upon background, genetics, previous medical history, application of exercises, posture, motivation to follow physical therapy advice, and various other physical factors. It is impossible to give a 100% accurate diagnosis and prognosis without a thorough physical examination. Likewise, the advice given for management of an injury cannot be deemed fully accurate in the absence of an examination from one of the licensed physical therapists at Parker Physio.

Significant injury risk is possible if you do not follow due diligence and seek suitable professional advice about your injury. No guarantees of specific results are expressly made or implied in this book.

REFERENCES

1   Levy BR, Slade MD, Kasl SV. Longitudinal benefit of positive self-perceptions of aging on functional health. *J Gerontol B Psychol Sci Soc Sci*. 2002;57:409–417.

2   Brinjikji W, Luetmer PH, Comstock B, et al. Systematic Literature Review of Imaging Features of Spinal Degeneration in Asymptomatic Populations. *AJNR American journal of neuroradiology*. 2015;36(4):811-816. doi:10.3174/ajnr.A4173

3   McAlindon TE, LaValley MP, Harvey WF, et al. Effect of Intra-articular Triamcinolone vs Saline on Knee Cartilage Volume and Pain in Patients With Knee Osteoarthritis: A Randomized Clinical Trial. *JAMA*.2017;317(19):1967–1975. doi:10.1001/jama.2017.5283

4   Bogduk N. Management of chronic low back pain. Med J Aust . 2004;180(2):79-83.

5   Johannes CB, Le TK, Zhou X, Johnston JA, Dworkin RH. The prevalence of chronic pain in United States adults: results of an Internet-based survey. J Pain. 2010;11(11):1230-1239. doi: 10.1016/j.jpain.2010.07.002.

6   Relationship Between Mechanical Factors and Incidence of Low Back Pain. Mohammad Reza Nourbakhsh and Amir Massoud Arab. Journal of Orthopaedic & Sports Physical Therapy 2002 32:9, 447-460

7   Felson DT, Zhang Y, Anthony JM, Naimark A, Anderson JJ. Weight Loss Reduces the Risk for Symptomatic Knee Osteoarthritis in Women: The Framingham Study. Ann Intern Med. 1992;116:535–539. doi: 10.7326/0003-4819-116-7-535

8   Katz, Jeffrey N., et al. "Surgery versus physical therapy for a meniscal tear and osteoarthritis." *New England Journal of Medicine* 368.18 (2013): 1675-1684.

9 Sihvonen, Raine, et al. "Arthroscopic partial meniscectomy versus sham surgery for a degenerative meniscal tear." *New England Journal of Medicine* 369.26 (2013): 2515-2524.

10 Yamamoto, Atsushi, et al. "Prevalence and risk factors of a rotator cuff tear in the general population." *Journal of Shoulder and Elbow Surgery* 19.1 (2010): 116-120.

11 Tempelhof, Siegbert, Stefan Rupp, and Romain Seil. "Age-related prevalence of rotator cuff tears in asymptomatic shoulders." *Journal of shoulder and elbow surgery* 8.4 (1999): 296-299.

12 Miller MB. The cervical spine: physical therapy patient management utilizing current evidence. Wilmarth MA, ed. ISC 21.2.6, Current Concepts of Orthopaedic Physical Therapy. 3rd ed. La Crosse, WI: Orthopaedic Section, APTA; 2011.

13 Cleland JA, Childs JD, McRae M, Palmer JA, Stowell T. Immediate effects of thoracic manipulation in patients with neck pain: a randomized clinical trial. Man Ther. 2005;10(2):127-135.

14 Rosenfeld M, Gunnarsson R, Borenstein P. Early intervention in whiplash associated disorders: a comparison of two treatment protocols. Spine 2000;25:1782.

15 Aggarwal BB, Shishodia S, Sandur SK, Pandey MK, Sethi G. Inflammation and cancer: How hot is the link? Biochem Pharmacol. 2006;72:1605–21.

16 Giugliano D, Ceriello A, Esposito K. The effects of diet on inflammation - Emphasis on the metabolic syndrome. J Am Coll Cardiol. 2006;48:677–85.

17 Kenney, W. Larry, and Percy Chiu. "Influence of age on thirst and fluid intake." *Medicine and science in sports and exercise*33.9 (2001): 1524-1532.

18 Grossman, Paul, et al. "Mindfulness-based stress reduction and health benefits: A meta-analysis." *Journal of psychosomatic research* 57.1 (2004): 35-43.

19 Lally, Phillippa, et al. "How are habits formed: Modelling habit formation in the real world." *European journal of social psychology* 40.6 (2010): 998-1009.

20   Williamson, Ann M., and Anne-Marie Feyer. "Moderate sleep deprivation produces impairments in cognitive and motor performance equivalent to legally prescribed levels of alcohol intoxication." *Occupational and environmental medicine* 57.10 (2000): 649-655.

21   Milewski, Matthew D., et al. "Chronic lack of sleep is associated with increased sports injuries in adolescent athletes." *Journal of Pediatric Orthopaedics* 34.2 (2014): 129-133.

22   Brooks, Amber, and Leon Lack. "A brief afternoon nap following nocturnal sleep restriction: which nap duration is most recuperative?." *Sleep* 29.6 (2006): 831-840.

23   Fritz, Julie M., et al. "Primary care referral of patients with low back pain to physical therapy: impact on future health care utilization and costs." *Spine* 37.25 (2012): 2114-2121.

LL

3307
KRESSLER
AFTER 3

Made in the USA
Coppell, TX
19 October 2019